D1617435

GERMANY'S NEW CONSERVATISM

Its History and Dilemma
in the Twentieth Century

Germany's New Conservatism

Its History and Dilemma in the Twentieth Century

BY KLEMENS VON KLEMPERER

Foreword by Sigmund Neumann

PRINCETON, NEW JERSEY
PRINCETON UNIVERSITY PRESS

KLEMENS VON KLEMPERER is L. Clark Seelye Professor of History at Smith College. He is a native of Berlin, studied at the University of Vienna, and obtained his doctor's degree from Harvard University.

The 1968 printing includes a Postscript by the author.

Printed in the United States of America
By Princeton University Press, Princeton, New Jersey

TO THE GOOD PEOPLE IN
PLANDOME, L.I.—NORFOLK, CONN.
CLAREMONT, N.H.
WHO SAW THIS BOOK GROW

FOREWORD

CONSERVATISM: NEW AND OLD

by Sigmund Neumann

CONSERVATISM is the fashion of the day. Only a generation ago a derogatory design, if not the death nail for any politically ambitious man of affairs, it seems to have become suddenly a mark of distinction and the open-sesame to wise statesmanship. While some lone stalwarts of way back may rejoice in such belated recognition and renown of a much maligned notion, this is truly the time to save it from its own newly won enthusiasts in order to salvage its historical entity.

Political concepts indeed have their ways and days. They are most endangered when they catch the popular fancy. Like coins, passed from hand to hand, their imprint gets worn, their deeper meaning is blurred, their pre-conceptions and consequences are cheapened and lost in mouth-to-mouth transactions. Thus they may well lose their original value. If one does not want to discard them altogether, one must re-press, re-furbish, re-define them.

Such a task is doubly called for in a time of transition (and what time is not in such a radical transformation?). Historical reality often changes without having yet managed to create its new language. In the clash of present-day, fast-changing systems, a continuous conceptual house-cleaning becomes a necessity. In fact, one could well argue that a time-lag usually exists between historical reality and its conceptualization, especially in a revolutionary age when the political vocabulary is quickly outdated and thus full of misnomers. We are still living within an ideological framework of a hundred years back and naturally cannot master our present-day political conflicts with such obsolete and often romantic stereotypes. This is a time when a meaningful historical comparison is called for. More than that: a theoretical clarification becomes a paramount preliminary for appropriate strategies of proper political action. All fundamental concepts must therefore be re-defined in the light of a new reality. On this basis alone can theory become, as it should, a guide to proper political action, a compass through chaos.

Conservatism and liberalism, the time-honored twins of ideological confrontation, are a case in question. In the confusion of their contemporary abuse, one may be inclined to dismiss them despairingly as adequate tools of conceptual clarification; yet one will still be left with the need for proper yardsticks in the present-day political labyrinth. True, an examination of their real meaning will reveal that the accustomed classifications of political ideologies and movements in terms of conservatism, liberalism, socialism, communism, fascism, etc., are misleading, to say the least. Not only have innumerable combinations (such as liberal conservatism, conservative socialism, National Bolshevism, the people's democracy) confused the political fronts, but the fundamental concepts themselves have shifted their original meaning under the impact of radical social changes. One may even doubt the simple contrast between right- and left-wing movements. Originally "radical" groups, such as the Parti Radical Socialiste, have been pushed to the right under the pressure of newly appearing leftist movements. At the same time frequent attempts at bridging right- and left-wing radical organizations, insignificant though the attempts may be in view of long-range developments, point to similar psychological attitudes even among deadly political opponents.

The full recognition of these difficulties should not lead to the easy dismissal of ideological concepts altogether, as is frequently suggested by short-sighted "realists" in politics. On the contrary, ideologies cannot be taken seriously enough in the vacuum of a spiritual crisis when the underlying unity of Christian European traditions is challenged by a counter-church, when uncompromising political conflicts along petrified political fronts are threatening, and when the drives for fundamental reorientation are of primary importance in the final line-up of the peoples—at least wherever they still remain free to choose.

* * *

It is against the background of such urgent conceptual considerations that this study by Klemens von Klemperer should be evaluated. It can serve a threefold purpose. In the first place, it presents a significant case study of a little-known and complex chapter of conservative contribution: the story of twentieth century German neo-conservatism, which incidentally throws new light on the ill-fated Weimar Republic.

Secondly, in this crushing and fatal surrender of a proud and productive position, vis-à-vis National Socialism, an historical drama is unfolded that reflects a tragic failure of European traditionalism to cope with the radical forces of threatening nihilism. This warning signal in the life-and-death struggle of the Western world gives the German theme its world-wide weight and ominous omen. In fact, one may wonder, viewing its present-day aspiration, whether a new conservatism can postulate an adequate mid-twentieth century political philosophy; yet that is exactly what is demanded by a new generation, grown up amid the fulfillment of, and therefore skeptical about, the classic concepts of the last century's ideologies. For such a proud program, conservatism must above all recognize the proper historical position in which it finds itself and respond to the issues and needs of the time. It may constitutionally find it difficult to detect the tender tendencies of promising breakthroughs and may easily revert instead to patterns of the past, thus turning a refreshing opening into a fruitless reaction. The popular identification of conservatism with the mere defense of the *status quo* or, worse than that, with an outdated order thus might find a renewed confirmation. It would be as misleading as the equally prevalent descriptions of liberalism as continuous change for change's sake.

The third and most important function of a present-day analysis of conservatism, therefore, is an attempt at a basic definition which would confront the contemporary usage with the often misinterpreted historical images and with a timeless classification of the term. In short, the student of modern ideologies must ask himself whether there are general notions of conservatism and liberalism which, though rarely existent in their pure manifestations, may still serve as "ideal types" against which the mixed reality can be measured. It is on this level that the von Klemperer book makes a special contribution and therefore reaches far beyond a useful case study to a most timely conceptual clarification.

*　　*　　*

There is no need for a rehearsal of the book's revealing record. What might be useful, however, by way of introduction is to single out some of the significant issues that are evoked by this presentation and to draw upon its findings for their past perspective, their portentous presence, their future implications. The book does not suggest any easy solutions, yet for this very reason it may represent a clarion call for fruitful follow-ups. What better recommendation could one give for a thought-provoking task than the confidence that it will serve as a trail blazer for other expeditions into the *terra incognita*?

German conservatism entered the twentieth century (the historical stage of the subsequent study) with a host of past liabilities and contemporary complexities. Awakening as it was from tacit traditionalism under the impact of the world challenge of the French Revolution and its ensuing liberal-radical ideas, its first articulate response in the early nineteenth century was naturally a reactionary retreat to the position of the imperilled *status quo*. But while this reaction characteristically remained a mainstay of Continental conservatives, there were certainly other alternatives and, in all fairness to the sincerity of the diehards, more constructive answers to the revolutionary provocation. In fact one may say that the future of conservatism as a meaningful and effective ideology depended on a dynamic widening of its vista in order to absorb the shock of revolutionary change.

The German conservatives were often altogether unaware of the real issue of the nineteenth century, namely the conflict between state and society, the adjustment of an old power system to the new social forces of the Industrial Revolution. This failure to strike a proper balance in Prussia-Germany was of serious consequence. It foreshadowed the frustrations of Weimar.

Different from the straight middle class victory in Western Europe, the German attempt followed three stages— romantic, liberal, and realistic—which were reflected in the subsequent responses of the old ruling class. Romantic conservatism did not want to recognize the new forces at all. King Frederick William IV, "the Romanticist on the Throne," tried, after a short and unhappy bow to the Political Revolution, to turn the clock back. The reactionary government of General Manteuffel, although accepted for a time by the frightened middle class, was still no answer for Prussia-Germany, if it were to attain a position of power in society. Yet the Junkers were adamant in their rejection of any reforms, a position they held even in the late days of Weimar. It was no coincidence that the Republic's grave-digger von Papen (chancellor of 1932's Midsummer Night's Dream) unearthed Manteuffel's speeches and used them practically verbatim in his governmental declarations when path-finding for Hitler's twentieth century autocracy.

The tragedy of the old German ruling class was that it did not recognize the dynamics of modern society. True, throughout the nineteenth and twentieth centuries some open-minded conservatives made themselves the vanguard of the rising social forces; but this group always remained a small elite at the periphery of events. "Tory democracy," rejuvenating British conservatism by absorbing newly emerging strata of society, could never reach the core of German conservatism, which isolated itself from the progressive forces and thus became sterile.

The liberal-minded among the conservative aristocracy were few. From the great reformers under Freiherrn vom Stein and Generals Boyen, Scharnhorst, and Gneisenau in the age of the War of Liberation, to the Wochenblattpartei of von Bethmann and Joseph Maria von Radowitz, hapless adviser to his stubborn royal friend, Frederick William, in the days of 1848, to the *Freikonservative* in the Second Empire and the *Volkskonservative* of the Weimar Republic, to the rightist opposition against National Socialism which ended with the futile attempt on Hitler's life in 1944—this was a continuous line involving largely the same families, who tried to bring a New Deal to Germany. Only a few fleeting moments in German history, e.g. the New Era of 1857 to 1862, indicated what they might have meant to a liberal Germany.

This short interlude was interrupted by the Prussian constitutional conflict in 1862 when King William finally called Bismarck to power. The argument between the Crown and the Parliament spelled the second defeat of the German middle class and its parliamentary majority. Not only did the chancellor completely disregard the Parliament's persistent rejection of the budget but he broke its resistance by "blood and iron" in his victories in the Danish War (1864), the Prussian-Austrian conflict (1866), and the Franco-Prussian War (1871), the crowning event of unification. It was a bad omen for the politicians of the German bourgeoisie. Although Bismarck in an astute gesture bowed to the parliamentary majority after his victory over Austria by introducing the "law of indemnity," which exonerated him for his unconstitutional action, it was in reality the middle class that acquiesced in a feudalized society.

This was the Bismarckian compromise of a realistic conservatism. In contrast to Britain, where the middle class forced the aristocracy to accept new standards of society, in Germany it was the bourgeoisie that became feudalized. In a division of labor Bismarck forced it to accept the political rule of the Junkers although he left the middle class in control of economic life. This realistic conservatism in short neither accepted the romantic rejection of the Industrial Revolution nor did it follow the liberal claim of a Tory democracy for leadership of this new society. Bismarck realized that the young capitalism was needed in the power struggle of the new nationalism, and thus he pledged to the middle class the government's full support. The burgher, in return for the promise of protective tariffs, colonial expansion, and of assurance against the proletarian threat, surrendered his political birthrights to the feudal guarantors of "law and order." The German *Rechtstaat* indeed endeared itself to the middle class, which under the protection of law and order could grow rich and smug. This was a high price to pay. It meant the political abdication of a proud middle class and its degradation to an irresponsible bourgeoisie. The group now had no recourse except to go to "Father State" and ask for help—for colonial markets, for economic monopolies, for factory controls—without regard for the domestic (including the social) and the international consequences of these policies. It was only after the breakdown of the Second Empire that the serious effects of such a political surrender became evident.

Much of the last chapter of German conservatism, as reported by von Klemperer, was already foredoomed by the preceding decisions, which gave the movement its fatal turn. Thus the core movement at crucial moments of history shied away from seizing priceless opportunities and from recruiting new adherents for conservatism. The few in its camp who recognized the signs of the time remained officers without an army, prophets without a following, and finally a small cohort of courageous conspirators in a lost cause. To probe into the why of that failure would necessitate a comprehensive, comparative, and coherent analysis of this era of missed opportunities. It would be worth the trouble. The last act of a tragedy does not seem to leave much scope to its protagonists; they become marionettes of an inevitable finale.

Or do they really? History again and again allows breakthroughs for a courageous leadership and for a sound people cognizant of the full meaning of an experienced crisis. The Weimar Republic in the honeymoon of the armistice period, and more so during the high noon of the Stresemann era of reconstruction, and even as late as during the desperate doom of its waning evening, was open to such breakthroughs. It did not have to end with the Nazi fiasco. The von Klemperer study, seen in this dramatic sequence, might serve as a sobering reminder of history's many-dimensional design and thus as a much-needed corrective to the unilinear intellectual analysis, that simpleton's postscript to an experienced past.

That the story took the tragic turn of an "inevitable" Greek tragedy had much to do with the conservatives' misjudgment of times and tides. It is often not primarily the attacker's purpose and power but the defender's lack of foresight and forcefulness that decides the outcome of a revolution.

* * *

It is at this point that the von Klemperer analysis reaches out to explore the fundamental nature of the contemporary crisis and its great exploiter: modern totalitarianism. Even ten years after the demise of fascism and National Socialism, their meaning and menace have not yet been fully grasped. What the thoughtful observer, however, realizes is the fact that their real threat could not be met by the dictator's defeat on the battlefield or even by their ignoble end, but only by the clear recognition and the consequent destruction of all those elements of unrest which constitute the totalitarian states' mass basis and omnipresent appeal. Theirs is a never-ending threat, and it is most certainly not reserved to those nations which were once afflicted by the disease. "It is one of the Devil's wiles to make us believe he is Hitler," Denis de Rougemont rightly stated a decade ago. It is still true today. For wherever the contemporary crisis reaches the core of our existence—international, national, personal—the peril is present.

The neo-conservative spokesmen, passed in review in this

volume, were children of the crisis. They were indeed serious about it and in this sense can well serve as guides to burning problems of our time. Their tragedy was not merely that many of them were "second-rate thinkers" peddling a pseudo-conservatism of a "poor-man's Nietzsche," but that they understood neither the deeper roots nor the demonic dynamics of the revolution around them. They were caught therefore in its deluge. This had a great deal to do with the intellectuals' peculiar plight in this "land of poets and thinkers." The tragic historical split between *Macht* and *Geist* did not allow the proper emergence of the *homme de lettres* and of a responsible intelligentsia. Through crucial centuries separated from the vital stream of social forces and the center of policy decisions, they arrogantly and naïvely misjudged their own strength and the signs of the time. Eventually they entered a fatal "marriage of convenience" with the unprincipled powers of a "permanent revolution" which they meant to harness with the past mastery of venerable traditionalism. If they had read carefully Jakob Burckhardt, the prophetic Swiss sage of an earlier revolutionary era, they would have been forewarned against the coming terrible *"simplificateurs"* and against the fate of the weaker revolution, ruthlessly consumed in its clash with the stronger one. Because that was exactly what they were facing and where they were failing. Their romantic attachment to the past did not make them grasp the completely changed structure and strategy of a polyform upheaval in this age of several coexisting revolutions—national, cultural, political, and economic-social. These contemporary revolutions are interwoven and inextricably mixed in patterns and politics. Still, every era has its predominant type and the stronger revolution sets the style. The pathetic document *What We Expect of National Socialism*, written by a number of conservative intellectuals who on the eve of the National Socialist breakthrough manifested their hopes and aspirations in respect to the coming revolution, showed their utter lack of understanding of the revolutionary reality.

The Great Debate over neo-conservatism which is developing in this country should heed the dilemmas of these German conservatives and at the same time beware of easy transfers of altogether different traditions. There is about the land a genuine desire for a new orientation, caused not least by the national adoption and absorption of the New Deal philosophy. On this generally accepted new plateau both major parties are groping for a more adequate expression of the nation's next aspirations. This is a time for redefining basic ideological planks. Yet any attempts at wholesale importation of British or Continental "makes" will only lead to pseudo-revivals and outright false interpretations of Burke, Burckhardt, Max Weber—an injuring injustice to the old masters and an even more deceiving disservice to a serious spiritual awakening in this nation.

It is certainly too early to state here where this quest will find its fruitful articulation, what party its standard bearer will be, what definite forms it will take, and what pitfalls it must avoid if it is not to fall into the dilemmas of its confrères. Surely it will have to take into account the specific American climate, its basically liberal tradition, its present position, and its future aspirations. There is an abundant literature about an artificial reconstruction of the past, a literature creating a respectable array of ancestors and introducing a very strange intellectual lineage. If conservatism is to take hold in this country, it must be *sui generis*.

*　　*　　*

All this is only to say that conservatism like all meaningful social science concepts must be spelled out in time and space, both in the concept's specific historical situation and in its local representation. The neglect of this elementary truth has led to many misunderstandings and confusing confrontations. Thus budding beginners in the social science labyrinth may be disturbed by the obvious fact that liberal tenets of the mid-nineteenth century John Stuart Mill might well serve as conservative bases in a mid-twentieth century setting. Yesterday's liberal may well be today's conservative.

In fact, viewed in long-range historical perspective, contemporary antagonists may often appear much closer to each other in their competition over similar issues and for the same clientele than their ideological predecessors through the ages, confronted with altogether different programs and peoples.

This clear focusing of social science notions forewarns against any premature generalizations, if one does not want to blur their concrete character until they lose body and shape. Which does not prevent the inquisitive mind from seeking out yardsticks of over-all definitions. This, however, must be done in the full knowledge of their increasing remoteness from reality, the more ambitious they are in encompassing wider circles of acceptance in time and space. Such a caveat is especially in order in respect to ideological concepts, which by their very nature will have an even shorter wave length due to their double feature of being rational constructs and aims of political ambitions at the same time.

Von Klemperer is fully aware of this flexible, even ambiguous, nature of the phenomenon when he describes the author's double role as observer and participant and the subject matter's twin approach to the logic and politics of conservatism. And yet despite these obvious limitations, the search for archetypes of political ideologies remains the consistent and proud endeavor of systematic scholarship. The study of conservatism must be raised to this third level if it is to serve as a compass through the contemporary chaos of conceptual confusion. In this respect also the study opens valuable avenues for further pursuit.

Such a typology of prevailing ideas may never produce any conclusive and consistent philosophy but only relative concepts of human predispositions, yet it should be possible, and it has remained a perennial challenge, to conceive a catalog of basic attitudes toward human nature, social structure, and the historical process for whatever use may be derived from such basic categories.

The four major concepts of change, freedom, irrationalism, and pessimism, developed by the author, may serve as an ideal springboard for such a pointed analysis. This four-fold circumscription for one does away with the usual identification of conservatism with the reactionary view. It allows for a more realistic differentiation of the alive variations in action, liberty, human reason, and world outlook and reveals at the same time the common concern and common ground of diverse ideological camps in the Western society, which alone makes it possible for contesting contemporaries to live in the same world and to speak the same language.

The concrete confrontation of the prevailing ideologies thus draws a picture not simply in black and white but in shades of gray. Gradations of transition offer a lifeline which permits an eventual and indeed continuous confluence of these warring creeds.

Still, for an ideal typology one may start out with a bipolar position, which puts conservatism at the societal end and liberalism at the opposite, personal pole, the one regarding the group as the prime mover and the individual as a mere member of the greater whole, while the other sees in man the driving force, directive, and justification of state and society, making them solely functioning arms of his well-being.

From those divergent starting points flow some basically contrasting attitudes toward the purpose and plans of politics. The conservative will not only be suspicious of ambitious aims of quick transformations, but will also question their motives and motions, if they derive from individual schemes and abstract reasoning. He will see justification in action only if it is rooted in a traditional pattern making the present a portent bridge from the past to the future. Such an approach by necessity does not give high priority to change, and where it permits it, it calls for patience, perseverance, and a minimalization of individual initiative.

This is exactly the point from which the liberal launches his action. His trust in human ingenuity and capabilities is based on a belief in (what his opponent would denounce as arrogant usurpation of) man's mind; yet his confidence is paired with the liberal faith in all-persuasive reason, which will prevent an anarchy of individual wills and guarantee the flow of continuous progress toward universal perfectibility.

It was this power (or one might say religion) of rationalism which initiated the liberalism of the French Revolution and aroused its conservative counter. This remained the spiritual shibboleth in the following two centuries. It addressed itself to the fundamental nature of man and society whether it be rational or irrational.

From such presuppositions flow consequential attitudes toward governmental planning and individual training. While the conservative naturally places state and community high on his priority list, he will be hesitant in accepting far-reaching, man-made schemes that may destroy the slowly grown fiber of time-honored customs and groups. In this sense he may well become the staunch defender of the autonomy and variety of his historical institutions in a pluralistic society and even of the established freedoms of the individual himself.

The liberal, on the other hand, out of his trust in man's original intellect will assign to him the architect's master plans for a better morrow. In the pursuit of this breakthrough to a better world, he may even find the organized state the only reliable ally strong enough to pierce privileged positions and to prevent the seizure of *Lebensraum* by powerful individuals.

Thus, superficially at least, the roles of the traditional antagonists may be reversed as they so often are in our time—the liberal posing as the guardian of the strong protective state and the conservative as the last line of defense of individualism, engulfed by the forces of modern mechanized mass society.

Such confusion may be clarified if one measures man's worth in terms of the expectations of the individual's education. Its proud function in the conservative catechism consists in the preparation of an oncoming generation for the persistent responsibilities and disciplined controls of a fundamentally fixed order. This "contract with the past" demands a continuous rediscovery and renewal of traditional values, into which the living person has to be integrated. The liberal philosophy of education, by contrast, will emphasize the unlimited possibilities for the individual mind to extend the frontiers of the known world and, in his liberation from custom's chains, to find new avenues of progressive self-expression. Underneath these contrasting educational approaches may easily be detected fundamental divergences in philosophical outlook. The historical process, in the liberal view, presents itself as an assertion of the freedom of the individual and through him mankind's march toward perfecting progress. The life process, to the conservative, becomes a continuous unfolding and fulfillment of a predestined present (which is past and future at the same time) finding its full and sufficient meaning in vital existence itself. If such a conservatism is articulating a philosophy of history at all, it may be conceived as a cyclical pattern which defines the developmental process as a mere renewal of constants.

From such differing vantage points, the whole concept of man presents itself in contrasting contours. An essentially optimistic philosophy of liberalism will push forward even in the sight of recognized human and environmental difficulties (or may be heartened by these very hindrances) to a utopian's perfect state. The conservative, with a fundamentally pessimistic view of the nature of man—his "original sin," his eternal religious bounds, his temporary preconceived position—will naturally be cynical about the mortal's ability to make a new and better world and indeed will categorically reject such ambitious and unreal claims.

Even such cursory confrontation of absolute ideologies suggests that the reality of political fronts as presented by statesmen and social philosophers through the ages shows a much more interrelated image of convictions. Who is a conservative through and through? Who is such a liberal? The world beware of meeting the ideal types in the flesh!

It is one of the special qualities of the von Klemperer
analysis that while approaching the subject with the systematic fervor of a disciplined scholar it never loses sight of
reality's rich blendings. Maybe one reason for the successful
fulfillment of this difficult task is simply the fact that the
author, in his dual role as a participant-observer, is an ideal
student of his subject. Because if any field of our discipline
demands the seemingly impossible from its investigator—a
sense of subjective involvement, commitment, and ever-
present sympathetic understanding paralleled by an attitude
of aloof distance, cool comparison, and critical evaluation
from without—it is the history of ideas, especially if it en-
compasses the scholar's own intellectual world. It calls for
constant, concrete circumscription, and at the same time
for concise concepts. Yet its notions must be fluid and flexible and of a very life-quality. This is no easy assignment.
If it is well done, it is well worth recording.

PREFACE

THIS book is concerned with recent history through which, in part, I myself have lived. I have faced my task in a dual capacity, from within and from without, as one who is intellectually involved and as a scholar. But such is, in one way or another, the condition of every historian. If I have succeeded at all in doing justice to both senses of value, the human and the historical, I owe it to my teachers and friends. Professor William L. Langer of Harvard University has guided this work through its initial phases. I am indebted to Professors Sidney B. Fay of Harvard University, Hajo Holborn of Yale University, and Sigmund Neumann of Wesleyan University for the interest they have shown in my work and the help they have given me. Dr. Fritz T. Epstein of the Library of Congress was a never-exhausted source of advice and information. Through interview or correspondence I have obtained valuable information from Professor Heinrich Brüning, Dr. Georg Franz, Mr. Heinrich von Gleichen, Dr. Hildegard Kornhardt, Dr. Rudolf Pechel, Mr. Friedrich Vorwerk, and Mr. Hans Zehrer. The editors of the *Review of Politics* have permitted me to reprint the major part of an article which originally appeared in that journal. I owe thanks to Mrs. Donald Chrisman for giving me editorial help, Mrs. Michael S. Olmsted for typing the manuscript, and above all to my wife, Betty, for her constant encouragement and for always reminding me that good thinking is dependent on perfection of style and form.

1957

In this new edition of my book I should like to express my indebtedness to my long-standing friendship and scholarly companionship with Klaus Epstein. He has been abruptly taken away from us, but he will be long remembered.

1968

CONTENTS

CONTENTS

GERMANY'S NEW CONSERVATISM

Its History and Dilemma
in the Twentieth Century

INTRODUCTION

ONE of the most challenging difficulties which confront the historian of ideas is the fact that ideas are subject to varying interpretations and to change. Though he may like to think that the ideas with which he is dealing have an absolute, objective reality of their own, he finds that they are relative and, indeed, fragile. However exciting, however much calling for serious commitment, they have an elusive quality. And as the historian, in search of a given idea and its workings, moves his telescope, he finds that he holds a kaleidoscope with always-changing patterns. Ideas, then, which move men often to a point of sacrifice and which we like to think of as undying, are, after all, only kaleidoscopic formations and transitory flashes. They take on a new meaning everywhere and all the time.

The fundamental issue, the dilemma between what amounts to existence and non-existence of an idea, cannot be explained away. We cannot ignore the reality of experience which went in the early nineteenth century with such an idea as nationalism. Neither can we ignore the fact that there were, in fact, nationalisms evolving in different national and social settings and at different times. At best, then, the historian might distinguish between the content and form of an idea. Each idea has not only its "contents" (Cassirer) or "basic intention" (Mannheim), but also its "dynamics" (Cassirer). And we might well reconcile ourselves to a conflict between the two. The primary task of the historian of ideas is, after all, to follow up the working of an idea through time and space. His *métier* is the fallacy of men as well as of ideas, not theory but life, not logic but trial and error.

This book is a peculiar story of trial and error. It is a chapter in the history of an idea—conservatism—whose workings have not merely developed away from the original "basic intention" but have come in conflict with it. This, then, is the story of an extreme dilemma between the logic

3

of conservatism and the politics of conservatism, or, in other words, of conservatism against itself. Our test case will be Germany and our focus will be on the revival of conservative thinking in Germany since the end of the nineteenth century, a process which came to a climax in the years following the first World War. Rightly or wrongly historians have come to speak of a veritable "conservative revolution" in the twentieth century Germany. However spectacular this revival was, we cannot help going back to the beginnings of conservatism at the time of the French Revolution and comparing the problems of conservatism then and those of conservatism a century later. This comparison will give us the standards for measuring the intensity of the dilemma of conservatism and enable us to judge the true nature of the new twentieth century German conservatism.

One facet of the initial situation of conservatism may be anticipated here. Conservatism was originally formulated in the heat of the argument for and against the French Revolution. It was a "heart idea," stressing the irrational, as against the "head ideas" of the eighteenth century, stressing the rational. Nonetheless, conservatism was launched into an age, the nineteenth century—the "golden age of the bourgeoisie"[1]—in which many notions of the "arrogant" or, as de Maistre called it, "foolish"[2] eighteenth century had become common coinage. Nineteenth century society saw progress on all levels. It was the age which tried to translate the eighteenth century premise of reason—"one-eyed reason," as we are reminded by Whitehead[3]—into reality. In one way or other it became the executor of the French Revolution and was, so it seemed, well on the way toward solving its three main

[1] Thomas Mann, "The Years of My Life," *Harper's Magazine*, CCI (October 1950), 252.

[2] "Age of follies": Joseph de Maistre, *Essay on the Generative Principle of Political Constitutions* (Boston, 1847), 48.

[3] Alfred North Whitehead, *Science and the Modern World* (Pelican edn., New York, 1948), 60.

political tasks: popular representation, the nationality question, and the social problem. It witnessed vast strides in the fields of science and technology. No wonder, therefore, that part of its creed was the assumption that mankind was "over the hump," beyond barbarism and catastrophe, that man could achieve mastery over nature.

Most of the nineteenth century political thought was subject to such notions. They were shared not only by the liberals, who, after all, were the avowed disciples of the eighteenth century *philosophes;* conservative thinking was also affected by them. Even conservatives like Hegel and Ranke, while they carefully qualified the idea of progress—they called it "evolution"—were part of the climate of optimism. Indeed, liberals and conservatives were, if not brothers, cousins. They were related to each other by a spirit of gentlemen's agreement. Neither liberalism nor conservatism was what de Tocqueville called an "absolutist system."[4] Neither had an orthodoxy of its own. While liberalism was not altogether the party of change and freedom, conservatism was not altogether the party of reaction and despotism. Both were dedicated to the causes of change and freedom. They represented but different approaches to these problems. They were tentative attitudes which complemented, influenced, and tolerated each other. It was precisely this sense of tolerance—or call it irony—which was the social cement of the nineteenth century. It saved liberalism from sheer utopianism, and conservatism from the extreme of fierce reaction. It enabled conservatism to rejuvenate itself.

But long before the first catastrophe of our century, the first World War, smote the theories of progress, dissenters made themselves heard, men who turned altogether against their own times. To them the nineteenth century, precisely due to its sense of irony, lacked depth. Dostoevsky called it "characterless" and he wrote about "our unhappy

[4] Alexis de Tocqueville, *Recollections* (ed. J. P. Mayer, London, 1948), 68.

nineteenth century." It appeared as a this-worldly conspiracy which tended to forget the reality of the invisible
and irrational. It tended to overlook man's primitive past
as well as to dispense with religion. It emancipated man
but left him uprooted. From his "sulking corner" in Basle
the great Jakob Burckhardt turned against the easy optimism of his age. The over-all philosophic attack against the
"decadence" of the century came from Friedrich Nietzsche.
Both Burckhardt and Nietzsche were watching with particular concern the developments in Imperial Germany,
where the so-called *Gründerjahre* (founders' years) produced a mood of economic and political materialism in
which ideas and ideals receded before the lure of success
and power.

It was finally the generation of Freud and Pareto whose
thought called for a final disengagement from the "Vic-
torian compromise." They challenged progress altogether.
Pushing forward the frontiers of knowledge they emerged
with an honestly and irrevocably pessimistic view of human
nature. At last the findings of "science" and the eighteenth
century ideals were openly in conflict. The study of psychology and of the social sciences came to shock a world
which had seemed so plainly geared for a rule of reason
and for always more popular government, with the findings
that man is irrational and that society is essentially static
and controlled by tradition and myth. Progress, Georges
Sorel summed up bluntly, was but an illusion.

The reaction against the climate of optimism in the
nineteenth century became a dominant note of the twentieth century intellectual and political scene. Men like
Burckhardt and Nietzsche established a distinct precedent
for the twentieth century revulsion against the so-called
"bourgeois" values. While Marx's protest led into the various Leftist protest movements of our day, from the re-
formist social democracy to communism, and while Kierkegaard led into contemporary theological existentialism, the
tradition emanating from Burckhardt and Nietzsche found

its way into an anti-rationalist movement which was particularly strong in Germany. The last movement is the subject of this study. It was essentially conservative in its rejection of rationalism and liberalism, in its rediscovery of the irrational, and in its search, however vague, for faith and tradition. It constituted an articulate Rightist protest against an age of secularization, against the bourgeois world.

However, in Germany, the always "protesting Germany," where rationalism never really had found a secure home, such a position had dangers. A critique of rationalism threatened to lead into a wholesale negation of reason, of the mind, as an alien "Western" importation. A critique of the nineteenth century threatened to lead into complete rejection. Might not the hostility to the predominant features of the century hide a tiredness with civilization as a whole? The new conservatism moved into close proximity to a nihilism which threatened to do away with our cultural traditions as such. Specifically, in rejecting the nineteenth century tradition, it jeopardized the heritage of freedom. It suggested a conservatism no more concerned with the problem of freedom. The new conservatism was clearly heading into a dilemma between conserving and destroying, between a positive attitude toward our civilization and nihilism.

The social changes in Germany since the end of the century helped only to deepen the dilemma. The workings of industrialization produced the mass man, who became alienated from society. Defeat, revolution, and inflation marked the crumbling of old institutions—of monarchy and aristocracy—and the gradual weakening of the authority of the organized churches and the family. The blessing of emancipation and secularization had turned into the curse of proletarization, and, alas, the middle classes themselves fell victim to this process. The little man was faced with the "what-now" situation. All too late it became clear that man could not and did not want to live in isolation and that man could not do without loyalties and needed to be reintegrated with society. But could the old loyalties be recreated? It was Disraeli who had warned of the effects of the destruction of the "traditionary influences" and who foresaw the revenge which "outraged tradition" would take.[5] The first half of the twentieth century in Germany has proven to be the period of "outraged tradition." And where would the quest for ties on the part of the new mass man lead to? Would he acknowledge the heritage of freedom which had been a vital part of nineteenth century conservatism? Or would he dispense with it? Jakob Burckhardt predicted the coming of an age of lawless despotism. "What we see before us is a general levelling down, and we might declare the rise of great individuals an impossibility if our prophetic souls did not warn us that . . . the 'right man' may appear overnight—and all the world will follow in his train."[6] And to his friend Friedrich von Preen he confided his premonitions of "the *terribles simplificateurs* who will come over our old Europe."[7] While the "disorganizing principles,"[8] as Nietzsche put it, of the nineteenth century thus were clearly evident, there was all the more need for a revival of tradition and authority— in brief, for a new conservatism. But the great question remained whether any restated principles of conservatism could compete for the ear of the masses with the blast of the new leaders. Was conservative thought flexible enough to revitalize the old allegiances or to create new ones in their place? All the above questions suggest the depth of

[5] William F. Monypenny and George E. Buckle, *The Life of Benjamin Disraeli* (New York, 1914), III, 181, quoted in Peter Viereck, *Conservatism Revisited* (New York, London, 1949) , 128.

[6] Jakob Burckhardt, *Force and Freedom: Reflections on History* (ed. James Hastings Nichols, New York, 1943), 345.

[7] Letter of Burckhardt to Preen, July 24, 1889, Jakob Burckhardt, *Briefe an seinen Freund Friedrich von Preen, 1864-1893* (Stuttgart, Berlin, 1922), 248.

[8] Friedrich Nietzsche, "The Will to Power," *The Complete Works of Friedrich Nietzsche* (ed. Oscar Levy, 2nd edn., New York, London, 1910), XIV, 60.

the dilemma of the conservative in twentieth century Germany.

Early in the year 1927 the Austrian poet Hugo von Hofmannsthal, in his now famous address to the students of the University of Munich, called attention to the new conservatism in twentieth century Germany by referring to what he called the "conservative revolution."[9] In a discussion of letters as the "spiritual voice of the nation," Hofmannsthal pointed to a crisis of the German mind. Alluding to the well-known separation in German society between the intellectual and the political sphere, of "mind" and "life," he deplored that German writing, in the past, had functioned in a vacuum. It was "not truly representative or establishing a tradition."[10] It was symptomatic of a crisis of a civilization which had lost its contacts with life. In turn, Hofmannsthal talked about the "legion of seekers" throughout the country who were striving for the reestablishment of faith and tradition and whose aim was not freedom but "allegiance." And he concluded thus: "The process of which I am speaking is nothing less than a conservative revolution on such a scale as the history of Europe has never known. Its object is form, a new German reality, in which the whole nation will share."[11]

The whole speech was something like a twentieth century romantic manifesto, a restatement of Novalis's *Die Christenheit oder Europa,* which in its day had been one of the finest and most spontaneous apologies for the conservative position. One was reminded of Dostoevsky's fiercer and more alarming surrender to "miracle, mystery, and authority." Actually Hofmannsthal as an observer of the German scene of his day spoke on good evidence. There was the Youth Movement, adolescent and vague, but sincere in its longing for new spiritual and social forms, a

[9] Hugo von Hofmannsthal, *Das Schrifttum als geistiger Raum der Nation* (Munich, 1927).
[10] *Ibid.,* 16.   [11] *Ibid.,* 31.

factor in German life since the early years of the century which no man of Hofmannsthal's sensitivity could ignore. There were many self-searching interpretations of Germany's role during the first World War which pointed toward a new concern with the problem of conservatism. The war may have dealt a death blow to the monarchy throughout Central Europe, but from the ashes of the old conservatism rose the phoenix of a new one. There were the founding fathers of the Republic, men like Max Weber, to whom the survival of the new state was dependent on its being conservative. And, finally, there were the innumerable popular political philosophers and prophets of the type of Moeller van den Bruck, Spengler, and Ernst Jünger who, increasingly critical of the Republic and what it stood for, formed their political clubs, circles, movements, and fraternal organizations *(Bünde)* on the periphery of political life. Skilled pamphleteers, they swamped the periodical market with their semi-political, semi-philosophic, semi-religious, often close to apocalyptic jargon, and they found access to the "respectable" public. They became self-styled heralds of a new revolution which came to be commonly referred to in Germany as the "conservative revolution," the "revolution from the right," or the "national revolution."

Ever since Hofmannsthal's address historians have gone to work on the new conservatism in Germany. Except for an early cautious and thoughtful interpretation by Waldemar Gurian,[12] most approaches to the problem have been either of an accusing or of an apologetic nature. In the first category are the stimulating studies by Aurel Kolnai, Edmond Vermeil, and Friedrich Hayek.[13] These authors

[12] Walter Gerhart (pseud. for Waldemar Gurian), *Um des Reiches Zukunft. Nationale Wiedergeburt oder politische Reaktion?* (Freiburg, Br., 1932).

[13] Aurel Kolnai, *The War against the West* (New York, 1938); Edmond Vermeil, *Doctrinaires de la Révolution Allemande 1918-1938* (Paris, 1938); Friedrich A. Hayek, *The Road to Serfdom* (4th edn., Chicago, 1945), 167-180.

have a tendency to throw the new conservatives together with Nazism. The new conservatives were, in short, the "doctrinaires" of the Nazi revolution.[14] In the second category are the works by authors who, like Hermann Rauschning and Armin Mohler,[15] were and are themselves deeply involved in the new conservatism. More directly inspired by Hofmannsthal's address than the other group, they emerge with a rigid differentiation between the "conservative revolution" and the Nazi revolution, the "revolution of nihilism."[16] According to them conservatism is a well-defined view of life designed to make the Western world conscious of its traditions and to equip it with purpose in its fight against fascism and, for that matter, communism.

If this study goes its own way, it is not for the purpose of seeking a middle ground and not for fear of commitment. My primary difference with both the above groups lies in the field of method. Both have prejudged their case in terms of their fundamental assessment of the German conservative tradition. The history of conservatism is to them the history of an idea with which they agree or disagree. Handed down from one thinker to another, it is

[14] Indicative of the widespread acceptance, in particular outside Germany, of this viewpoint is E. H. Carr's recent reference to Moeller van den Bruck as "the intellectual of the Nazi movement" and to the June Club magazine *Gewissen* as a "National Socialist journal"; Edward Hallett Carr, *The Interregnum, 1923-1924* (New York, 1954), 181, 177.

[15] Hermann Rauschning, *The Revolution of Nihilism. Warning to the West* (New York, 1939) and *The Conservative Revolution* (New York, 1941); Armin Mohler, *Die Konservative Revolution in Deutschland 1918-1932. Grundriss ihrer Weltanschauungen* (Stuttgart, 1950). Cf. also Walter Görlitz, "Die konservative Revolution," *Sonntagsblatt* (Hamburg), No. 9 (February 28, 1954).

[16] It is interesting that evidently Hofmannsthal himself was unconcerned with the possibility that his speech might have been interpreted as encouragement to the Nazis. Referring to the speech, Thomas Mann wrote in a letter dated December 4, 1946 to the late Professor Karl Viëtor of Harvard: "I remember well that when Hofmannsthal's speech appeared, I warned him in a conversation of the impending threat, to which he to some extent had thus given support. With some uneasiness he passed over the subject."

to them a sovereign idea, so to speak, with its own definite impact upon society. In reality, as we have seen, the history of as complex a phenomenon as conservatism has to be sought in the changing context of society. For better or worse there is neither a paved "road to serfdom" nor a self-acting "conservative revolution." While conservatism has its "basic intention" it also has its "dynamism." This study sets out to explore the conflict between both, or, in other words, the gap between the logic of conservatism and its politics.

My focus on the new conservatism is merely the focus on what seems to me the best test case for the dilemma of conservatism.[17] Though a study of the old-fashioned German black-white-red conservatism as represented politically in the Republic by the German Nationals of the German National People's Party (D.N.V.P.) naturally would have had some bearing on our problem, it would have yielded only the predictable negative result that the turning back of the wheel of history is never a solution for any political and social problem. The D.N.V.P. with its reactionary social policy and its Hohenzollern attachments never stood a chance of capturing the imagination of the Germans. This book is the story of those in twentieth century Germany who, in particular after the days of the first World War, were faced with the "uprootedness" of their people. They were the people who saw that the new Republic needed not only more popular government but also more roots, more allegiances. In their opposition to rationalism they may well have been motivated by the "loftiest tenets of culture."[18] We shall see that initially their attitude toward the Weimar Republic was a positive one. In the light of this fact historians of the Weimar Republic

[17] From the innumerable representatives of the new conservatism—be they individuals or groups—I have selected representative examples to demonstrate the problem of the dilemma of conservatism. For an exhaustive listing see Mohler, *Die konservative Revolution*.

[18] Mann, "The Years of My Life," *Harper's Magazine*, 258.

might revise their verdict on its weaknesses and on the causes of its decline. Whether or not the Republic was liberal enough or socialistic enough, it is suggested here that it was not conservative enough.

However, the process of alienation from the Republic brought out the worst in the conservative position. Did a Moeller van den Bruck still consider himself committed to the conservative heritage of freedom? By appealing to the masses, to "youth," by slandering the "nineteenth century," "reason," the "West," did not the neo-conservatives sacrifice their principles to mere *élan* and, thereby, surrender to National Socialism?

In tracing the problems of conservatism in modern German society this book seeks to throw light, however indirectly, on the society itself. The dilemma of conservatism, it is suggested here, is a symptom of crisis not merely of conservatism but also of any middle-of-the-road position. Probing the dilemma may help explain from the angle of conservatism how and why the "vital center" of our civilization is threatened. Ultimately this book tries to disentangle one paradox: Why is it that in the twentieth century the German-speaking world produced some of the most penetrating diagnoses of the illnesses of our civilization, and, at the same time, gave birth to the most devastating movement to end all civilization? We assume that these two phenomena are interrelated.

PART I

THE NINETEENTH CENTURY
BACKGROUND

CHAPTER I

TOWARD A DEFINITION
OF CONSERVATISM

No Orthodoxy

NO GREAT conservative of the past has left us a definition of conservatism. There have been types of conservatism, but no schools of conservatism; there are expressions of conservatism, but there is no theory of conservatism. Going back to its origins in the nineteenth century, we find signs of conservatism in the most diverse quarters. There were, of course, the "classics" of conservatism. But instead of constituting a united front, their authors reflected a wide variety of views, depending on the generation to which they belonged, on their religious affiliations, on their national backgrounds, or on other factors. One might say that most of the early conservatives were still sufficiently rooted in the medieval Thomistic tradition to agree on a general law of nature applicable to all men; but then Ranke and Savigny introduced the conflicting notion of history as a factor of conservative policy. While de Maistre, the Savoyard, and Karl Ludwig Haller, the Swiss, were among the most rigorous defenders of the old order, and while they were eminently influential, they were actively opposed within their own camp. The infallibility of de Maistre's Catholicism was bound to be challenged by Protestant conservatives. And even the great Metternich, chancellor of the strongest Catholic power in Europe, came to blows with de Maistre, who never forgave him for allowing the Congress of Vienna to violate the principle of legitimacy. In turn, Haller's theories of private property as the basis of power soon appeared archaic in the century in which the state was to play such an important role; they were squarely opposed by most of the Prussian thinkers, for whom the state was coming to be considered the source of power. And then there was Edmund Burke, the least theoretical of the conservatives. Trained in the country of Locke and of Hume, this great mind was turned primarily on practical issues: there was nothing academic about it.[1] Taking "sound, well-understood principles" for granted, Burke always reinforced his advice with the urgency of a particular situation—such as the issue of the taxation of the American colonies, or that of the French Revolution— and with the persuasiveness of his oratory. The empiricist Burke became at last the most influential conservative on the Continent as well as in England.

All these expressions of conservatism were but signs of an attitude which in one form or another was evident in almost all social strata throughout Europe. There were men deeply committed in the struggle against the French Revolution—the émigrés, like de Maistre himself, whose lives had been most directly affected by the events since 1789. They represented, as we now know, a fair section of the French population, that is, all three estates.[2] But there were also virtually millions who had no axe to grind, yet whose lives, once the storm of revolution and war had subsided, fell back into their customary quiet. This happened particularly in the small German principalities, where the prince once more commanded the loyalty of his people, high and low. One might also look into the ranks of the lower French provincial aristocracy as represented by Stendhal's M. Rênal, the mayor of Verrières, who identified the prosperity of his town with "the King's interests, those of the Monarchy and above all those of our holy religion."[3] For the mayor and his kind conservatism was simply a form of respectability. In a stranger way, conservatism owed some of its strength to many disenchanted revolutionaries,

[1] Cf. Metternich as a "professor" in Peter Viereck, *Conservatism Revisited*, 4.

[2] Cf. Donald Greer, *The Incidence of the Emigration during the French Revolution* (Cambridge, Mass., 1951).

[3] Marie-Henri Beyle (de Stendhal), *The Red and the Black* (Modern Library edn., New York, 1926), 129.

ranging from the always irresponsible romanticists to Balzac's tragic Père Goriot, the one-time profiteer from the Revolution who became the selfless champion of the family and fatherhood. A random sampling of conservative types might even include Goncharov's Oblomov, the Russian country squire whose loyalty to his backward world was part and parcel of his indolence.

Conservatism, then, was anything from high-minded inspiration to frustrated revolution, from religious revivalism to Babbitry and inertia. But in the last analysis it was formed and held together by attitudes which had stemmed from the French Revolution and then turned against it. Except perhaps in England conservatism was, like liberalism, a child of the French Revolution. There had been no conservatism in the Ancien Régime. The latter, though it had had its theoretical foundations—such as the divine right theories of Bishop Bossuet—needed no apology. The Ancien Régime took itself for granted and did not have to justify itself before men. It was largely the Revolution which spurred men to take sides—for and against—and which in turn challenged its enemies to reassess the values of the old order. For only through the French Revolution did conservatism become conscious of itself and royalism become conservatism. One might say that conservatism was sophisticated royalism.

The Ancien Régime, then, had been merely the prehistory of conservatism. While the former was identified with institutions like monarchy and aristocracy, conservatism, as the expression of a new generation, was not committed to them. The conservative principles were, so Metternich assured Guizot, "applicable to the most diverse situations."[4] Indeed the conservative might join the liberal, as Taine did, in criticizing the political ills of the Ancien Régime. And Burke wrote: "I believe, no creature now

[4] Letter of Metternich to Guizot, Vienna, June 15, 1847; Metternich, *Mémoires* (Paris, 1883), VII, 402, quoted in Viereck, *Conservatism Revisited*, 3.

maintains 'that the crown is held by divine, hereditary and indefeasible right.' "[5] There was no denying that the Revolution had set things in motion; there was no escape from its basic impact on the climate of Europe. Even de Maistre accepted the Revolution, much as a Christian accepts the fall of man. Thus he could argue that the Revolution but proved the presence of God: it was a grand and collective atonement of mankind for its sins.

The conservative criticism of the Revolution was directed fundamentally against the "presumption" of modern man, as Metternich put it,[6] who thought that he could remake the world in his own image. The course of the Revolution seemed to have shown that not even the glamorous new theories of liberty were immune to being turned into tyranny; moreover, in the eyes of the conservative, they had been proven fallacious. For the conservative saw that no man-made blueprint could redress the ills of this world, and that no policy could lead to Utopia. The new experience was thus mainly a religious one, an acceptance of a higher order. Conservatism became a philosophy of acceptance. The conservative learned the hard way that man must live, as Burke wrote, "in a just correspondence and symmetry with the order of the world."[7] Instead of creating a new order, he aimed at discovering the order already inherent in things. This faith in the firmness of the created order was the common ground of all conservatives.

It appears, then, that although conservatism had no orthodoxy of its own, all expressions of conservatism derived from the acceptance of a created order. For the conservative this was a basic assumption, just as faith in reason and man was a basic one for the liberal. In short, conservatism had its logic. This we shall analyze by discussing the four central attributes of conservatism: the

[5] Edmund Burke, *Reflections on the Revolution in France, Works* (5th edn., Boston, 1877) , III, 265.

[6] Metternich, *Profession de Foi Politique, Mémoires* (Paris, 1881), III, 430.

[7] Burke, *Reflections, Works*, III, 275.

concept of change, the concept of freedom, irrationalism, and pessimism. Such an analysis will not help us reconstruct the perfect conservative—for he has never existed—but it should help us to understand the general set of values inherent in the conservative point of view and, especially, to measure the distance between it and the fascist position.

The Logic of Conservatism

A. THE CONSERVATIVE CONCEPT OF CHANGE

No major "revision" of history is needed to correct the old-fashioned Whig historian's view that conservatism entails dire reaction and oppression. The last thirty years have yielded a number of impressive historical studies vindicating the achievement of nineteenth century conservative statesmanship and thought. We have become better judges of the nineteenth century. We now realize that the argument between Right and Left has been a productive one. While Ranke, the conservative, saw liberalism as a "ferment of life,"[8] John Stuart Mill, the radical, reiterated the "commonplace" that "a party of order or stability and a party of progress are both necessarily elements of a healthy state of political life."[9] The nineteenth century parliament was the clearest expression of the unity of assumptions and interests that underlay an obvious diversity.[10]

Change was one of the assumptions shared by conservative and liberal alike. In this connection Lord Eldon, the leader of the Ultra-Tories, was an oddity even among the

[8] Leopold von Ranke, *Neue Briefe* (ed. Hans Herzfeld, Hamburg, 1949), 445.
[9] John Stuart Mill, *On Liberty* (ed. Alburey Castell, New York, 1947), 47.
[10] In his *Table Talk* Samuel Taylor Coleridge, holding forth on the "Ideal Tory and Whig," said that "they both agreed in the ultimate preservation of the balance [of the three estates]; and accordingly they might each, under certain circumstances, without the slightest inconsistency pass from one side to the other, as the ultimate object required it." Samuel Taylor Coleridge, *Table Talk* (London, 1835), 143f.

conservatives. Coming from him, the saying that man is a "creature of habit" was an understatement,[11] for he was opposed on principle to all innovation. In this connection, moreover, the controversial and perhaps too much revisited Metternich must be tentatively relegated, along with Eldon, to a special category of "reactionaries."[12] It has been rightly pointed out that the role which his system assigned to Austria did not conform to the actual resources of the Empire.[13] Metternich was one of the fiercest and most tragic opponents of the *Zeitgeist* and all its aspects. But it should be said in defense of the Eldons and Metternichs that they never had to resort to such desperately "reactionary" thoughts as Mirabeau, whose dying words de Maistre quoted with fitting malice. Had he lived longer, sighed Mirabeau, he would have pieced the fragments of the old monarchy together again.[14] Here the noted revolutionary was the greatest of all "reactionaries."

In his attitude toward change, we find that the conservative temperamentally prefers the known to the unknown. He may look backward rather than forward. He may also, with Metternich, instinctively "detest every change of the year."[15] It is in the past that he finds the context by which

[11] Cf. the amusing essay, John Clive, "Lord Eldon Revisited," *Partisan Review*, xvi (December 1949), 1255ff.

[12] Metternich once wrote: "I was born into an unfortunate age. I was born either too early or too late; now I feel good for nothing. Earlier I would have enjoyed my days, later I would have helped to reconstruct. Now I am spending my life supporting the decaying edifices. I should have been born in the year 1900 with the twentieth century ahead of me." Quoted in Franz Schnabel, *Deutsche Geschichte im Neunzehnten Jahrhundert* (2nd edn., Freiburg, 1949), ii, 64. Peter Viereck in *Conservatism Revisited* vindicates his hero Metternich too exclusively in the light of our twentieth century experience. There still remains Metternich the eighteenth century man dedicated to the old Europe, a backward-looking and ultimately tragic statesman.

[13] Franz Schnabel, *Deutsche Geschichte*, ii, 60f.

[14] Joseph de Maistre, *Considérations sur la France* (Lyon, Paris, 1855), 8.

[15] Quoted in Heinrich von Srbik, *Metternich. Der Staatsmann und der Mensch* (Munich, 1925), i, 272.

the course of change is to be charted. This may seem paradoxical. But some measure of retrospection in no way contradicts a positive attitude toward change. As Whitehead remarked, "mere change without conservation is a passage from nothing to nothing."[16] In other words, if there is no firm standard by which change can be measured, there may be flux, but there is logically no change. To the conservative, therefore, the problem of change demands an awareness of the past, and "conservation and correction"[17] are twin principles. If, then, the conservative was opposed to revolutions, he was not necessarily opposed to change. When Burke emphasized the "dislike"[18] he felt for revolutions, he was referring to the French Revolution. At the same time he defended the Glorious Revolution, "the Revolution which we revere."[19] Burke, of course, would have rejected sudden change, for the conservative preferred evolution to revolution. More fundamentally, Burke wanted England to maintain its old laws and institutions. It was James II who had broken these laws; and the Glorious Revolution stood for the "true principles"[20] as expressed in the Declaration of Right. The French Revolution, on the other hand, wrought change without precedent, "stripped of every relation, in all the nakedness and solitude of metaphysical abstraction."[21]

The conservative reacted to written constitutions and codifications much as he reacted to revolutions. While Carl Friedrich von Savigny opposed a codification of the German law and while Frederick William IV in a dramatic gesture rejected in 1849 the new Frankfurt constitution as a "shred of paper," they did not condemn change as such. For conservatives, law was something found and not made. To them unwritten law was the real living constitution of the land,[22] more basic than the written law: a mode of

16 Whitehead, *Science and the Modern World,* 201.
17 Burke, *Reflections, Works,* III, 259.   18 *Ibid.,* 264.
19 *Ibid.,* 252.   20 *Ibid.,* 252.   21 *Ibid.,* 240.
22 "The constitution is the work of circumstances"; de Maistre, *Essay on the Generative Principle,* 46.

behavior, a code of rules which were generally understood. They distrusted written guarantees as a priori impositions stifling organic growth. It seemed a risky thing, to say the least, to entrust a country's destinies to the will of a lawmaker. Organic growth and tradition thus appeared as a protection against arbitrary rule, against the Robespierres and Napoleons, as well as against tyrants to come.

B. THE CONSERVATIVE CONCEPT OF FREEDOM

Corresponding to the nineteenth century conservative's concept of change was his concept of freedom. The conservative position was not, as has been too often assumed, a denial of freedom, but rather a redefinition of freedom in the light of the revolutionary events. The nineteenth century conservative was as much concerned with freedom as was the liberal; the two differed merely in their interpretations. "Of all the loose terms in the world," Burke wrote to a French acquaintance of his, "liberty is the most indefinite."[23]

According to the conservative, freedom, like change, must be understood within a context. There is no such thing as abstract, undefined freedom. Moreover, for the conservative, freedom requires a basic measure of authority. Quite clearly freedom is not anarchy. Once more the conservative position seems paradoxical, because man, whose actions are determined by authority, or the past, does not seem free to act. But this proposition must be tested in the workings of society. Does not every free society devise rules to prevent its members from encroaching upon each other's freedom? And presumably all men are subject to these rules. With great eloquence Burke turned against the "liberty in the abstract" brought about by the French Revolution: "Abstractedly speaking, government, as well as liberty, is good; yet could I, in common sense, ten years ago have felicitated France on her enjoyment of a govern-

[23] Letter of the Burke to M. Dupont, October, 1789; Edmund Burke, *Correspondence* (London, 1844), III, 106.

ment . . . without inquiry what the nature of that government was, or how it was administered? Can I now congratulate the same nation upon its freedom? Is it because liberty in the abstract may be classed among the blessings of mankind that I am seriously to felicitate a madman who has escaped from the protecting restraint and wholesome darkness of his cell on his restoration to the enjoyment of light and liberty? Am I to congratulate a highwayman and murderer who has broken prison upon the recovery of his natural rights?"[24] Eighteenth and nineteenth century conservatives thus saw freedom within the context of society. It was freedom according to the laws of the countries; it was "social freedom."[25]

Furthermore, these conservatives argued that the French Revolution in the name of abstract freedom left France with a rigidly centralized and powerful state. The ideas of 1789 produced an easy opening for tyranny by imposing a general norm on established rights and customs, and sacrificed the old liberties to a liberty which struck conservatives as a meaningless "philosophic theory."[26] Haller was not a hypocrite in claiming to be an apostle of freedom. In his eyes the all-inclusive prerogatives of the modern state constituted a real danger. The state interfered with society, which was based on private relationships, and force threatened to take the place of "love," "good will,"[27] and spontaneous growth. De Maistre, too, had a good case against the state which claimed the whole life and thought of its citizens. He emphasized the autonomy of religion and in particular the rights of the Church. The spiritual liberties of the citizen, he said, transcended the political authority of the state. Therefore de Maistre could call the

[24] Burke, *Reflections, Works,* III, 240f.
[25] Letter to M. Dupont, Burke, *Correspondence,* III, 106.
[26] Carl Ludwig Haller, *Restauration der Staatswissenschaft oder Theorie des natürlich-geselligen Zustandes der Chimäre des künstlich-bürgerlichen entgegengesetzt* (2nd edn., Winterthur, 1820-1825), I, xii.
[27] *Ibid.,* I, xxii.

popes the "natural protectors of civil freedom" and "enemies of despotism."[28] Like Haller, he sought a practical approach to freedom. At any rate, they both made a good case for freedom by defending diversity against the encroachments of a leveling state.

Their positive attitude toward freedom placed the early conservatives uncomfortably between, as they often expressed it, the Scylla of absolutism and the Charybdis of constitutionalism.[29] On one hand it meant a vigilant criticism of the absolutism of the Ancien Régime. In rejecting absolutism the conservative was the ally of the liberal[30]— a fact which the historian might do well to recall. On the other hand the conservative found himself in opposition to the liberal—and often in a working alliance with absolutism—when it came to facing the dangers of revolution. But in both situations the conservative acted as guardian of freedom as he understood it. On this score he differed more with the reactionary, who sought refuge in the past for its own sake, than with the liberal. Between the conservative and the liberal the difference was one of semantics: for one, freedom was essentially a concrete task; for the other, an abstract ideal. As a consequence the conservative excelled as the administrator of liberty, and the liberal as its advocate. And ultimately the interaction of both accounts for the history of liberty in the nineteenth century.

C. IRRATIONALISM

Conservatism is often likened to fascism because both appear as part of the great "revolt against the revolt" and

[28] Joseph de Maistre, *Du Pape* (8th edn., Lyon, 1849), 482.

[29] Haller, *Restauration*, I, lvi; Ernst Ludwig von Gerlach, *Aufzeichnungen aus seinem Leben und Wirken 1795-1877* (ed. Jakob von Gerlach, Schwerin in Meckl., 1903), II, 104.

[30] Cf. on this subject the excellent contribution by Alfred von Martin, "Weltanschauliche Motive im altkonservativen Denken," *Deutscher Staat und deutsche Parteien. Beiträge zur deutschen Partei- und Ideengeschichte. Friedrich Meinecke zum 60. Geburtstag dargebracht* (Munich, Berlin, 1922), 342ff.

in particular as reactions against the theoretical nature of the ideas which originated with the Enlightenment and which found their expression in nineteenth century liberalism. Unlike the liberal, whose thought was abstract, the thought of the conservative and the fascist tended to be concrete. While the liberal conceived of man and society as they ought to be, static, ascertainable, and as proper objects of rational inquiry, the conservative and fascist approached man and society as they are, subjective, mysterious, dynamic, and, in the last analysis, defying rational definition. In this both the conservative and the fascist can trace their lineage back to romanticism. Both conservatism and fascism are forms of irrationalism. In the warfare between "reason" and "life" they side with the latter. "Life" was once described as a "conservative" idea:[31] undoubtedly it is a fascist idea also. Irrationalism, however, covers a multitude of sins. Edmund Burke's attack on the tedious "metaphysical distinctions" that Lord North's government brought to bear on the American question[32] was irrational, as was the Nazi policy of "blood and soil." But while the conservative distaste for reason and theory had a variety of motives—love of tradition, an awareness of the complexity of life, and, plainly, fear of God—the fascist's self-advertised "indifference toward all theories"[33] amounted to an *élan* unguided by principles. Fascism was an extreme form of anti-intellectualism, mere intuition translated into violent action. In effect, then, a closer inquiry into the irrationalist premises of conservatism and fascism points toward the fundamental difference between the two positions. In Germany's critical time, just before 1933, this difference was clearly understood by one of the most penetrating observers of the scene—Ernst

[31] Thomas Mann, *Betrachtungen eines Unpolitischen* (15th-18th edn., Berlin, 1920) , 608.

[32] Edmund Burke, *Speech on American Taxation, Works*, II, 73.

[33] For a discussion of this subject cf. Franz Neumann, *Behemoth, The Structure and Practice of National Socialism 1933-1944* (Toronto, New York, London, 1944), 462ff.

Robert Curtius—who called irrationalism a "double-edged weapon" standing for what is higher than reason and theory as well as lower. In Germany the question was precisely whether irrationalism was to take one form or the other, the form of tradition or the form of "revolutionary chaos."[34]

D. PESSIMISM

It has also been said that conservatism and fascism have in common a pessimistic view of human nature.[35] In this respect also they are both at variance with liberalism. The liberal position is built on the assumption of the supremacy of man, who is endowed with reason and, therefore, in a position to lift himself above the past. The liberal explained the sufferings and inconsistencies on this earth in terms of ignorance and superstition, which can be overcome by education. The liberal believed in progress. Looking on liberalism from the perspective of this dark century we become aware of the sweeping assumptions which underlie the liberal's optimism. He had a firm faith in a better future. His Utopia was on this earth. On the other hand, both the conservative and the fascist tended to be realistic. They argued that the liberal mistook what man should be for what he is, that he made of him an "artificial creature"[36] and confounded ethics with psychology, ethics with politics. In fact, they regarded the liberal as an unbearable and boring moralizer. The conservative shared with the fascist a more or less negative view of man. According to this view, man is neither rational nor supreme, and his history is the history of suffering rather than action. And in one way or another, religiously or mystically, the debunkers of the Enlightenment would subject man's fate to a larger plan— to God, or to some anonymous "wave of the future." From

[34] Ernst Robert Curtius, *Deutscher Geist in Gefahr* (Stuttgart, Berlin, 1932), 20f.

[35] Cf. Franz Neumann, *Behemoth*, 460f.

[36] Edmund Burke, *A Letter to a Member of the National Assembly, Works*, IV, 28.

his exile in Russia the most misanthropic of all conservatives, de Maistre, could thus witness the French Revolution
with an air of superiority. Even at this moment of extreme
action men were but "simple instruments."[37] The Revolution was but a punishment imposed by God. Man was
an "instrument of God." Likewise, in his heathen way,
Adolf Hitler believed in an "iron law of historical development"[38] to which man was subject.

But once more the analogy between conservatism and
fascism ends just below the surface. The conservative's
opposition to a one-sidedly optimistic faith in man was
connected with his organic view of life. Man was not an
isolated atom. The eighteenth century, so de Maistre
charged, had forgotten man's "dependence."[39] Man was
shaped by his past and, therefore, subject to tradition. In
defense of this position Burke gave his celebrated definition
of the social contract in terms of "a partnership not only
between those who are living, but between those who are
living, those who are dead, and those who are to be born."
Moreover man was under God and dependent on "the
great primeval contract of eternal society . . . connecting
the visible and invisible world."[40] The conservative image
of man thus entailed a perception of depth; and though
man, according to the conservative, did not hold his destinies in his own hands, he emerged enriched by partaking
in an infinite chain of relationships.

The nature of conservative pessimism should be still
further qualified. It admitted no perfection in this world.
No human effort, no politics could ultimately remedy the
ills of the world. Politics had merely a limited function,
it was the "art of the possible" and an attempt to cope with
an existing order. The conservative, therefore, who has
generally been called "unpolitical," at the same time was

[37] De Maistre, *Considérations*, 5.
[38] Hermann Rauschning, *Hitler Speaks* (London, 1939), 47.
[39] De Maistre, *Essay on the Generative Principle*, 42.
[40] Burke, *Reflections, Works*, III, 359.

likely to be a religious man. As Burke wrote: "We know, and it is our pride to know, that man is by his constitution a religious animal."[41] Whereas, if things went wrong, the liberal tended to have a sense of guilt, the conservative tended to have a sense of sin. It might be suggested, therefore, that the difference between the liberal and the conservative concepts of man and society narrowed down to one between secularism and an essentially religious view. It was a difference also between monism and dualism, between non-acceptance and acceptance of a given order. The conservative, to be sure, also had a Utopia, but it was not of this world.

The pessimistic aspects of National Socialism stem more directly from its pattern of domination than from an elaborate rationale. Its negative view of man, instead of placing man into the setting of past, present, and future and instead of relating the visible and the invisible world, aimed at leveling man. In this connection we might remember that National Socialism was not simply an old-fashioned dictatorship. It was, strictly speaking, not a dictatorship over the masses, but one supported by the masses. It ruled not only by force but by intoxication. It therefore had to aim at the destruction of the individual, that is, at "depersonalization," and it maintained itself by an adroit manipulation of the masses. The most frightening aspect of Nazism was indeed its volunteer basis which accomplished the obliteration of the thinking individual by mass psychology, and of tradition by a new myth. With National Socialism, pessimism in fact had lost its function as a vital corrective, as an antidote to optimism; it was, to use a phrase from Nietzsche, a "preparatory state to nihilism."[42] In contrast to the conservative, the fascist had no Utopia at all, unless it was a deceptive euphoria.

[41] *Ibid.*, 351.

[42] Friedrich Nietzsche, "The Will to Power," *The Complete Works of Friedrich Nietzsche* (ed. Oscar Levy, 2nd edn., New York, London, 1910), xiv, 11.

On the count of pessimism the difference between conservatism and fascism thus becomes all the more blatant. Where the former opened up new worlds of experience, the latter leveled. Truth was for the conservative, as it was for de Tocqueville, a "rare and precious"[43] thing; for the fascist it was simply something manufactured at will. And in the last analysis National Socialism rejected the appeal to the eighteenth century man-made ideals as well as the appeal to God. Behind a façade of sacrosanctity it was only a new form of secularism, behind a façade of authoritarianism it rejected all authority. While conservatism emerged as a philosophy of acceptance, fascism was in essence a revolutionary movement standing for arbitrary rule.

E. CONCLUSION

The German students who burnt Haller's works during the memorable Wartburg festival in 1817 would hardly have subscribed to our vindication of conservatism. Their claims, as well as the outcries of those who were persecuted in one way or another by the French Restoration, can be as little explained away as the sufferings of those who, a generation earlier, had died under the guillotine of the Revolution. They were, we admit, victims of the idea of freedom. They were all living testimony of the fact that no system of thought is immune against being twisted into a justification for tyranny. But this does not invalidate the "basic intention" of the respective system of thought. It has, therefore, been important to underscore that conservatism, like liberalism, was part of that *"hortus inclusus* of the nineteenth century,"[44] a forward-looking century which believed in freedom and the dignity of man. In turn the ideological differences between conservatism and fascism had to be stressed. However, this vindication of

[43] Alexis de Tocqueville, *Recollections* (ed. J. P. Mayer, London, 1948), 93.
[44] Isaiah Berlin, "Political Ideas in the Twentieth Century," *Foreign Affairs*, xxviii (April 1950), 374.

31

conservatism means only the beginning of our investigation. It has sharpened for us the dilemma of conservatism in twentieth century Germany. It calls all the more for an explanation of the twentieth century associations between conservatism and National Socialism.

CHAPTER II

THE GENESIS OF THE DILEMMA

Nineteenth Century German Conservatism at a Dead End

WHEN Count Westarp, one of the leaders of German conservatism before and after the first World War, reminisced that conservatism in Germany became a "problem" after the dissolution of the Conservative Party in 1918,[1] he overlooked the danger signs which had been apparent long before. The "crisis of conservatism"[2] in Germany goes back to the middle of the nineteenth century. As early as that time we encounter some of the symptoms which account for the weak position in which the conservative forces of the Weimar Republic found themselves when faced with the challenge of fascism.

Partly due to its disunities pre-Bismarckian Germany was a natural ground for a spontaneous development of conservative thought. Indeed, Prussian conservatism out of which German conservatism grew, was started by a group of landowners and middle class intellectuals who freely criticized the crown as well as the new theories of the sovereignty of the people. They criticized a vague cosmopolitanism as well as the new nationalism. Altogether they were an unafraid lot of aristocrats, by birth or intellect, a balance between the stubbornness of royalism and the fashionability of the *Zeitgeist*.

But it might be remembered that from its very beginnings German conservatism was oriented toward the East rather than the West. It was on the Holy Alliance circuit, so to speak, rather than on the Burkian one. Although Burke had found his entry into Germany through Gentz, the spirit of Burke never really caught on in Germany.

[1] Graf Westarp, *Konservative Politik im letzten Jahrzehnt des Kaiserreiches* (Berlin, 1935-1936), II, 671.
[2] Cf. von Martin, "Weltanschauliche Motive," *Deutscher Staat*, 378.

The German conservatives did not live up to the Burkian balance between principles and expediency. They tended to be either unbending idealists like Adam Müller, the self-styled disciple of Burke, or insensitive realists like the great Bismarck. Furthermore, like German society at large, German conservatism was static and inflexible, more dedicated to a defense of an old order than to representing conservative principles within a changing world. The formula "Tory men and Whig measures"[3] was little known in Germany. Karl Mannheim argued that the distinguishing mark of German conservatism was the process of "thinking through to the end." Germany "achieved for the ideology of conservatism what France did for the Enlightenment—she exploited it to the fullest extent of its logical conclusions."[4] In Germany, in other words, conservatism acquired an orthodoxy of a sort not seen elsewhere. It was unbending and doctrinaire, and when finally it was faced by the challenge of the Bismarckian power state, it surrendered its principles to expediency.

The issue which precipitated the "crisis of conservatism" in Germany was unification. It was inevitable that sooner or later German conservatism should broaden its basis and adjust itself to the concept of national unity. However, no Burkian solution, no easy transition was found. There was only the alternative between principle and expediency. A small minority among the conservatives, represented by Ernst Ludwig von Gerlach, stood up for their principles.[5] Gerlach, who had been one of the founders of the Prussian Conservative Party in 1848, held out resolutely against the new forces of nationalism. They were, like democracy itself, part of the spirit of revolution. On the other side there was the overpowering Bismarck, who, sensitive to the trend of the times, was determined to achieve German unification

[3] R. J. White, *The Conservative Tradition* (London, 1950), 17.

[4] Karl Mannheim, "Conservative Thought," *Essays on Sociology and Social Psychology* (ed. Paul Kecskemeti, London, 1953), 82.

[5] For a lengthy discussion of Gerlach's position see Hans Joachim Schoeps, *Das andere Preussen* (Stuttgart, 1952).

at all costs. The break between Gerlach and Bismarck, which took place in 1866, occurred ultimately over the issue of "right versus might." Gerlach wrote in his declaration of war against Bismarck: "Let us beware of the abominable misconception according to which God's holy commandments do not apply to the fields of politics, diplomacy, and war, as if these areas recognized no higher law than patriotic egoism. *Justitia fundamentum regnorum!*"[6]

With Bismarck conservatism was forced into a strait jacket. It became part of that "fortress" Berlin, about which Lord Acton had so observingly complained.[7] The intellectual resources of conservatism were thus reduced to the statist tradition represented by Hegel, Stahl, and Ranke. Hegel had been the great exponent of a conservatism rooted in the state. For him conservatism had become identical with an uncritical acquiescence to the realities of the Prussian state. He had, one might say, succumbed to the paradox of conservatism, combining authority with freedom by reducing the margin of freedom to the freedom to obey. His casuistry was impressive, his sense of humor nil. But this questionable giant reduced German conservatism to a position of subservience. Through him the German conservatives became, as the witty Alexander Herzen called them, "Berlin Buddhists."[8] Stahl and Ranke reinforced this tendency. The development of Ranke's thought is an example of the degradation of conservatism under the influence of Bismarck. Ranke's well-founded opposition to the unification of Germany did not survive the *annus fatalis* of 1866. Like so many other German intellectuals, Ranke surrendered to success. Later he wrote to Bismarck: "The historian has much to learn from you."[9] Due to

[6] Ernst Ludwig von Gerlach, "Krieg und Bundes-Reform," *Kreuzzeitung* (May 8, 1866), quoted in *ibid.*, 46.

[7] Lord Acton, "German Schools of History," *Historical Essays and Studies* (London, 1919), 378.

[8] Alexander Herzen, *My Past and Thoughts* (London, 1924), II, 120.

[9] Letter of Ranke to Bismarck, February 22, 1877, Leopold von Ranke, *Das Briefwerk* (ed. W. P. Fuchs, Hamburg, 1949), 546f.

Hegel the difference between acceptance and acquiescence became blurred in Germany.

And as conservatism became "official" in Bismarck's Germany, it lost whatever vigor it had previously had. Still in 1866 the Conservative Party opposed Bismarck on the indemnity issue, which led to a splintering of the Party, with the Free Conservatives establishing themselves as a group in support of the chancellor. By 1876, however, the Conservative Party itself was forced into submission and its reorganization as the German Conservative Party indicated a willingness on the part of the younger generation of conservatives to accept the Bismarckian solution, including its constitutional basis. This concession meant, however, that from an admittedly fierce but independent Junker party it turned into a docile vehicle of the state. Without men like Ernst Ludwig von Gerlach, conservatism in Germany became more and more nearly identical with statism and nationalism and it turned into a sabre-rattling, blood-and-iron type of realism which was devoid of the ethics and the religious orientations of true conservatism.

Nietzsche, Conservative and Nihilist

There is still another trend which made itself felt in nineteenth century German conservatism and accounts for the latter's subsequent vulnerability. It had no connection with the "official" conservatism. In fact, it came from the camp of the so-called "cultural opposition" against the Second Reich. It emanated from a thinker—Friedrich Nietzsche—who is not commonly ranked among "conservatives," but whose influence among twentieth century German conservatives has become singular. He belongs to those men of letters in the nineteenth century who rebelled against their age. He was Burckhardt's *enfant terrible*. While Burckhardt, with the worst premonitions about his age, escaped to the aristocratic isolation of his scholarly world, Nietzsche waged open battle against the "decadence" of Western civilization. He exchanged the seclusion of

Burckhardt's Basle—where he himself had taught for ten years—for the exposure of Don Quixote's windmills.

An exegesis of Nietzsche has become a veritable problem. He has been accepted all too literally as the "good European." Also, all too literally has he been taken as a "proto-fascist." Nietzsche himself is his worst enemy in this respect. His work is a chain of brilliant insights veiled in over-statement, paradox, and metaphor. The growing intensity and emphasis of Nietzsche's untimeliness might have to be traced to his approaching insanity. The reader of Nietzsche is bound to ask whether the nineteenth century was really decadent beyond resurrection. And he must not preclude the possibility that Nietzsche himself loved that century, loved it dearly—and that he would have liked to save it.

Nietzsche's *Zeitkritik* was launched from the position of a philosophic conservative. The German problem, the object of his early polemics,[10] served merely as a test case— a steppingstone for the grand assault against his time. Nietzsche's thoughts were "thoughts out of season." He turned conservatism against Hegel, who had made the Germans subservient to history at the expense of "the other spiritual powers, art and religion."[11] He turned conservatism against Bismarck's achievement. Along with Burckhardt he became the focus of the "cultural opposition" against the Second Reich. He scolded the "abuse of success" after the war of 1870-1871,[12] which had spelled spiritual sterility. More important than the political unification was the "unity of the German spirit and life."[13] More vital than the unwelcome and superimposed state was the "unity of artistic style in every outward expression

[10] Friedrich Nietzsche, "David Strauss, the Confessor and the Writer," *Works* (3rd edn., New York, London, n.d.), IV, 1ff. and "The Use and Abuse of History," *Works* (3rd edn., New York, London, n.d.), V, 1ff.
[11] Nietzsche, "Use and Abuse," *Works*, V, 71.
[12] Nietzsche, "David Strauss," *Works*, IV, 6.
[13] Nietzsche, "Use and Abuse," *Works*, V, 38.

of the people's life."[14] Precisely in this preoccupation with history and politics and in the exuberant identification of politics with progress, Germany had become an index for what was happening all over Europe. The European man, Nietzsche charged, by an excessive trust in historical necessity and by turning to the state and society for the solution of his problems, surrendered his own individuality. He abdicated life while turning into a shallow mass man.

Nietzsche's answer to the age of Hegel and Bismarck was his philosophy of life. It made him the father of modern irrationalism. The *memento vivere* which he opposed to the *memento mori*[15] breathed the exuberance of new insights. By breaking through the conventions and deceptions of the "decadent" civilization it overcame the alienation of man from himself. The Nietzschean man was again himself. He had the "will" to live, or as Nietzsche called it, the "will to power." His sense of values was underived, spontaneous, aristocratic. Toward the end of his life Nietzsche summarized his position as follows: "Concerning the strength of the nineteenth century—we are more medieval than the eighteenth century; not only more inquisitive or more susceptible to the strange and the rare. We have revolted against the revolution. . . . We have freed ourselves from the fear of reason. . . ."[16] Thus far Thomas Mann was right when he assessed Nietzsche's position as "anti-nihilistic" and "eminently conservative."[17]

But the Nietzschean emphasis was, as Mann also learned later,[18] more complex, more questionable, more bedeviling. Nietzsche's later work in particular brought conservatism and nihilism into close and dangerous neighborhood. The genesis of Nietzsche's nihilism was the philosophic pessimism of the late century. His own increasing fear of the

14 *Ibid.*, 34.

15 *Ibid.*, 66f.

16 Nietzsche, "The Will to Power," *Works*, xv, 394.

17 Mann, *Betrachtungen*, 48.

18 Thomas Mann, "Nietzsches Philosophie im Lichte unserer Erfahrung," *Die Neue Rundschau* (Achtes Heft, Herbst, 1947), 359-389.

emergence of the mass man in a coming age of democracy and socialism led him to the conclusion that our civilization was dead beyond resurrection. Nietzsche thus moved to a position of despair, and his "transvaluation of values" threatened to turn against all tradition. Nietzsche's Zarathustra saying, "I love the great despisers, because they are the great adorers,"[19] leaves us in uncertainty. In his paradoxical position between conservatism and nihilism, between conserving and destroying, Nietzsche anticipated the dilemma of conservatism, the problem of the twentieth century conservatives.

Nietzsche's impact upon later generations has been repeatedly examined.[20] During most of his lifetime he lived in isolation and found no recognition. But in the 1890's, when Nietzsche existed in complete mental alienation under the care of his mother and sister, a voluminous Nietzsche literature sprang up. Tributes from the eminent Dane Georg Brandes, who discovered in Nietzsche's philosophy the marks of "aristocratic radicalism,"[21] and from a few young scholars like Georg Simmel and Max Scheler, were confronted by a host of pamphlets written by enraged Christian apologists. While Nietzsche continued to be contested abroad, he became more and more accepted in Germany itself. Whether "gentle Nietzscheans" or "tough Nietzscheans"[22] the Germans were Nietzscheans. Among the "tough" variety are found the twentieth century German conservatives. Nietzsche became their patron saint

[19] Friedrich Nietzsche, "Thus Spake Zarathustra," *Works* (6th edn., New York, London, 1930), xi, 9.

[20] Cf. Crane Brinton, *Nietzsche* (Cambridge, Mass., 1941), Chaps. viiff; Gisela Deesz, *Die Entwicklung des Nietzsche-Bildes in Deutschland* (diss., Würzburg, 1933); Friedrich Würzbach, "Nietzsche. Ein Gesamtüberblick über die bisherige Nietzsche-Literatur," *Literarische Berichte aus dem Gebiete der Philosophie*, Erfurt, xix/xx, xxvi, 1929, 1932; Walter A. Kaufmann, *Nietzsche: Philosopher, Psychologist, Antichrist* (Princeton, 1950), Epilogue.

[21] Georg Brandes, "Aristokratischer Radicalismus. Eine Abhandlung über Friedrich Nietzsche," *Deutsche Rundschau*, lxiii (1890), 52-89.

[22] These are Mr. Brinton's terms.

along with lesser lights—such as Paul de Lagarde and the "Rembrandt-German" Julius Langbehn.[23] Both directly and indirectly he reached the younger generation, a group which was more profoundly disturbed than any German generation since the Napoleonic period. Its confusion and its questioning were expressed in the Youth Movement, which adopted a Nietzschean viewpoint. Nietzsche's influence finally extended to the war and post-war periods, when, as never before in German history, the old values were shaken and questioned.

Challenges to Conservatism:
The Workers and the Proletarianized
Middle Classes

The most critical challenge to conservatism came from the changing social pattern of the late nineteenth century. The progress of industrialization brought about a completely novel relationship between man and society, man and nature, man and God. It gave rise to a new mass personality which threatened to encompass all social layers. With large-scale industrialization came the proletarian, the man who did not know from where he came or where he was going, the man who lived a hand-to-mouth existence with, at best, the ambition to buy a "movie ticket" from his salary.[24] He was the man of whom Burckhardt warned and whose "slave morality" Nietzsche exposed.

The immediate challenge to conservatism—as to liberalism—was the absorption of the laboring class into society. While in the nineteenth century, German conservatism had become increasingly a middle class venture, it had to broaden its basis still further in order to survive. Unlike England, Germany did not have a "Tory democracy" or a similar vigorous political adaptation of conservative

[23] Paul de Lagarde, *Deutsche Schriften* (3rd edn., Munich, 1937), in particular "Konservativ?" (1853); Julius Langbehn, *Rembrandt als Erzieher. Von einem Deutschen* (85th-90th edn., Stuttgart, 1936).

[24] This image is borrowed from Wilhelm Röpke, "Die proletarisierte Gesellschaft," *Der Monat,* II (June 1950), 228.

theory. Bismarck's social legislation did not win over the workers. For the kaiser the workers remained "fellows without fatherland." Thus the conservatism of the Conservative Party and the crown became petrified and the crown moved close to becoming a meaningless and unbeloved symbol. It is necessary to look elsewhere, into the ranks of the opposition to Bismarck, for a more searching conservatism. The persistent policy of Friedrich Naumann —backed by Max Weber—advocated an alliance between monarchy and workers and was, in the best sense of the word, conservative. But these men were outsiders in politics.

Of still more far-reaching significance was the spiritual and social task of making liberty meaningful to the new mass man. The advance of technology quite clearly could not be stopped. But it had produced a type, the mass man, to whom the old freedoms as well as the old forms of allegiance had become incomprehensible. Burke once wrote that "to be attached to the subdivision, to love the little platoon we belong to in society is the first principle . . . of public affections."[25] Yet the "little platoons" to which Burke had referred vanished rapidly: the family, the neighborhoods, the provincial connections, "resting places" all. The workings of the government became meaningless and distant, and life in general a harassing experience. The average man lost his sense of participation. It is no wonder that freedom came to be thought of as an intolerable burden and bondage a blessing, that the search for truth which seemed so tenuous and remote gave way to a ready acceptance of the myth.

While the proletarianized workers tended to become Marxists of one form or another, the proletarianized middle classes turned toward fascism. Such was the situation in twentieth century Germany. Defeat, the abolishment of the monarchy, and finally the inflation undermined the

[25] Burke, *Reflections, Works,* III, 292.

foundations of the middle classes.[26] If the mark of the bourgeois during the days of the Second Reich had been "culture and property," property, on the whole, was gone by the late twenties. What was left of culture was turned into a frantic expression of hurt pride. National Socialism became eventually a vehicle by which the degraded bourgeois could and did assert his lost respectability by revolutionary means. It was his plunge into unreality.

Out of this background grew the dilemma of the German conservative of the twentieth century. From the very start Germany did not have an altogether healthy conservative tradition. The logic of conservatism, which we have traced earlier and which should have been the measure for the reviving conservatism of the twentieth century, were already distorted by the mid-nineteenth century. And while the Nietzschean forecast of the European crisis already indicated the thin dividing line between conservatism and nihilism, the social changes since the late nineteenth century put an increasing premium on extremism in politics, on chauvinism, force, and totalitarianism. For the rest, the dilemma of the German conservative of the twentieth century was indeed essentially one between the logic and the politics of conservatism. For even if he abided by the tenets of conservatism, what were the possibilities of making conservative policy attractive to the masses? The challenge to conservatism was considerable. It was a test of its vitality and ingenuity in the face of a serious crisis.

[26] Cf. Hendrik de Man, *Sozialismus und Nationalfascismus* (Potsdam, 1931); Erich Fromm, *Escape from Freedom* (New York, 1941). It is regrettable that Fromm in his analysis of the modern German's need to "belong" points toward an inevitable escape into fascism. The alternative escape into conservatism is not explored. This shortcoming of Fromm's otherwise-penetrating work is due to his failure to distinguish between conservatism and National Socialism. Authoritarianism is identified with National Socialism (*ibid.*, 5, 221) and indeed Moeller van den Bruck is labeled "one of the ideological fathers of National Socialism" (*ibid.*, 171f).

CHAPTER III

THE REVIVAL OF GERMAN CONSERVATISM IN THE YOUTH MOVEMENT AND DURING THE FIRST WORLD WAR

The Youth Movement

THE German Youth Movement takes an important place in the changing intellectual and social world around the turn of the nineteenth century. The eccentricities of Nietzsche could easily have been written off, for the time being at least, as more or less isolated phenomena. The developments in the social sciences, as sketched earlier, could have been dismissed as academic theories. Even the threat from the ever-growing Social Democratic Party could have been disposed of in terms of coming from an outside class—the workers. The smugness and self-righteousness of the middle classes were, in the long run, more effectively shaken by the emergence of the Youth Movement. The average *Bürger* did not quite know what to think of these strange adolescents of the Wandervogel who left their homes and schools to rediscover the countryside and whose every expression was rebellion. But it was perturbing that these youngsters should have found themselves spontaneously in protest against society, and, more so, that most of them came from middle class homes. One could not quite laugh them off. Perhaps, all too seriously, some people discovered in them the makings of an "invisible revolution."[1] When, however, it became fashionable for educators of renown, men like Dilthey, Troeltsch, and Spranger, to take an interest in the Youth Movement and to encourage its activities, there seemed good ground for the average *Bürger* to

[1] Cf. Frank Thiess, *Wiedergeburt der Liebe. Die unsichtbare Revolution* (Berlin, Vienna, Leipzig, 1931), passim, particularly 96ff.

reexamine his own values and institutions in the light of this "symptom of . . . crisis."[2]

The basic experience of the Youth Movement was the conflict between the bourgeois world and individual life. It was also a conflict between generations, in which, strangely enough, the fathers were the liberals and the sons the conservatives. This was a marked reversal since the days of the earlier youth movement—the *Burschenschaften* of 1815. Then the new generation, which had fought in the Wars of Liberation, was in the fore in the struggle for a unified German state and for constitutionalism. Now liberalism, so it seemed to the sons, had lost its vitality and had come to stand for a world of confinement and convention. The young generation was tired of the state and tired of constitutions just as the early conservatives had been distrustful of them. In the Youth Movement there was a touch of the anarchic. It was anti-authoritarian, but it was also in search of authority and allegiances. This was its conservatism.

The Youth Movement derived its conservatism from Nietzsche and the traditions of nineteenth century irrationalism. Nietzsche, Lagarde, Stefan George became its heroes and were read, quoted, imitated, and freely plagiarized. They had given sanction to the struggle between the generations. Nietzsche had called upon the "first generation of fighters and dragon-slayers" to establish the "Reich of Youth."[3] Lagarde had defended German youth against the complaint that it lacked idealism: "I do not complain that our youth lacks ideals: I accuse those men, the statesmen above all, who do not offer ideals to the young generation."[4] To a searching youth, the irrationalists, all experimenters in conservatism, pointed a way to a conservatism

[2] Eduard Spranger, quoted in Georg Steinhausen, *Deutsche Geistes- und Kulturgeschichte von 1870 bis zur Gegenwart* (Halle, 1931), 473.
[3] Nietzsche, "Use and Abuse," *Works*, v, 97.
[4] Lagarde, "Über die Klage, dass der deutschen Jugend der Idealismus fehle," *Deutsche Schriften*, 439.

through rebellion and radicalism,[5] thus setting the tone for a revolutionary conservatism. Hegel and Bismarck were squarely repudiated. And Nietzsche, in lieu of traditions long lost, postulated the "will of tradition,"[6] a variation only of the ominous "will of power," as the foundation of a new conservatism. All the more did Stefan George's symbolism appeal to the young. They learned to see themselves as the "new nobility" of a "new Reich":

> New nobility you wanted
> Does not hail from crown or scutcheon!
> Men of whatsoever level
> Show their lust in venial glances,
> Show their greeds in ribald glances . . .
> Scions rare of rank intrinsic
> Grow from matter, not from peerage,
> And you will detect your kindred
> By the light within their eyes.[7]

Twentieth century knights were they, united by secret codes. They claimed to be dedicated to a "mission"; more correctly they were in search of one. Heinrich Heine, had he lived to see those Wandervögel, would have called them "armed Nietzscheans."

The revolutionary temper of the Youth Movement is evident from its famous declaration, formulated at a meeting near Kassel on the Hohen Meissner hill in October 1913. It stated that "Free German Youth,[8] on their own

[5] Lagarde, in an early pamphlet, characterized himself as "too conservative not to be radical." Lagarde, "Konservativ?" (1853), *Deutsche Schriften*, 9.

[6] Nietzsche, "The Will to Power," *Works*, xiv, 59.

[7] Stefan George, *Poems* (tr. Carol North Valhope and Ernst Morwitz, New York, 1943), 212-213. The poem is from *The Star of the Covenant*, which appeared in 1913.

[8] This was the newly found name for all the groups, including the Wandervogel, which convened. By 1913 the movement was spread all over Germany and the German parts of the Austro-Hungarian monarchy, and had a total membership amounting to roughly fifty to sixty thousand. For details on the history of the Freideutsche Jugend see A. Messer, *Die freideutsche Jugendbewegung. (Ihr Ver-*

initiative, under their own responsibility, and with deep sincerity, are determined independently to shape their own lives. For the sake of this inner freedom they will under any and all circumstances take united action. . . ."[9]

Revolution was written all over the declaration. And there was the very source of the dilemma of the Youth Movement. On one hand, the emphasis on "inner freedom" was an encouraging note to find in a German climate where, for a century, it was chiefly freedom against the outside world that had been stressed. Indeed, the meeting reflected a healthy aversion against the awkward beer-hall patriotism of the Germans and was a warning against the hollow and meaningless devotion to national slogans.[10] On the other hand, an adolescent search for an ideal society took the place of concrete political thinking in the Youth Movement. It turned, however understandably, against the political parties and declared itself "unpolitical" and "nonpartisan." But it had, as yet, little to offer instead but memories of medieval corporative life. In its opposition to the capitalistic order the Youth Movement put itself on record as an early experiment of middle class socialism. It was neither proletarian nor Marxist. It was "conscience-stricken" and disturbed by the grey anonymity of the cities. But the social program of the movement remained indefinite.[11] On the whole the movement was a mere symptom of restlessness: it displayed an excess of passion but as yet little ability to mold its beliefs into new forms. It contributed toward undermining the middle classes from within rather than rejuvenating them.

---

lauf von 1913-1919) (Langensalza, 1920). For above figures see Howard Becker, *German Youth: Bond or Free* (London, 1946), 94.

[9] Translation taken over from Becker, *German Youth*, 100. The words "on their own initiative" and the last sentence were omitted following a meeting at Marburg in March 1914 in which a moderate majority prevailed. Messer, *Freideutsche*, 27ff.

[10] Messer, *Freideutsche*, 19.

[11] Even proposals concerning redistribution of land (*Siedlung*) and cooperatives, which were presented at the meeting by two students, were ignored. *Ibid.*, 22f.

It should be remembered that the same generation which celebrated on the Hohen Meissner in 1913 gave most of the volunteers in 1914. At the front the Freideutsche Jugend merged with the anonymous "field-grey" army and the so-called "war experience" became its central idea. So much had it become representative in the eyes of the public of the "front generation" that the storming of Langemarck in Belgium in the winter of 1914 became accredited to it. The same generation emerged from the war as the "tragic generation"; it lost roughly one million out of its original five and a half million[12] and carried its ideals into a changed world of defeat and poverty. It was this very generation which asked the questions about the survival of its ideals and, alas, about the meaning of the war.[13] Finally, this generation later came to accept war and revolution as solutions in themselves.

The Ideas of 1914

Lenin once called the first World War a "mighty accelerator of events."[14] The outbreak of the war in 1914 brought out in Germany the realization that the new century called for a new thinking. The nineteenth century suddenly moved into perspective. Now, in the manner in which the Youth Movement had, somewhat ungratefully, put the older generation on the shelf, the nation took a whole century to task. Ernst Troeltsch wrote about "the great abyss which separates us from the pre-war days."[15] Nietzsche seemed vindicated. "Nietzsche's criticism of the past century," Thomas Mann exclaimed in his much-disputed war book, ". . . appeared never more magnificently

[12] E. Günther Gründel, *Die Sendung der jungen Generation. Versuch einer umfassenden revolutionären Sinndeutung der Krise* (3rd edn., Munich, 1933), 27f.

[13] *Sinn des Krieges.*

[14] V. I. Lenin, "Letters from Afar," *Handbook of Marxism* (ed. Emile Burns, New York, 1935), 762.

[15] Ernst Troeltsch, "Die Ideen von 1914" (1916), *Deutscher Geist und Westeuropa* (ed. Hans Baron, Tübingen, 1925), 35.

fitting."[16] In retrospect the nineteenth century appeared "little generous and intellectually hardly gallant."[17] It looked thoroughly "bourgeois" and despicably unheroic. It looked like a century without faith.

The German situation during the early years of the war could not have been more fittingly reflected than in Mann's statement that the twentieth century, in contrast to the nineteenth century, "has faith—or at least it teaches that one should have faith."[18] In the beginning of the war a leaflet composed by Gottfried Traub, a defrocked but popular Protestant pastor, proclaimed, "Germany prays." Troeltsch reiterated, "Germany prays."[19] The poet Rudolf Binding commented upon the "great religiosity *(Gläubigkeit)*"[20] which came over the people. But while some prayed to the Christian God, others prayed to a German god. While some believed, others merely wanted to believe. The new wave of "religiosity" was more a sociological than a religious phenomenon. It was oriented more toward the nation than toward the world beyond. One might simply say that Germany was looking for an "idea." In a historical perspective it appears that, unlike the majority of the French, whose faith was rooted in their revolutionary tradition, the Germans never had been thrilled by the thought of barricades. Unlike the English, to whom the crown was a living symbol, the Germans were not held together by the kaiser. The Germans had reason to feel unhappy about themselves.[21] Therefore, the outbreak of war was met in

---

[16] Mann, *Betrachtungen,* xxv. Troeltsch observed that through the "war experience" Nietzsche's thought had finally become purified of its sickly and exaggerated elements and thus had set "new aims" for the German people. Troeltsch, "Der metaphysische und religiöse Geist der deutschen Kultur," *Deutscher Geist,* 75.

[17] Mann, *Betrachtungen,* xxv.   [18] *Ibid.,* xxviii.

[19] Troeltsch, "Die Ideen von 1914," *Deutscher Geist,* 38.

[20] Rudolf Binding, *Erlebtes Leben* (Frankfurt/M, 1928), 237, quoted in Hanna Hafkesbrink, *Unknown Germany. An Inner Chronicle of the First World War based on Letters and Diaries* (New Haven, 1948), 35.

[21] For the awareness on the part of leading German intellectuals

Germany with an unequaled enthusiasm.[22] It meant a release from the "lazy peace." The so-called "war experience" was mainly an introspective German affair. The intellectuals, spearheading the upsurge of emotions, busied themselves in interpreting the war as a "German Revolution,"[23] as a victory, primarily within the German soul, of the "ideas of 1914" over the "ideas of 1789." It was this search for an idea, for the meaning of the war, which led many German intellectuals to a rethinking of the problems of conservatism and produced, in effect, various formulations of a wartime conservatism.

The "ideas of 1914" were an ideological counterpart to the *Burgfriede* which the kaiser proclaimed on August 4, 1914. They constituted a rallying point for intellectuals, whatever their political background, whatever their views concerning specific war aims. Two organizations in particular dedicated themselves to a formulation of the "ideas of 1914," one of which was the Association of German Scholars and Artists (Bund deutscher Gelehrter und Künstler) with headquarters in the Akademie der Wissenschaften in Berlin. It had a membership of about one thousand intellectuals from the Right to the majority Social Democracy,[24] and under the leadership of Heinrich von Gleichen-Russwurm it assumed the functions of a German psychological warfare agency of sorts. Socially more exclusive and meeting in the elegant Pringsheim Palais in the Wilhelm-

that Germany was unprepared to wage war on the level of ideas cf. Karl Pribram, "Deutscher Nationalismus und deutscher Sozialismus," *Archiv für Sozialwissenschaft und Sozialpolitik*, IL (1922), 325.

[22] Cf. Hafkesbrink, *Unknown Germany*.

[23] Johann Plenge, *Der Krieg und die Volkswirtschaft* (Münster/W, 1915), 171. Cf. also Paul Lensch, *Drei Jahre Weltrevolution* (Berlin, 1917), 8f; Ernst Jünger, ed., *Krieg und Krieger* (Berlin, 1930), 11.

[24] For a partial membership list see *Briefwechsel zwischen den Herren Yves Guyot und Daniel Bellet und Herrn Lujo Brentano* (ed. Kulturbund deutscher Gelehrter und Künstler, Berlin, n.d.), n.p. For the executive committee see *Deutsche Volkskraft nach zwei Kriegsjahren* (ed. Bund deutscher Gelehrter und Künstler, Leipzig, Berlin, 1916), appendix.

Strasse was the influential Deutsche Gesellschaft 1914 under the chairmanship of the colonial secretary of state, Wilhelm Solf. Its membership included men from all professions. Among the intellectuals were the historians Friedrich Meinecke and Ernst Troeltsch, the industrialist Walther Rathenau, and the socialists Paul Lensch and August Winnig.[25] Altogether the membership of the two associations was motley. And much of the tenor of their discussions as well as of their publications was bound to be of a traditional patriotic and nationalistic nature. They served at the same time as forums for the expression of the new experience suggested by the concept "ideas of 1914."

The term itself, the "ideas of 1914," was coined by Johann Plenge, a sociologist at the University of Münster.[26] He was known as a neo-Hegelian who had greatly influenced the revival of Hegelianism among Marxists. He was a scholar of Marx, yet not a Marxist himself; a Hegelian, yet not much of a scholar of Hegel. An outsider by all descriptions, he was a vigorous and vain stylist with a marked tendency toward moralizing and prophesying. The Swedish geopolitician Rudolf Kjellén, a highly respected neutral, gave added prestige to the new concept by advertising it as a "world historical perspective."[27] Among its leading interpreters were also the philosopher Max Scheler, Thomas Mann, and the historians Friedrich Meinecke and Ernst Troeltsch.[28] Friedrich Naumann, *sui generis,* contributed his momentous Central Europe idea.[29]

[25] Cf. Friedrich Meinecke, *Strassburg, Freiburg, Berlin 1901-1919. Erinnerungen* (Stuttgart, 1949), 157f.; Hans W. Gatzke, *Germany's Drive to the West* (Baltimore, 1950), 136f.

[26] Cf. Johann Plenge, *Der Krieg und die Volkswirtschaft* (Münster/W, 1915) and *1789 und 1914. Die symbolischen Jahre in der Geschichte des deutschen Geistes* (Berlin, 1916).

[27] Rudolf Kjellén, *Die Ideen von 1914. Eine Weltgeschichtliche Perspektive* (Leipzig, 1915).

[28] Max Scheler, *Der Genius des Krieges und der deutsche Krieg* (Leipzig, 1915); Thomas Mann, *Betrachtungen eines Unpolitischen* (Berlin, 1918); *Die deutsche Freiheit* (ed. Bund deutscher Gelehrter und Künstler, Gotha, 1917), containing among others contributions

The sudden outburst of professorial activity seemed to justify Richard Wagner's famous but questionable statement that "the German is conservative." The German people was told by Plenge that its war was really a war against the "destructive liberalism of the eighteenth century."[30] "The German mind has always been conservative and will remain so forever," Thomas Mann echoed.[31] He was among the many German intellectuals for whom the "meaning of the hour" was "allegiance," rather than "liberation, more and more liberation."[32]

For some thinkers like Max Scheler, "liberation" was overcome by war as an inner experience. The "genius of war" itself had "re-established" the "broken contact between individual, people, nation, world and God."[33] With this glorification of war Scheler formulated a position which became a pattern with many of the younger generation, notably Ernst Jünger. Jünger in his youth had made an unsuccessful attempt to join the French Foreign Legion in search of the horizons which he could not find in "bourgeois Germany."[34] In 1914 he was among the volunteers. And he experienced war as the grand alternative to bourgeois existence. Jünger in the post-war years became a fascinating interpreter of a sophisticated militarism for a generation—it was the generation of the original Youth Movement—on which the war had left a strong imprint.

Thomas Mann gave a more ideological emphasis to the

by Meinecke and Troeltsch; Ernst Troeltsch, *Deutscher Geist und Westeuropa* (ed. Hans Baron, Tübingen, 1925); Otto Hintze, Friedrich Meinecke, Hermann Oncken, Hermann Schumacher, eds., *Deutschland und der Weltkrieg* (Leipzig, 1915), containing among others contributions by Meinecke and Troeltsch; Friedrich Meinecke, *Die deutsche Erhebung* (2nd-5th edn., Stuttgart, Berlin, 1914).

[29] Friedrich Naumann, *Mitteleuropa* (Berlin, 1915).
[30] Plenge, *Der Krieg und die Volkswirtschaft*, 171.
[31] Mann, *Betrachtungen*, 605.
[32] *Ibid.*, 527f.
[33] Scheler, *Der Genius des Krieges*, 2, quoted in Hafkesbrink, *Unknown Germany*, 37.
[34] Cf. Wulf Dieter Müller, *Ernst Jünger* (Berlin, 1934), 16f.

"ideas of 1914" in his *Betrachtungen,* which he considered his war service.[35] He had been all artist, all observer when he wrote his first great novel, *Buddenbrooks* (1901). Its theme, the decline of an old patrician family, the conflict between virility and refinement, between life and the mind, nature and art, left him uncommitted. The war, however, called for a greater degree of involvement even on the part of the artist. In fact the war, with its seemingly cosmic issues, called for an "either-or." And from then on, the story of the Buddenbrooks appeared to Mann clearly as a "symptom of national degeneracy."[36] And he wrote the *Betrachtungen* in search of a corrective to refinement, as an effort to overcome the *fin de siècle* and to return to the roots. The *Betrachtungen* was a Nietzschean book as well as a Burckhardtian and Lagardean one.[37] Nietzsche's idea of life became the intoxicating—in Nietzsche's terms, "dithyrambic"—antidote to decline. A "conservative" idea, it gained "national importance"[38] through Mann.

Thomas Mann called his conservatism "truly revolutionary."[39] It was a new-old experience. It had outlived the fallacies of the "ideas of 1789." The new conservatism was "unpolitical," for it emphasized spiritual—indeed religious—values as against mere political ones. It represented a rejection of an excess of freedom and at the same time a quest for an "inner tyrant," for "absolute values,"[40] for religion. To Mann politics and religion, freedom and religion were alternatives. So far Mann's "revolutionary" conservatism was well in line with the nineteenth century conservative tradition.

However, Thomas Mann called for religion knowing that he himself had none.[41] His *Betrachtungen* was at best a searching book, a monologue which perhaps never should have been printed. And in lieu of religion Mann took ref-

35 Cf. Mann, *Betrachtungen,* ix.
36 *Ibid.,* 608.
37 Cf. *ibid.,* 605, 260ff.
38 *Ibid.,* 608.
39 *Ibid.,* 347.
40 *Ibid.,* 529.
41 Cf. *ibid.,* 551.

uge in nationalism. He reduced conservatism to nationalism. "Conservative and national," Mann boasted, "are one and the same thing."[42] The *Betrachtungen,* in other words, was *ersatz* ware.

Finally, Nietzsche, the "good European," was used against Europe. Mann's Germany was Dostoevsky's "protesting"[43] Germany, whose history had been separate from the history of Europe, whose soul was mysterious to the world. While the sociologist Werner Sombart in his patriotic exercise had called Germany the country of "heroes" in contrast to England, the country of "traders,"[44] Mann established the dichotomy between German *Kultur* and Western civilization. Under the impact of the war Mann stressed the anti-Western position of German conservatism. He differentiated sharply between the conservatism of the West—the "conservatism of the 'eternal principles' "—and Germany's own "inner conservatism."[45] In effect, he denied the cosmopolitan traditions of German conservatism in favor of an Eastern orientation. And through Mann Russia became one of the great attractions to German conservatism.

Even Ernst Troeltsch, in politics a liberal, persuaded himself to say in a lecture to the Deutsche Gesellschaft that the Germans had "outgrown European liberalism."[46] As might be expected, his slant on the "ideas of 1914" was considerably more level-headed than that of the militarists and nationalists. The often-used argument that the war was fought in defense of a German concept of freedom[47] became meaningful through him.[48] Even in the writings of his friend Meinecke this concept was still drowned by plain

[42] *Ibid.*, 247.   [43] *Ibid.*, 1ff.

[44] Werner Sombart, *Händler und Helden. Patriotische Besinnungen* (Munich, Leipzig, 1915).

[45] Mann, *Betrachtungen*, 347.

[46] Troeltsch, "Die Ideen von 1914" (1916) , *Deutscher Geist*, 32.

[47] Cf. Plenge, *1789 und 1914*, 9; Meinecke, "Die deutsche Freiheit" (1916), *Die deutsche Freiheit*, 14ff.

[48] Cf. Troeltsch, "Die deutsche Idee von der Freiheit," *Deutscher Geist*, 80ff.

jingoism. But Troeltsch carefully outlined a position which led away from the "individualistic-liberal age"[49] as well as the Wilhelmian past. Differentiating between the abstract ideas of 1789 and the organic German idea of freedom, he led up to outlining a middle way between authoritarianism and equalitarianism.[50] This position was analogous to that of the early nineteenth century conservatives who had tried to steer their way between absolutism and constitutionalism. Furthermore, this was a reasonable position for patriotic men to assume in hoping for reforms in post-war Germany.

The tenor of the spirit of 1914 was no doubt right-of-center. It was anti-liberal as well as irrational. But though this wartime conservatism reflected basically the position of the early nineteenth century conservatives, it showed some novel and perturbing signs of extremism in the form of an anti-Western nationalism and of outright anti-intellectualism. Much of this extremism might be attributed to the temper of the times. Even the formulators themselves of the "ideas of 1914" were aware of its dangers. Beneath the surface of patriotic zest, undertones of caution could be detected. Troeltsch, while elaborating the distinction between the "spirit of German culture" and the West, warned against the isolation of the German mind from the West. Was the German position to amount to a "war against the West"? Even Thomas Mann himself emerged with warnings against an extremist position. They constituted an afterthought to his otherwise ferocious *Betrachtungen*. After all, Mann shied away from an "either-or" and arrived at a position which he called "ironical." Irony is the ability to not take one's own position too seriously; its essence is detachment. Applying it to the Nietzschean problem of life versus mind, Mann finally explained that life without mind appeared to him as a "nihilistic Utopia"; he added

---

[49] Troeltsch, "Privatmoral und Staatsmoral" (1916), *ibid.*, 161.
[50] Troeltsch, "Die Ideen von 1914," *ibid.*, 44.

that "life too needs mind."[51] Irony and not a one-sided radicalism, Mann stressed, was "the spirit of conservatism."[52] Thus irony, even though stated as a mere reservation, as an afterthought, became a vital part of the wartime conservatism. It was the one basis on which a humanist could represent the "ideas of 1914." It should have become the Magna Charta of twentieth century German conservatism.

CENTRAL EUROPE

One of the tangible points on which almost all proponents of the "ideas of 1914" agreed was the idea of Central Europe as interpreted by Friedrich Naumann. Central Europe was a reality in German history before it became an issue. The Holy Roman Empire and the Germanic Confederation of 1815 were essentially Central European inasmuch as they established, each in its own way, a supernational order under German leadership between the Western national monarchies and the Russian Empire. Central Europe became an issue when the old order was challenged in 1848 by the twin forces of nationalism and liberalism. And when the German question was settled by Bismarck in 1871 on strictly statist lines, the Central European idea became one of the main arguments of the conservative "enemies of Bismarck." In particular, Constantin Frantz and Lagarde attacked the Iron Chancellor for Prussianizing Germany. He had, so they claimed, in effect surrendered to French rationalism; his Germany was merely a replica of France, "an Eastern France."[53] Frantz and Lagarde stressed in the name of diversity the "European character" of Prussia and Austria[54] and agitated for a fed-

---

[51] Mann, *Betrachtungen*, 588.   [52] *Ibid.*, 604.

[53] Constantin Frantz, *Die nationale Rechtseinheit und das Reichsgericht* (Augsburg, 1873), 2, 7, quoted in Louis Sauzin, "The Political Thought of Constantin Frantz," in *The Third Reich* (London, 1955), 117.

[54] Constantin Frantz, *Deutschland und der Föderalismus* (Hellerau, 1917), 71. The first edition of the work appeared under the title *Der*

eration—a true Reich—in Central Europe. It ought to be
stressed, however, that this Central Europe idea, however
genuinely conservative, did have its expansive, indeed im-
perialist, aspects, inasmuch as it served as a justification
for a renewed German *Drang nach Osten*.

Naumann's spectacular *Mitteleuropa* revived the idea of
Central Europe at the moment when Germany and Austria
went to war together. It became one of the most widely
read war books. It was a vision of a bloc of Central powers
based on a union between Germany and the Austro-Hungarian Monarchy. Naumann's emphasis was economic
rather than political, and defensive—he wrote about a "defensive alliance"[55]—rather than expansionist.[56] In long-
range terms, he was concerned with bringing order into the
vital and troublesome core of Europe. "We shall emerge
from the war as Mid-Europeans . . . . Mid-Europe is the
fruit of the war. We have sat together in the war's economic
prison, we have fought together, we are determined to live
together."[57] It was this scheme of Naumann's which was
praised by Troeltsch as "one of the great experiences of
this war" and as "a political idea, which can give clarity,
aim, energy, and assurance to our actions, since in recent
years we have had no idea at all . . . ."[58] Later, in the post-
war years, it found a revival in the literature of the neo-
conservative movement, notably in the *Tat* magazine.

THE MEETING BETWEEN CONSERVATISM AND SOCIALISM

One of the most interesting aspects of the "war experience" was its socialist orientation. Indeed, socialism be-

---

*Föderalismus als das leitende Prinzip für die soziale, staatliche und
internationale Organisation, unter besonderer Bezugnahme auf
Deutschland* (Mainz, 1879).

[55] Friedrich Naumann, *Central Europe* (tr. C. M. Meredith, New
York, 1917), 11.

[56] Cf., for this interpretation, Gatzke, *Germany's Drive to the West*,
105f; Henry Cord Meyer, *Mitteleuropa in German Thought and Action*
(The Hague, 1955), 198ff.

[57] Naumann, *Central Europe*, 282-283.

[58] Troeltsch, "Die Ideen von 1914," *Deutscher Geist*, 51, 53.

came a vital feature of the "ideas of 1914." Designated as "German socialism," "national socialism," "conservative socialism," it had little to do with the mainstream of European socialism, be it Utopian or Marxian. It was not concerned with the worker, or indeed with any one class, but it was a direct outgrowth of a general national feeling of solidarity. The affinity between conservatism and socialism, which Karl Mannheim pointed out,[59] was clearly evident in the wartime socialism. While the wartime conservatism was an expression of protest against the alienation of the individual from an original irrational order by the forces of rationalism and liberalism, the wartime socialism was a protest against the alienation of man from nature and society by the machine and by capitalism. The protest of the new socialism was essentially derived from the conservative one. Its aim, the overcoming of the alienation between classes, the reestablishment of a just and natural economic and social order among the Germans, was inherently conservative.

The new socialism had no one lawgiver like Karl Marx. It had, however, some precedents in German history.[60] Its architects, no doubt, were conscious of Fichte's legacy and above all of his concept of the "closed economy."[61] Friedrich List, the German antagonist of Adam Smith, had educated the Germans to think in terms of their national

[59] Karl Mannheim, "Conservative Thought," *Essays on Sociology and Social Psychology*, 84ff. Cf. also a discussion of the "congruity of human behavior in conservatism and socialism" in Sigmund Neumann, *Die Stufen des preussischen Konservatismus. Ein Beitrag zum Staats- und Gesellschaftsbild Deutschlands im 19. Jahrhundert* (Berlin, 1928), 74.

[60] Karl Pribram considered the wartime socialism as "a return of the German people to its noblest and best traditions." Pribram, "Deutscher Nationalismus und deutscher Sozialismus," *Archiv*, IL (1922), 299.

[61] Troeltsch: "Germany has turned into a closed economy" Troeltsch, "Die Ideen von 1914," *Deutscher Geist*, 44. Cf. also Wichard von Moellendorff, *Von Einst zu Einst (Deutsche Gemeinwirtschaft Pamphlet 1)* (Jena, 1917.)

economy and protectionism. Even the strange Bismarck-Lassalle deal, although abortive, remained an inspiring example for later generations. Since the 1870's a group of so-called "Socialists of the Chair" (Kathedersozialisten) had formulated an anti-Marxist and an anti-liberal conservative socialism. Their main objective was a limited one, that is, to stem the rise of Marxism, and it was reached in August 1914 when the German workers lined up with the fatherland. Nevertheless, the leading minds among the "Socialists of the Chair," Adolf Wagner and Gustav Schmoller, directly affected the development of social thought during the war. Also, going back to the period of the "Socialists of the Chair," there was Adolf Stöcker's Christian Social Movement, which, in a working alliance with the Conservative Party, aimed at reaching the workers through anti-capitalistic and anti-Semitic slogans. Stöcker, who had a decisive influence upon German conservatism of the late nineteenth century, upon the kaiser as well as Friedrich Naumann, also was one of the main precursors of National Socialism. The affinity between the new conservatism of the twentieth century and National Socialism, insofar as it existed, was already foreshadowed in him.[62]

On the whole, however, the new socialism was the result of the immediate political and social situation which Germany faced during the war. Naumann's "community of the

---

[62] With some imagination, even Nietzsche's life philosophy could be interpreted in terms of socialism. Though Nietzsche despised socialism for its "slave-morality," various aphorisms from "The Will to Power" indicate that he was willing to think of the worker as part of his aristocratic world. For example: *"Concerning the future of the workingman.*—Workingmen should learn to regard their duties as *soldiers* do. They receive emoluments, incomes, but they do not get wages!" And "The workingmen ought one day live as the *Bürger* do now—but *above* them, distinguishing themselves by simplicity of their wants—the *superior* caste will then live in a poorer and simpler way and yet be in possession of power." (Italics in the original.) Nietzsche, "The Will to Power," *Works*, xv, 208f. Already by October 1900 the *Sozialistische Monatshefte* claimed Nietzsche for socialism; cf. Brinton, *Nietzsche*, 189.

trenches" (*Schützengrabenbündnis*) was the expression of a widely felt political as well as social unity.[63] Sacrifices were required of everybody for the cause of German victory. In general, the war made the Germans increasingly aware of the fact, which had been only vaguely felt in the Youth Movement, of the decline of the middle class society,[64] of the end of *laissez faire*, and of the need for a policy of planning. At the same time it made all the more relevant the problem raised by Burckhardt whether freedom could survive in a world of uniformity. Here again was the dilemma of conservatism in Germany.

THE WAR ECONOMY AND THE IDEAS OF WALTHER
RATHENAU AND WICHARD VON MOELLENDORFF

The German war economy was the testing ground for the new socialism. Climaxed by the Hindenburg Program of 1916, the arrangements were, by themselves, of a makeshift character. They were agreements, compromises generally, between the government, capital, and labor. They were designed to cope efficiently with an emergency. Those, however, who were most instrumental in preparing the economic planning, Walther Rathenau and Wichard von Moellendorff, saw in it not merely an isolated and temporary phenomenon. They looked toward Lloyd George's England to discover an "alliance between a mature conservatism and a moderate socialism."[65] More basically, they saw themselves as agents of the new century of social responsibilities. The ready popular acceptance of restrictive

63 Cf. also Meinecke's extolling of the "communal spirit" (*soziale Gemeingeist*), Meinecke, "Die deutsche Freiheit," *Die deutsche Freiheit*, 36, and Troeltsch's concept of "pure socialism," Troeltsch, "Privatmoral und Staatsmoral," *Deutscher Geist*, 160.

64 Walther Rathenau, "Von kommenden Dingen," *Gesammelte Schriften* (Berlin, 1918), III, 294 and "Die neue Wirtschaft," *Schriften*, v, 187.

65 Rudolf Wissell and Wichard von Moellendorff, *Wirtschaftliche Selbstverwaltung. Zwei Kundgebungen des Reichwirtschaftsministeriums* (*Deutsche Gemeinwirtschaft* Pamphlet 10) (Jena, 1919), 24. Cf. Moellendorff, *Von Einst zu Einst*, 27.

regulations of all sorts seemed an assurance to these men that the war economy was but a prelude to a twentieth century style of living.

Walther Rathenau was one of the most puzzling and complex figures in German public life in the twentieth century. The son of Emil Rathenau, who founded the great German electrical concern, the A.E.G., and his father's successor as head of the A.E.G., Walther Rathenau was a powerful German industrialist. During the last years of the Hohenzollern Monarchy as well as during the early phase of the Weimar Republic he was in no less a position of influence as a writer, economist, public servant, and politician. Over all, his life appears as a struggle of Rathenau contra Rathenau. Though he was an industrialist and organizer he protested against the mechanization of his age; though a capitalist of the first order, he was a socialist. He was a bitter critic of his age, and yet he was its representative. Though a man of action, he approached the problems of his times from the perspective of an artist torn by inner conflicts which are never quite overcome. The dualism between life and mind which has been so vital to the literary generations since Nietzsche was Rathenau's problem too.[66] Rathenau can hardly be associated with any one political camp or creed. During the Monarchy and the foundation of the Republic he was forced to remain aloof, to remain completely himself, a wild torrent of ideas. His doubts, like the paradoxes of Nietzsche, were never quite resolved. For this very reason Rathenau was one of the most stirring minds of his generation.

Moellendorff was an engineer and economist by profes-

[66] In his early philosophic work *Reflexionen* (Leipzig, 1908) Rathenau discussed courage and fear as the basic "polarity" dominating human thought. This distinction had a pathetic anti-Semitic overtone (cf. *ibid.*, 228, 237f.), according to which courage was a virtue exercised by the Nordic peoples, and fear a vice peculiar to the Jewish world. Rathenau in his later works dealt in broader terms with the dichotomy between the soul and the intellect and stressed the importance of controlling the intellect by the soul.

sion. Born in 1881 in Hongkong, the son of the German consul von Moellendorff, he went to school and then studied engineering in Berlin. From 1906 on he worked in the A.E.G., where he met both Emil and Walther Rathenau. The acquaintance with Walther Rathenau decisively influenced Moellendorff's career. He rose higher in the A.E.G. until at the outbreak of the war he became Rathenau's right-hand man in the organization of the German war economy.

The initiative toward the establishment of the war economy, though generally attributed to Rathenau, came from Moellendorff.[67] Upon his recommendation "to induce the Ministry of War to review conditions and to initiate a thrifty budget [*sparsamen Haushalt*] under a central authority,"[68] Rathenau conferred with the authorities. As a result the minister of war, von Falkenhayn, entrusted Rathenau, together with a retired colonel, with the direction of the War Raw Materials Division (Kriegsrohstoffabteilung, or K.R.A.) which was established as part of the Ministry of War. Working with men like Moellendorff he succeeded in bringing under his control all materials which were needed for the defense of the state. Through the commandeering of vital raw materials and by means of newly created War Industrial Companies which coordinated supply he achieved the organization of a "closed economy in a closed industrial state."[69]

In the spring of 1915 Rathenau resigned from office in view of the opposition which he had faced in the pursuit

[67] He was, according to Rathenau, "the first one" who, "in the course of friendly conversations," pointed out the "serious shortcomings" of the German economic structure; Rathenau, "Deutsche Rohstoffversorgung. Vortrag gehalten in der 'Deutschen Gesellschaft 1914' am 20. Dezember 1915," *Schriften*, v, 29f.

[68] Letter of Moellendorff to Rathenau, August 8, 1914, quoted in Otto Goebel, *Deutsche Rohstoffwirtschaft im Weltkrieg einschliesslich des Hindenburg Programms* (Stuttgart, Berlin, Leipzig, New Haven, 1930), 20.

[69] Rathenau, "Deutsche Rohstoffversorgung," *Schriften*, v, 53.

of his plans; he was replaced by Major Josef Koeth,[70] who followed in his footsteps, but who, for personal reasons chiefly, was more acceptable to the military hierarchy. Moellendorff stayed in public office longer than Rathenau, first as director of the coordinating War Agency for Chemicals (Kriegschemikaliengesellschaft) and subsequently as adviser to various other war agencies. He was opposed to the Hindenburg Program as a compromise solution, and finally retired in the spring of 1918 to a professorship of economics in Hanover.

Both Rathenau and Moellendorff had been only "guests in office," as Moellendorff put it. Their withdrawal from public office revealed, apart from the personal isolation in which Rathenau had found himself, the extent of their variance with the official war program. Their respective schemes exceeded the official policy, not only in extent, but in character. They were intellectual and part of a broader vision. They were responses to the German quest for the new "idea."

For Rathenau retirement in 1915 meant that he could devote himself freely to his philosophy and social thought. The speeches given and books written during the remaining war years are the most genuine and important legacy of this singularly sensitive statesman. He wrote with the pen of a Jewish prophet, and, like the Jewish prophets, he never abandoned his personal isolation and independence. The unique success of his writings proves that he raised problems which vitally concerned the German reading public.[71]

Rathenau's main problem was the evil of mechanization.

[70] Later Colonel Koeth; for more detailed information on Koeth cf. Fritz Redlich, "German Economic Planning for War and Peace," *Review of Politics*, vi (1944), 315-335.

[71] *Von kommenden Dingen* (Berlin, 1917) reached an edition of 24,000 three months after publication, and 65,000 by the middle of 1918. *Die neue Wirtschaft* (Berlin, 1918) scored an edition of 30,000 one month after publication. Count Harry Kessler, *Walther Rathenau. His Life and Work* (New York, 1930), 212f.

No one saw more clearly than he that mechanization threatened to deprive man of his active sense of participation in society and to degrade him to a role of anonymity. The bondage of the industrial man appeared to Rathenau potentially much more thorough and oppressive than any other known form of servitude. Essentially, mechanization was a challenge to freedom.

The defense of freedom, however, did not imply for Rathenau a return to *laissez faire*. It became clear from his two addresses to the Deutsche Gesellschaft 1914 that this was the ground on which he was in conflict with official opinion.[72] He talked about the "dim era of free economy,"[73] and his criticism of what he called the "fragments of European morals"[74] was unsparing.

Rathenau considered himself a part of the "counterforces"[75] which emerged out of the mechanistic era and which aimed at the regeneration of faith and the soul. But to him the escapism of the Youth Movement—be it into a medieval way of life or away from the city into nature—could be no solution. The industrialist Rathenau had to recognize mechanization as the "destiny of mankind,"[76] while the moralist Rathenau set out to outline a way to overcome it: "Only mechanization itself can lead us beyond mechanization."[77]

To a greater degree than Rathenau, Moellendorff was fascinated by mechanization. He was greatly impressed by American "technocracy,"[78] which he called a "lesson of

[72] Cf. Rathenau, "Deutsche Rohstoffversorgung," *Schriften*, v, 53ff. and "Probleme der Friedenswirtschaft. Vortrag gehalten in der 'Deutschen Gesellschaft 1914' am 18. Dezember 1916," *Schriften*, v, 66, passim.

[73] Rathenau, "Probleme der Friedenswirtschaft," *Schriften*, v, 93.

[74] "*Europäische Restmoral*"; Rathenau, "Von kommenden Dingen," *Schriften*, III, 178.

[75] *Ibid.*, 175.   [76] *Ibid.*, 33.

[77] Rathenau, *Briefe* (2nd edn., Dresden, 1926), I, 280.

[78] "Technocracy"—often called "Taylorism"—was a movement founded by the American F. W. Taylor (1856-1915) which aimed at improving industrial efficiency through competent industrial leader-

America,"[79] He extolled the "open, regulated [*gebun-denen*], well-meaning, and obliging aspects"[80] of mechanization in contrast to the evils of capitalism. Mechanization, in the last analysis, was a challenge which could be met by socialism.

Rathenau had the courage to interpret the economic planning of the war years as "an economic occurrence which borders closely on the methods of socialism and communism."[81] "We shall without hesitation wander part of our way alongside the road of socialism and still reject its objectives."[82] The Marxian answer, Rathenau thought, got stuck in the "sensualistic-mechanistic order."[83] Marxism was materialism, Moellendorff argued, which regulated relations between men and goods, but not between men and men.[84] The Marxian proletarian was the mass man who had lost his faith and his freedoms and was merely bargaining for material advantages. Rathenau summed up his views on Marx shortly after the war in a conversation with Karl Radek: "Marx merely gave the theory of destruction. From my works you will derive the theory of constructive socialism. . . ."[85]

Rathenau's and Moellendorff's socialism came to be known as "social economy" (*Deutsche Gemeinwirtschaft*). The term goes back to a wartime publication of Moellendorff's.[86] According to a somewhat demonstrative and epi-

---

ship and organization. One of the most challenging points provided for the replacement of businessmen by technicians and engineers in the management of industry. The movement was most influential in the early 1930's.

[79] Wichard von Moellendorff, *Konservativer Sozialismus* (ed. Hermann Curth, Hamburg, 1932), 56, 264.

[80] *Ibid.*, 63.

[81] Rathenau, "Deutsche Rohstoffversorgung," *Schriften*, v, 25.

[82] Rathenau, "Von kommenden Dingen," *Schriften*, iii, 74f.

[83] *Ibid.*, 37.

[84] Cf. Moellendorff, *Konservativer Sozialismus*, 64.

[85] Edward Hallett Carr, "Radek's 'Political Salon' in Berlin 1919," *Soviet Studies*, iii (1951/1952), 420.

[86] Moellendorff, *Deutsche Gemeinwirtschaft* (Berlin, 1916). Though the tract did not reach the general public, it is stated that it was

grammatic definition, the *Gemeinwirtschaft* is "not concerned with confiscation [*Wegnahme*] but with sacrifice [*Hingabe*], not with rights but with duties, not with liberties but with loyalties [*Gebundenheiten*]."[87] However, even though "duties" and "loyalties" were the vogue of the "war experience," "rights" and "liberties" had their place in the *Gemeinwirtschaft*. Rathenau balanced "social justice" against "civil freedom,"[88] and both Rathenau and Moellendorff took pains to differentiate between doctrinaire socialism and their own. The "practical socialist" does not have to resort to the elimination of private property. Indeed, he should not interfere with inventiveness and private initiative.[89] Socialism should mean subordinating private interest to the good of the whole. Rathenau, therefore, provided for semi-public professional associations which were to supervise the national economy. And Moellendorff revived an old plan of Bismarck's[90] in advocating the creation of a National Economic Council (Volkswirtschaftsrat) which was to supplement, if not to supplant, the work of the Reichstag.[91]

In theory as well as in practice Rathenau and Moellendorff worked on the reintegration of the individual into an industrial society. They were romanticists in a technological age, as retrospective as they were forward-looking, as idealistic as hard-hitting. It might be said of them, in criticism, that they banked all too heavily on the momen-

circulated "in ministries and imperial departments, in the offices of large enterprises and in various political clubs." F. Glum, "Das Problem des Reichswirtschaftsrats," *Recht und Wirtschaft*, x (1921), 36.

[87] Moellendorff, *Von Einst zu Einst*, 3f.

[88] Rathenau, "Probleme der Friedenswirtschaft," *Schriften*, v, 93.

[89] Cf. Moellendorff, *Konservativer Sozialismus*, 108.

[90] Cf. Glum, "Das Problem des Reichswirtschaftsrats," *Recht und Wirtschaft*, x (1921), 36.

[91] For a detailed account of the plans as projected in *Die neue Wirtschaft* (Berlin, 1918) and *Deutsche Gemeinwirtschaft* (Berlin, 1916) see Ralph H. Bowen, *German Theories of the Corporate State* (New York, London, 1947), 172ff. and 184ff.

tary receding of party and caste feeling as a result of the "war experience." For, as Rathenau assumed, would the department head of an enterprise, given the choice of doubling his income or of becoming a director, have forfeited the former alternative?[92] And could the profit motive ever be checked by idealism? But the great merit of Rathenau's and Moellendorff's concept lies in its good measure. It was devoid of any radical solution. It had no revolutionary message, no easy solution. It was neither violently nationalistic nor anti-intellectual. While it might have chosen the path of bourgeois baiting, it aimed at the reestablishment of a "rejuvenated middle class."[93] The new socialism of Rathenau and Moellendorff was a matter of reemphasizing traditions and redefining freedoms.

THE CRISIS OF SOCIAL DEMOCRACY
AND THE LITERATURE OF DISENCHANTMENT

The new socialism was also nourished from the Marxist camp. Its basis was broadened by defections from Social Democracy caused by the dilemma with which German Marxism was faced at the outset of the war. The response to the *Burgfriede* was bound to become a point of major disagreement within the rank and file of the German socialist movement. While on August 4, 1914 Hugo Haase read before the Reichstag the declaration of the Sozialdemokratische Partei Deutschlands acknowledging the Party's role in safeguarding "the *Kultur* and the independence"[94] of Germany, the "fellows without fatherland" were ready to do their duty, to fight and die for their country. The decision of the S.P.D. to support the German war effort, however, was the beginning of a fatal crisis within the Party.

It had become evident in the meeting of the S.P.D. leaders on August 3 that within the Party grave dissension

92 Rathenau, "Von kommenden Dingen," *Schriften*, III, 155.

93 Moellendorff, *Konservativer Sozialismus*, 186.

94 Edwyn Bevan, *German Social Democracy during the War* (London, 1918), 21.

existed on the attitude toward the war, and it was only party discipline that prevented fourteen dissenting votes against the war and war credits from going on record during the next day's Reichstag session. They represented the voice of Marxian orthodoxy and the interests of the Second International. They warned the workers against getting involved in a nationalistic war. As the war went on, the dissenters, the so-called Minority Socialists, became increasingly strong until they seceded under the leadership of Haase and founded, in the spring of 1917, the Independent Social Democratic Party (Unabhängige Sozialdemokratische Partei or U.S.P.).

The patriotic argument among the Majority Socialists was presented by its leading men, such as Heinrich Cunow, Eduard David, Konrad Haenisch, and the Austrian Karl Renner. They set out to prove that there was no conflict between the interests of the proletariat and those of the nation; indeed, the nation was considered the protector of the working class. A synthesis between the nation and the International was sought.[95] In the process of this reexamination of Marxism the Majority Socialists came close to the position taken by Rathenau and Moellendorff.

The era of good will which was marked by the "Policy of the Fourth of August" did not last. After the summer of 1916 the Majority Socialists saw themselves forced to conduct a more rigorous policy for peace. In July 1917, by

[95] Cf. the following writings: Heinrich Cunow, *Parteienzusammenbruch? Ein offenes Wort zum inneren Parteistreit* (Berlin, 1915); Eduard David, *Die Sozialdemokratie im Weltkrieg* (Berlin, 1915) and *Aus Deutschlands schwerster Zeit. Schriften und Reden aus den Jahren 1914-1919* (Berlin, 1927); Konrad Haenisch, *Die deutsche Sozialdemokratie in und nach dem Weltkrieg* (Berlin, 1916); Karl Renner, *Marxismus, Krieg und Internationale. Kritische Studien über offene Probleme des wissenschaftlichen und praktischen Sozialismus in und nach dem Weltkrieg* (Stuttgart, 1917). The patriotic course of the Majority Socialists was supported by two leading Social Democratic periodicals, the *Sozialistische Monatshefte*, a mouthpiece of former Revisionists who backed the war effort, and *Die Glocke*, which was founded in the fall of 1915 by an extreme Leftist Russian refugee named Alexander Helphand (pseudonym: "Parvus").

backing Erzberger's peace resolution along with the Center Party and the Progressives, they moved into full opposition to the continuation of the war. With this reversal of policy the Majority Socialists approached the line originally taken by the Minority Socialists, but the rift between the two parties could no longer be bridged. Actually, the Independents, out of intransigence, voted against the peace resolution.

An opposition against the new course of the S.P.D. recruited itself from men who were at the extreme right of Social Democracy, among them Cunow, Haenisch, Alexander Helphand, Paul Lensch—all former Radicals—and the union leader August Winnig. Plenge also belonged to this group. The *Glocke* became their mouthpiece. By continuing to back the German war effort these men isolated themselves from the S.P.D., to which they came to be known as "social imperialists."[96] The group reflected a disillusionment with Marxism. Its writings amounted to a "literature of disenchantment" from within the ranks of Marxism.[97] The logic of their position drove them to search for a "true socialism,"[98] which stressed, as Lensch did, the "inseparable unity" of class consciousness and nation consciousness.[99] This point of view allowed the *Glocke* Circle to accept the war economy as its own platform.

It matters little that after the war some members of the *Glocke* Circle found their way back to the Social Democrats, or that Lensch and Winnig eventually broke away from the old Party. It does matter that Marxists shifted

[96] In two editorials of July 2 and 4, 1916, the *Vorwärts*, the official daily of the S.P.D., rejecting the theories of Lensch, labeled the views expressed by the *"Glocke* Circle" for the first time as "social imperialism"; Ludwig Quessel, "Sozialimperialismus," *Sozialistische Monatshefte*, xxii (1916), 741.

[97] The term is borrowed from Sidney Hook, "Literature of Disenchantment," *New York Times Book Review*, May 16, 1948.

[98] Plenge, *Zur Vertiefung des Sozialismus* (Leipzig, 1919), 132.

[99] Paul Lensch, *Die Sozialdemokratie und der Weltkrieg* (Berlin, 1915), 216.

their ground from their traditional "material revolution" to a "spiritual revolution."[100] They became concerned with the integration of the individual into society by an "education toward solidarity"[101] which was to transcend class consciousness. Their ideas on planning, or, as they called it, "organization," considerably influenced twentieth century German conservative thought.[102] And they were largely responsible for the fact that in the post-war period conservative thought continued to study the problems of socialism.

In summary, the war experience rejuvenated German conservatism and brought it as close as it ever came to representing the ideals of a Tory democracy. The war brought about an understanding of conservatism which was independent of the party-line conservatism of the Conservatives. And, in the face of the rising danger of Marxism, the wartime conservatism outlined its own practical way of solving the social problem. It was unfortunate that it took the war to further this development, because it was the impact of the war which gave the new conservatism its distinctly anti-Western note and tended to cut off German conservatism from any European ties.

[100] Paul Lensch, *Drei Jahre Weltrevolution* (Berlin, 1917), 38.
[101] Plenge, *1789 und 1914*, 110.
[102] *Ibid.*, 15; Lensch, *Drei Jahre*, 19, 41; Wissell and Moellendorff, *Wirtschaftliche Selbstverwaltung*, 24; Oswald Spengler, *Preussentum und Sozialismus* (Munich, 1920), 49.

PART II

THE NEO-CONSERVATIVE MOVEMENT

"THE wonderful message of August 4, 1914," Naumann wrote, "should not be lost even after the revolution."[1] Indeed, the historian might safely assume that the mentality which prevailed in the Youth Movement and which went with the "ideas of 1914" would have gained new actuality after 1918. After all, the uprootedness, the sense of alienation from nature and society which was so acutely felt in the Youth Movement and which plagued the German intellectuals when they were faced by war in 1914, had become inescapable reality in 1918. It had become unmistakably a problem of general concern. Defeat and the abolishment of the Monarchy, followed by inflation, brought about a vacuum in German life which represented the main challenge the new Republic had to face. Among its many tasks the most fundamental and far-reaching one was that of filling the political, the social, and—last but not least—the psychological vacuum. This meant the estab-

[1] Theodor Heuss, *Friedrich Naumann. Der Mann, das Werk, die Zeit* (2nd edn., Stuttgart, Tübingen, 1949), 458.

lishing of new allegiances. What was needed above all was a Republican mystique to take the place of defunct traditions. What was needed, in other words, was a healthy conservatism.

We know that the Republic failed to meet this challenge. It remained unbeloved. However, an excess of hindsight tends unduly to simplify the history of the period after 1918 into a conflict between, on the one hand, a doomed Republic, and, on the other hand, the extreme Left—namely, the Communists—and an intransigent Right represented by the German Nationals and the National Socialists. A more careful examination of the early years after the revolution indicates that, at that time, the Republic served to focus the hopes of the majority of Germans. While the workers, for their part, expected a millennium through socialization, large segments of the middle classes emerged from war and revolution looking to the Republic for the reestablishment of national greatness and unity as well as for the setting up of a new social order. The historian, therefore, cannot maintain that the Republic was doomed by the lack of backing by the populace. If anything, it was threatened by the variety of its support. It was a workers' republic as well as a middle class republic. And its final failure was the failure to encompass these groups. Like the kaiser's Germany the Republic was unable to elevate itself to a level transcending social and political rivalry. It did not become a symbol; it could not make itself loved. It was a monarchy *manquée*.

A closer study of the initial years of the Republic is, therefore, particularly important for an assessment of the ultimate debacle. These were the decisive years, years of contrast between expectations and achievements, years of struggle, years in which the ultimate fate of the Republic hung in the balance. It was the period before the irrevocable polarization toward the extreme Left and Right took place.

Arthur Rosenberg in his exciting studies of the Republic[2] has focused on its early years and explored the possibilities which lay in a truly revolutionary course based upon an alliance between Social Democrats, Independents, and Communists. He thought that this coalition would have brought about a genuinely German form of democracy and a strong revolutionary dynamism, even though power factors—such as Moscow's hold over the Kommunistische Partei Deutschlands, or the implacable opposition of the Reichswehr to a Left coalition—were working against such a form of government.

A corresponding study—as is proposed in the following pages—will show that the situation faced by the Right during the early Republican period was still a flexible one and that various forces were at work trying to shape within the framework of the Republic a truly conservative policy to fill the vacuum left by defeat, revolution, and inflation. Weimar and the subsequent failure of socialization interfered with their socialistic dreams, as did Versailles with their patriotic pride. Ultimately, however, the failure of these efforts was due to the inner weakness of the new conservatism and to its inability to define clearly its position toward National Socialism.

Quite clearly the new conservatism, which acknowledged the breakdown of the Second Reich and what it stood for, could find no home in the Deutschnationale Volkspartei (D.N.V.P.). No more than its predecessor, the Conservative Party of the Imperial era, could this party claim to represent truly conservative opinion in the country as a whole. The D.N.V.P. had initially made a gesture to the revolution by presenting itself in the elections for the National Assembly under a new name, as a "people's" party. It had tried to improve on the Conservative Party by aiming at a broad social following. Indeed, it had at first withheld its commitment to the Monarchy.[3] But, after the first revolu-

[2] Arthur Rosenberg, *The Birth of the German Republic* (London, 1931) and *A History of the German Republic* (London, 1936).

[3] Cf. Walter H. Kaufmann, *Monarchism in the Weimar Republic* (New York, 1953), 53ff., 61ff.

tionary shock it came to reaffirm the traditional position of the official conservatism and declared itself "conservative only in the sense of Luther, Bismarck, and Hindenburg."[4] It remained the party of landed interests and heavy industry. It became the party of restoration, withdrawing behind the false security of the Hohenzollern Monarchy, which was no longer a living symbol of German conservatism. As a party the D.N.V.P. did not even begin to face the dilemma of conservatism. The revolution, which might have shown it that new ideas and symbols were needed to reach the masses, left no visible mark on the Party. The reactionary nature of the D.N.V.P. became clearly evident when, beginning with the year 1928, those members who gravitated toward the new conservatism seceded from it one by one.

The final victory of National Socialism has obscured, in the treatment of the history of the early Republican period, the fact that there were a number of independent groups and individuals who were in their own ways concerned with establishing new allegiances. These were the neoconservatives. This group included such "elders" of the Republic as Max Weber, Naumann, Troeltsch, Meinecke, indeed Rathenau and Thomas Mann, as well as the self-styled "young ones" around Moeller van den Bruck (*Die Jungen*) and also Spengler, Ernst Jünger, the *Tat* Circle, and the Strasser brothers. Our collective designation for them as a "movement" should convey the fact that, in spite of the obvious differences between these men, they were all dedicated to the tradition of the Youth Movement and of the "ideas of 1914." Their conservatism was a forward-looking conservatism, Nietzschean rather than Bismarckian. For them the revolution of 1918 was a challenge: it opened the way for a policy that was truly conservative, though within a republic. In other words, it allowed for an imaginative redefinition of conservatism in a changed situation. Like

[4] *Politische Ziele und Anschauungen der Deutschnationalen Volkspartei. Flugschrift No. 13*, quoted in *ibid.*, 54.

the early nineteenth century conservatives who had been children of the French Revolution, the neo-conservatives now were children of the German November Revolution.

The neo-conservatives have been repeatedly called "officers without an army" and they have been criticized because they "wore themselves out in brotherhoods and conventicles, in true German fashion, with problems which led them far from the political issues of the day into a maze of esoteric ideologies and doctrines."[5] The fact that the neo-conservative movement never crystallized into one political organization should not, however, detract from its significance. In the years immediately following the war it became an important factor in molding public opinion by means of its frequent publications, its clubs and circles, and its network of personal relations cutting across party lines. A study of the movement and of its course not only introduces us to one of the most critical phases in the history of German conservatism but also raises for us the crucial problem of how and why the Weimar Republic came to be an orphan republic.

[5] Rauschning, *Revolution of Nihilism*, 111.

CHAPTER I

THE REVOLUTION OF 1918-1919 AND ITS CONSERVATIVE ASPECTS

The "Dreamland of the Armistice Period"

THERE was a moment during the early months after the armistice, roughly before the Treaty of Versailles was signed and the Weimar Constitution was adopted, when Germany was in flux. It was one of those short periods in history which seem to be completely uprooted from the past and which are pregnant with possibilities. For Germany it was a vital period in which nothing was needed more than statesmanship. It was a "transition period of immense value."[1] It was, as Troeltsch saw it, the "dreamland of the armistice period."[2] The impact of the emotional upsurge after the revolution tended toward obliteration of the traditional domestic line-up and toward political reorientation. It is safe to say that it affected all shades of political opinion except out-and-out monarchism. Even among ardent nationalists and conservatives the revolution was initially welcomed. Thus the *Tat* magazine in its first issue after November 9 greeted the revolution warmly; its editor, Eugen Diederichs, welcomed the fall of the "old regime" and committed the *Tat* to a "joyous 'yea' to the revolution."[3] Moeller van den Bruck even admitted that he saw "great possibilities" in the revolution, as in "every break with the past."[4] In short, in those few months of euphoria even the conservative turned revolutionary.

The psychology of defeat must be recaptured if we want

[1] Heuss, *Naumann*, 445.

[2] Ernst Troeltsch, *Spektator-Briefe. Aufsätze über die deutsche Revolution und die Weltpolitik, 1918-1922* (ed. H. Baron, Tübingen, 1924), 69.

[3] Eugen Diederichs, "Die deutsche Revolution," *Die Tat*, x (1918-1919), 726.

[4] Moeller, *Das dritte Reich*, 25.

to understand the reactions of the Germans in those early months after November 1918. It was a period in which no issue could be faced squarely, not even defeat itself. Defeat meant for the German "collapse," in which sobriety and routine gave way to a temper of intense emotion. One was amazed to see houses and trees still standing.[5] The awareness of catastrophe prevailed and found its outlet in either undue despair or undue hope. As the young Ernst von Salomon witnessed, the despair of the returning soldiers was matched by victory preparations by those who lined the streets back home to receive them.[6] Defeat could thus appear at the same time as a curse and as a blessing. Moeller's two contradictory reactions to it—the "stab-in-the-back" thesis and the view of defeat as a much-needed lesson—were but symptoms of a generally confused situation.[7] How, otherwise, could we understand the publication in the December 1918 issue of the *Tat* of a poem by Richard Dehmel entitled "Victory" (*Sieg*)?[8] As against the prevailing chaos the poet projected a glittering vision of peace. Defeat opened the gates toward the millennium. It produced in itself a mentality which was revolutionary.

It is interesting that the final exit of the kaiser was not much lamented even among conservatives. In the last years of the war the so-called *Kaiserfrage* had agitated the minds of German politicians and intellectuals, among whom the abdication of the kaiser as a means of salvaging the Monarchy had found increasing support. But August Winnig observed quite correctly that "when the Republic took the place of the Monarchy, nobody opposed the Republic, in order to die for the Monarchy."[9] Though the Republic was not widely welcomed in Germany, it was widely accepted. Many a conservative settled on its conservative pos-

[5] Cf. Troeltsch, *Spektator-Briefe*, 19.

[6] Ernst von Salomon, *Die Geächteten* (Berlin, 1930), 28.

[7] Cf. infra, 160.

[8] *Die Tat*, x (1918-1919), 685.

[9] August Winnig, *Das Reich als Republik, 1918-1928* (2nd edn., Stuttgart, Berlin, 1929), 54.

sibilities; the 1918 revolution was to be turned into Germany's "glorious revolution."[10] Indeed, a clear delineation between the old black-white-red conservatism and a new conservatism became imperative. Within the ranks of the political Right the "fight against the reaction" was as yet to be fought.[11] The monarchic principle disappeared as an integral feature of conservative thought. But the question remained, whether and how the new Republic could be made to command the loyalties of the German nation.

Socialism was a vital element in the mood of the "dreamland of the armistice period." It became a veritable fashion among the middle classes as well as the workers. A sociology of the revolution would register the greatest upset in the ranks of the middle classes rather than among the workers. "The war," Lensch had claimed in 1917, "is being waged at the expense of the middle classes."[12] Defeat and revolution carried this development still further. The discharged officers and soldiers did not come back into carefree and protected homes. They were "disinherited."[13] Economic security and careers seemed assured only to a very few of the returners, many of whom had the first taste of unemployment. This situation was reflected in the conservative literature in terms of various appeals to the *Bürgertum*; "it lives through the eleventh hour of its history." And Eugen Diederichs added that the *Bürger* was "on trial."[14]

The *Bürger* became more and more a glorified have-not. It has been said of him that he has been "intellectualized"

[10] Wilhelm Stapel, "Die Zukunft der nationalen Bewegung," *Deutsches Volkstum*, xxvi (1924), 5.

[11] Winnig, *Das Reich als Republik*, 344; cf. also Max Hildebert Boehm, *Was uns not tut* (Berlin, 1919), 11; Heinrich von Gleichen, *Freies Volk* (Charlottenburg, 1919), 13f.

[12] Lensch, *Drei Jahre Weltrevolution*, 12.

[13] Cf. E. Günther Gründel, *Die Sendung der jungen Generation* (3rd edn., Munich, 1933), 40f.

[14] Ernst Krieck, "Aufruf zur Selbsthilfe," *Die Tat*, x (1918-1919), 679; Eugen Diederichs, "Die deutsche Revolution," *Die Tat*, x (1918-1919), 726.

by war and revolution.[15] He was driven into higher learn-
ing often in lieu of a better opportunity. And if he was not
a proletarian, it was merely because he generally would not
want to be called such. Moeller claimed that a proletarian
is "only he who wants to be a proletarian."[16] Between the
Bürger and the proletarian was the element of pride. The
former became the proverbial *Herr Doktor*, a sorry shadow
of the once arrogant *Reserveoffizier*. Threatened with the
loss of status, he found his last refuge in respectability.

In 1918 the impoverished middle classes had, therefore,
good reason to talk socialism. Troeltsch commented upon
the conservatives who "dreamt" socialism.[17] They also
"dreamt" revolution. Of course, they rejected the Marxist
gospel. They would call themselves "idealists." They would
feed upon the traditions of the Youth Movement and the
"war experience." And they would name their socialism
"new," "German," "national," or "conservative." According to Moeller, socialism was "the only so far available collective term for the new problems which the war has
raised."[18] Indeed, it made him face the revolution with
anticipation.

A survey of the neo-conservative literature of the months
following the revolution thus throws a new light on this
critical period. It suggests that there were forces at the
right which gravitated toward revolution and socialism.
These forces were representative of wide segments among
the hard-hit middle classes. It is fair to say that the latter
were disposed to accept the events of November 1918. They
"would have accepted the revolution, had it been a full
substitute for victory, had it ended the four years of fighting by a new achievement."[19] This means that, initially

[15] Konrad Heiden, *Adolf Hitler, Das Zeitalter der Verantwortungs-
losigkeit. Eine Biographie* (Zurich, 1936), 93f.

[16] Moeller, *Das dritte Reich*, 123f.

[17] Troeltsch, *Spektator-Briefe*, 51.

[18] Moeller van den Bruck, "Die Sozialisierung der Aussenpolitik"
(March 1919), *Das Recht der jungen Völker* (ed. Hans Schwarz, Berlin, 1932) , 112.

[19] Heiden, *Hitler*, 94.

at least, the new Republic had a much wider potential support than is generally assumed.

But while the psychology of the revolutionary situation made conservatism compatible with republicanism, the expectations in the initial days of the Republic on the part of conservative opinion did not materialize. The Republic did not turn out to be a good soil for conservatism. The result was a gradual process of alienation between the Republic and the conservatives. The latter drifted more and more into an attitude of resentment and into sympathizing with an extremist position. The events after 1918, by being the seeding ground of extremism and, indeed, fascism, thus accentuated the dilemma of conservatism.

The End of the "Dreamland of the Armistice Period": (a) The Failure of the New Socialism

The stabilization of the Republic put an end to the revolution. And as the stabilization came about, the chances for socialism in Germany vanished. Socialism was the one idea produced by the revolution which could have served as a common denominator to the German people. In particular, socialization was the "magic formula"[20] for socialists of every kind during the early years of the Republic. But the defeat of the Independents' political and social program through the elections for the National Assembly and the failure of the Socialization Commissions—not to mention the defeats of both the Independents and the Spartacists all over Germany by the army—turned the extreme Left against the Republic.

The new socialism also suffered rejection by the Republic. After the war, even more than during the war, the fathers of the new socialism saw their field wide open. They wanted socialization. Late in 1918 in *Die Grenzboten* you might read how socialism had become an integral part of German society through the war, and therefore "the Right,

[20] Werner F. Bruck, *Social and Economic History of Germany from William II to Hitler, 1888-1938* (Cardiff, 1938), 155.

also, will sponsor an organic continuation of socialization by means of state socialism."[21] The forces behind the new socialism were, to be sure, less spectacular than the ones behind Marxian socialism. Yet they were considerable and often underrated in their impact upon the opinions of the "intellectuals." For its orientation, the new socialism of the post-war period fell back not only on the precedent of the war socialism, but also on the influences from the Marxian camp and the ideas of management of Rathenau and Hugo Stinnes, above all. In the midst of so many contradictory contacts, the new socialism was labeled by the capitalists as anti-capitalistic and by the Marxists as anti-socialistic. An examination of its main concepts, the *Arbeitsgemeinschaft*, and *Gemeinwirtschaft*, will establish its place in German social thought. And the story of its fate under the Republic explains a great deal about the alienation of conservative opinion from the Republic.

THE ARBEITSGEMEINSCHAFT

The *Arbeitsgemeinschaft*, hailed as "the new political idea of the Right,"[22] corresponded to the Council (*Räte*) idea of the Left. It was a spontaneous agreement on labor relations reached immediately after the revolution (on November 15, 1918) between capital and labor. Among the German industrialists, Stinnes and Rathenau, and among the trade union leaders, Karl Legien for the Free Trade Unions and Adam Stegerwald for the Christian Unions, were most instrumental in bringing about the agreement. It stipulated the recognition by management of the unions and provided for the discontinuation of the so-called "yellow unions," which were company unions; and the principle of collective bargaining was recognized. Furthermore, the eight-hour work day, which had already been pro-

[21] Max Hildebert Boehm, "Nationalversammlung und Parteien," *Die Grenzboten*, LXXVII, 4/4 (1918), 200.
[22] Eduard Stadtler, "Zum Parteitag der Deutschen Volkspartei," *Die Grenzboten*, LXXIX, 4/4 (1920), 299.

claimed by an appeal of the Representatives of the People on November 12th, was generally introduced. A central commission, the *Zentralarbeitsgemeinschaft,* composed of employers and workers, was to decide about questions concerning the reconstruction of the German economy.

The *Arbeitsgemeinschaft* was a significant milestone in the field of labor relations. A result of Stinnes' initiative, it was not an isolated case of what might paradoxically be called "entrepreneurial socialism."[23] In 1919 Stinnes wrote to Winnig: "We must solve the social question now, or else there is no salvation for Germany."[24] The November agreement constituted the maximum of socialism which the majority of industrialists were willing to concede and, in turn, a triumph of the unions' policy of collective bargaining. It accentuated the split between the S.P.D. and the U.S.P., with the former welcoming and the latter attacking the agreement. Though the *Arbeitsgemeinschaft* itself was short-lived, all of its terms found their way into the public law.

The November agreement was accepted by the Right because it meant the first application of the principle of solidarity[25] to the post-war economy. It was a case of an idealistic socialism. But it merely set the pattern; it set the

[23] Hugo Stinnes was responsible for the organization of the Rheinisch-Westfälisches Elektrizitätswerk, which provided the Rhenish and Westphalian industrial area with power. It was a so-called "mixed enterprise," a German version of the T.V.A., combining public and private interests. The municipalities were given shares of and supervisory powers over the new enterprise. First devised in 1905, the mixed enterprise became during the Weimar Republic the pattern for about half of the electricity works. Rathenau's War Industrial Companies were mixed enterprises according to the same pattern. Cf. Bruck, *Social and Economic History,* 198ff.

[24] August Winnig, *Heimkehr* (3rd edn., Hamburg, 1935), 313.

[25] The concept "solidarity" (*Solidarismus*), meaning the community of interests between town and country, employer and employee, between competitors, between supplier and buyer, producer and consumer, etc. (cf. Wissell and Moellendorff, *Wirtschaftliche Selbstverwaltung,* 23), originated with the nineteenth century Catholic social theory (Franz Hitze, 1851-1921; Heinrich Pesch, 1854-1926).

proper "example."[26] And it became an incentive for the formulation of further economic plans along similar lines.

GEMEINWIRTSCHAFT

Gemeinwirtschaft was the outstanding post-war contribution of the non-Marxists to social policy. Once more Rathenau and Moellendorff were its leading proponents, and its fortunes were closely followed among the conservatives, who, on the whole, identified themselves with it.

Rathenau tried to channel his ideas into the movement for socialization. Actually, his name was, over his violent protest to President Friedrich Ebert, struck from the roster of the first Socialization Commission, due to objections on the part of the Independents against his participation. Called together in December 1918, the members of the first Commission resigned in April 1919 in protest against their lack of powers. The second Commission, with Rathenau as a member, was nominated after the Kapp Putsch in 1920. While the Left was deadlocked over the question of whether German industry was "ripe" for immediate socialization, Rathenau produced the most concrete plan for socialization. It amounted to a restatement of the principles of the war economy. "It will be our task," the report stated, "to effect the transition to new forms of industry and to point out the paths from our present industrial ethics to a system based on community ethics."[27] The new economy, according to Rathenau's plan, was to be built on the basis of solidarity between capital and labor, with both groups being equally represented in industrial concerns as well as in corporative bodies. As a man of affairs he saw that socialization was a long-range matter and that such basic changes in society could be effected only gradually.

The failure of the second Socialization Commission

[26] Moellendorff, *Konservativer Sozialismus*, 162. Cf. also 148.
[27] Report of the Socialization Commission, dated July 31, 1920, p. 17, quoted in Kessler, *Walther Rathenau*, 256.

brought out clearly the limits of socialization as well as the inability and unwillingness of the government to apply even a reduced measure of socialism. Rathenau traveled the bitter road from disappointment to resigned acquiescence. Already, at the occasion of the first anniversary of the revolution he had complained that "it was not a revolution. . . . The first year has brought a certain measure of order; which was to be expected, for we are an orderly people. It has produced bourgeois measures, an old-fashioned republican constitution, and so forth; ideas and deeds it has not produced. . . ."[28] Rathenau's idealism was soon silenced. The last chapter of Rathenau's Utopia was written in 1919; it already contained a marked note of resignation.[29] No further books were written by Rathenau. Even the active support which he had had since the late war years from the Eugen Diederichs publishing house dwindled in 1920.[30] When Rathenau assumed the office of minister of reconstruction and, subsequently, that of minister of foreign affairs, he altogether abandoned the role of the reformer. He withdrew into his other self.

After the war Moellendorff was in an even better position than his friend to root their common idea of *Gemeinwirtschaft* in the Republic. Following the defeat, he accepted in December 1918 the position of under state secretary in the Reichswirtschaftsamt, which was elevated to the status of Ministry of Economics in February 1919. His immediate superiors were at first Dr. August Müller and, afterward, the minister, Rudolf Wissell, both Social

[28] *Welt am Montag* (November 10, 1919, No. 45), quoted in *ibid.*, 265f.

[29] Walther Rathenau, *Die neue Gesellschaft* (Berlin, 1919) and *Autonome Wirtschaft* (*Deutsche Gemeinwirtschaft* Pamphlet 16) (Jena, 1919).

[30] Cf. the columns of the *Tat* from 1918 to 1920 and the series of pamphlets called *Deutsche Gemeinwirtschaft* (1917-1920), which was brought out by Rathenau's editor Erich Schairer and which included among its eighteen titles works by Rathenau, Moellendorff, and writers with related views.

Democrats connected with the *Sozialistische Monatshefte*.[31] The whole legislation on socialization of the National Assembly goes back to Mollendorff, whose personality dominated the Ministry of Economics. But Articles 156 and 165 of the Constitution, as well as the laws of the year 1919 on socialization, remained in Moellendorff's own opinion a "half-hearted" farce,[32] or, as the *Tat* summed up later, "socialism on paper."[33]

The clearest statement on socialization coming from a non-Marxist appeared in Moellendorff's ill-fated *Denkschrift*.[34] It was thought of by Moellendorff and Wissell primarily as a memorandum for discussion and approval by the government, but it reached the public through an indiscretion in the *Vossische Zeitung* on May 24, 1919. Moellendorff's memorandum began with a sharp criticism of the government, which, though relying on a parliamentary majority, was "day by day losing more of its popular support."[35] The government was attacked for its lack of a clearly defined social policy: "for the benefit of the democratic principle, socialism has been seriously neglected. It is most urgent that this mistake be repaired, lest socialism be left to wild anarchistic experiments and, in addition, democracy itself should suffer."[36]

The *Denkschrift* was devised as an elaboration of the *Arbeitsgemeinschaft* idea, which Moellendorff referred to as "reflecting exactly my official policy."[37] Its main pro-

---

[31] The *Sozialistische Monatshefte*, under the direction of Joseph Bloch, Max Cohen-Reuss, and Julius Kaliski, was after the war an energetic advocate of socialization. The ideas expressed in the *Sozialistische Monatshefte* often coincided with Moellendorff's ideas.

[32] Moellendorff, *Konservativer Sozialismus*, 255.

[33] Wilhelm Rössle, "Sozialismus auf dem Papier," *Die Tat*. XXII (1930-1931), 903-913.

[34] *Der Aufbau der Gemeinwirtschaft. Denkschrift des Reichswirtschaftsministeriums vom 7. Mai 1919* (*Deutsche Gemeinwirtschaft* Pamphlet 9) (Jena, 1919).

[35] *Ibid.*, 2.   [36] *Ibid.*, 4.

[37] Moellendorff, *Konservativer Sozialismus*, 162. Cf. also Wissell and Moellendorff, *Wirtschaftliche Selbstverwaltung*, 8, 26.

visions were as follows: a twofold corporative representation, a regional and a vocational one, each organized on
the basis of equality between the interested social groups,
was to be established. These representations were to administer the economic and social affairs for a given region
and profession, respectively. They, in turn, were to send
representatives to the Reich Economic Council, which was
to be the highest organ of the German *Gemeinwirtschaft*.

Moellendorff was opposed to all plans for "full socialization" because they aimed at the complete elimination
of private property. He rejected Bolshevism—though he
was quite impressed by its development in Soviet Russia.
Altogether he had little use for the Marxist approach to
socialization. In an atmosphere of reviving party loyalties,
Moellendorff's plan stood out as the work of a devoted
public servant. With the constitution not yet decided upon,
the *Denkschrift* was kept deliberately flexible so as to fit
into any political framework. But, on the whole, Moellendorff remained oblivious to the political powers that be.

Moellendorff's plan met with hostility from almost every
side but the extreme Right.[38] Even Walther Rathenau
turned against it when it was first published. He had been
angered by the fact that during the debate on the socialization law in the National Assembly Wissell had failed to
give due credit to him. Rathenau now maintained that the
scheme was launched prematurely, since it could not count
on the necessary support to pass, and since neither the
workers nor the employers had acquired as yet the ethics
which were needed for the success of such a venture.[39] Both
Wissell and Moellendorff defended their proposals before
various meetings of German industrialists;[40] Wissell pre-

[38] Cf., for a detailed survey of opinions for and against the plan,
Bowen, *German Theories of the Corporative State*, 195ff.

[39] Cf. Kessler, *Walther Rathenau*, 254ff. Maintaining that the
Gemeinwirtschaft was inspired by himself, Rathenau launched a sharp
attack against the Moellendorff-Wissell plan in *Autonome Wirtschaft*
(*Deutsche Gemeinwirtschaft* Pamphlet 16) (Jena, 1919).

[40] Their addresses were reprinted in Wissell and Moellendorff,
Wirtschaftliche Selbstverwaltung.

sented the plan to the Party Convention of the S.P.D. in Weimar in June 1919. But the plan met strong opposition in both camps. The cabinet of Gustav Bauer finally rejected it on July 8, 1919 against one supporting vote, cast by Wissell. Soon afterward both Wissell and Moellendorff resigned from the Ministry of Economics.

With the rejection of the *Gemeinwirtschaft* the efforts toward socialization in Germany had failed. The effect of this failure upon public opinion, as foreseen by Wissell at the Party Convention in Weimar, was nothing less than devastating: "Despite the Revolution, the nation feels that its hopes have been disappointed. Those things which the people expected of the Government have not come to pass . . . . Essentially we have governed according to the old forms of our State life. We have only succeeded in breathing very little fresh life into these forms. We have not been able so to influence the Revolution that Germany seemed filled with a new spirit. The inner structure of German civilization, of social life, appears little altered. And even so, not for the better. The nation believes that the achievements of the Revolution are simply negative in character, that in place of one form of military and bureaucratic government by individuals another has been introduced, and that the principles of government do not differ essentially from those of the old regime. . . . I believe that the verdict of history upon the National Assembly and ourselves will be bitter."[41]

From the Right the criticism of the failure of socialization was no less violent. The Social Democracy had been disappointing. "Now that it was in power, it failed no less than the . . . capitalistic bourgeoisie," Gründel recalled.[42] And Spengler stressed that "the republican form of government has not the least in common with socialism."[43]

[41] Rosenberg, *A History of the German Republic,* 125f.

[42] Gründel, *Sendung,* 191.

[43] Oswald Spengler, *Preussentum und Sozialismus* (Munich, 1920), 13.

If on one hand, as Moeller had to admit, the ideas of *Gemeinwirtschaft* remained "literature"[44] because of the fault of the Republic, on the other hand they were not dead for him and those like him. It was, he pointed out, too deeply rooted in the traditions of the nation. Moellendorff left a deep impression upon Moeller's thought; he was, as Moeller phrased it, "conservative when there was need for conservatism, social when there was need for socialism."[45] The end of socialization did not put an end to the popular movement for socialization. Indeed, with men like Moeller and Spengler, socialism became a political myth.

The End of the "Dreamland of the Armistice Period": (b) Versailles

The end of the euphoria after November 1918 was marked also by Versailles. Before Versailles, Troeltsch observed, one could still hope "to incorporate the German Reich as a factor of peace and justice, of social reforms and spiritual rebirth, into the community of peoples."[46] Ernst von Salomon recalled the revolutionary character of the immediate post-war period—which for him extended far into the 1920's—when Germany had "opened its pores to absorb the ideas of the world."[47] Before Versailles the nationalist Moeller did not seem out of place when suggesting that Wilson support his new idea of the "young peoples,"[48] and that, in other words, America mediate in favor of Germany. While the German army was still somewhat intact, and while the trust in Wilson's Fourteen Points still prevailed, a "tolerable peace" was generally expected.

[44] Moeller, *Das dritte Reich*, 134.
[45] Moeller van den Bruck, *Der politische Mensch* (ed. Hans Schwarz, Breslau, 1933), 72.
[46] Troeltsch, *Spektator-Briefe*, 16f.
[47] Ernst von Salomon, *Nahe Geschichte. Ein Überblick* (Berlin, 1936), 121.
[48] Cf. infra, 158f.

To all Germans Versailles was a great disappointment dramatically expressed by the resignations of Chancellor Philipp Scheidemann and the foreign minister, Count Ulrich von Brockdorff-Rantzau. But Versailles, whether too severe or not, was part of an inevitable anatomy of war. It was the price of defeat. And, for the Germans, it meant that they had to live with the sober and unpleasant reality of defeat.

The signing of the Treaty of Versailles was the first act of the so-called Policy of Fulfillment, which became the foreign policy of the Weimar Republic, interrupted only by the unsuccessful passive resistance to the Ruhr occupation. The Policy of Fulfillment was, like the timid social policy of the Republic, thankless. Unpopularity was the price for stabilization. And the fact that the Republic had to sign and was made responsible for the humiliating treaty directed the wrath of the population at the new state. After Versailles Germany became a more and more divided house. The Weimar Republic had to contend not only with a hostile socialistic myth, but also with a hostile nationalistic myth. Brockdorff-Rantzau had clearly foreseen this double threat. While at Versailles, he had pointed to the danger which could originate for the peace of the world, *"if in place of a national capitalism a national socialism should originate,* if nationalism should use a thoroughly organized economy as its weapon, as its army."[49]

The appeal to the national traditions thus became the obsession of a sick people and, in particular, of the impoverished middle classes. The nationalistic argument gave those classes an illusion of strength. While on the economic level they were continually losing ground, this argument gave them a welcome foundation of respectability.[50] Nationalism acquired the taint of resentment. And the young

[49] Graf Brockdorff-Rantzau, *Dokumente* (Charlottenburg, 1920), 148f. Italics in the original.
[50] Cf. Hendrik de Man, *Sozialismus und Nationalfascismus* (Potsdam, 1931); Fromm, *Escape from Freedom*, 216f.

Republic, unable to control this nationalism, "abandoned the leadership of the nationalist movement to counter-revolutionary forces."[51]

In summary, the "dreamland of the armistice period" did not last long. Also, its reality was primarily of a psychological nature and only indirectly of a political nature. It was part of the fever of revolution which was bound to recede. And, compared with the Utopian expectations of the masses, the tasks of the government were immediate political ones. The foremost concern was the prevention of a complete economic and political disintegration of Germany. The maintenance of order was essential for the survival of Germany as a unit. Socialistic experiments of any kind seemed as out of place as a foreign policy of defiance. As regards the issue of socialization, the Revisionist training of the late nineteenth century Social Democracy had conditioned the party to a careful policy, But now the Allied intervention in Russia was a warning to the German government which might have carried the revolution to extremes and thus added to the chaos in Germany. Unlike Russia, Germany's location between the East and the West would have made her an easy prey for her neighbors. The government had, therefore, to choose a policy of order and moderation. In a public address in Berlin the Social Democrat Hermann Müller said: "It is a misfortune that our party received the portfolios of office at the time which is as unfavorable as possible for socialization. The entire economic life has collapsed. Almost all assumptions for socialization are lacking. . . . We do not dare experiment; we must proceed cautiously."[52]

On the other hand, the revolutionary months contained the seeds for a republican mystique in Germany which encompassed both the Left and the Right. Therefore, it is

[51] Rosenberg, *A History of the German Republic*, 131f.
[51] *Vorwärts* (April 7, 1919), quoted in Ralph Haswell Lutz, *The German Revolution 1918-1919* (Stanford University, 1922), 67.

possible to argue that the very psychological reality of the transition period might have been better exploited by the Republic. This is Arthur Rosenberg's argument as he stresses the failure of Social Democracy to satisfy the German workers. Conservative opinion was no less disappointed. As we have seen, conservatism cannot be simply considered a counter-revolutionary element in the Republic. Indeed, it had participated in the "November experience."[53] And only later did the process start which, as Konrad Haenisch charged, "drove the masses of the strongly nationalistic German intelligentsia out of the ranks of the Democracy."[54] "Order" became identical with the "deprivation of the fruits of the revolution."[55] The policy of law and order (*Ruhe und Ordnung*) stood against the psychology of revolution, an unkindly alternative, from which the whole course of the Weimar Republic suffered. The following sections will trace the gradual alienation of the neo-conservatives from the Republic. It is part of the story of how Germany became a "republic without republicans."

[53] Heinrich von Gleichen, "Das Politische Kolleg," *Deutsche Rundschau*, CLXXXVII (1921), 105.
[54] Quoted in Wilhelm Stapel, "Das geistige Deutschland und die Republik. Offener Brief an Konrad Haenisch," *Deutsches Volkstum*, XXIII (1921), 105.
[55] Troeltsch, *Spektator-Briefe*, 38.

CHAPTER II

THE FORMATIVE YEARS
OF THE REPUBLIC

The "Elders" of the Republic

THE Weimar Republic became, like the France of Louis
Philippe, one of those societies in modern history in which
people were "bored." It had an exemplary democratic
constitution and yet it never became a properly functioning democracy. It replaced the Monarchy by a legal structure which was little loved by the people. It was not able
to fill the vacuum left by defeat, and the euphoria of the
early days soon gave way to a grim awakening. The Weimar
Republic became a ready target for an unhappy nation.

In these circumstances it would be too easy to say that
the dilemma of German conservatism in the days of the
Republic was one between identification with the Republic and opposition. The legalism of the Weimar structure
was surely not conducive to a healthy conservatism. It was
in no way an answer to the emotional needs of an orphaned
people. The dilemma, then, was one between two kinds of
opposition. On one hand, there was a need for a realistic,
positive opposition to take into account the political predicament in which Germany found itself. It was necessary
to separate the element of tragedy in the early Republic
from the mistakes which were made by it. The former had
to be accepted realistically; the latter had to be repaired.
In particular, since the Monarchy had clearly disappeared,
the way for a conservative policy within the Republic was
open.

The other side of the dilemma was a purely negative
opposition—a policy of despair, tired of law and freedom
as well as of liberalism. This alternative tended to take
conservatism to an abyss beyond which there was nothing

but unreality and myth. It brought conservatism close to surrendering to fascism.

On the positive side of the ledger were some of the "elders" of the Republic, men like Max Weber, Meinecke, Naumann, Troeltsch, Rathenau, and, after his full recovery from the *Betrachtungen,* Thomas Mann. These were all men whose roots were in the nineteenth century. They might be called German liberals as well as conservatives, depending upon the way we look at them. They shifted their party allegiances as their conscience told them. And to them the struggle between Right and Left in itself was a vital condition for freedom. They carried with them the "happy feeling," as Meinecke called it,[1] of the basic understanding which underlay variety. In them Germany had a rare generation of intellectuals whose concern for their country was dictated by the broadest and most human considerations. The "elders" without exception had been supporters of the Hohenzollern Monarchy, though increasingly critical of the kaiser's personal regime. They had striven to liberalize the Empire. With Naumann as their leading spirit they had aimed at a reconciliation between the Monarchy and the workers. The Monarchy could not have had more loyal supporters. While the "elders" found their hopes in the Monarchy betrayed, they never became 100 percent republicans. Even after the revolution Max Weber still declared himself an adherent of a parliamentary monarchy.[2] And, if they became republicans after all, it was not out of enthusiasm but, as Meinecke expressed it, "out of good sense *(aus Vernunft).*"[3] They thought and acted like Louis Adolphe Thiers, who, in an analogous situation in France in 1871, as first president of the Third Republic, had said that "the Republic is the government

[1] Friedrich Meinecke, *Strassburg, Freiburg, Berlin 1901-1919. Erinnerungen* (Stuttgart, 1949), 245.

[2] Max Weber, "Deutschlands künftige Staatsform," *Gesammelte Politische Schriften* (Munich, 1921), 342.

[3] Friedrich Meinecke, *Republik, Bürgertum und Jugend* (Frankfurt, 1925), 19.

that divides us least," and "the Republic will be conservative or it will not be."[4]

While in the days of the Monarchy most of the "elders" were liberals, they were conservatives during the Republic.[5] In themselves they represented the parliamentary balance of the nineteenth century and were a corrective to the existing governmental structure, whether it was monarchic or republican.

There was nothing sentimental about the conservatism of the "elders." It was a conservatism of mature minds, the result of years of observation and insight into the workings of society. It came close to being a scholarly conservatism. It was based on elaborate reasoning such as is inherent in Max Weber's study of the types of authority.[6] Weber's distinction between "legal," "traditional," and "charismatic" authority led to an understanding of the needs of the new Republic. The latter showed the weaknesses of a purely legal authority and it tended to underrate the importance of traditional and irrational associations. It was, as Troeltsch complained, a mere "formal democracy" devoid of *élan* and of the "great ideas."[7] Like the French nobility of the early nineteenth century, which, according to de Tocqueville, had learned from the French Revolution "if not the truth, at least the social usefulness of belief,"[8] the "elders" were eminently conscious of the "social usefulness" of tradition and charisma. It was on these grounds that their criticism of the Republic was based.

A direct influence on the making of the Weimar Constitution can be traced back to this group of "elders." Among the things which they advocated were a federal structure

4 Cf. Meinecke's reference to Thiers in *ibid.*, 15.

5 This notwithstanding the fact that in their party allegiances or their voting they moved on the whole from the Right in pre-war days to the Left in post-war days.

6 Max Weber, *The Theory of Social and Economic Organization* (ed. Talcott Parsons, New York, 1947), 324ff.

7 Troeltsch, *Spektator-Briefe*, 48.

8 J. P. Mayer, ed., *The Recollections of Alexis de Tocqueville* (London, 1948), 120.

for a united Germany, and a strong presidency based upon popular elections. The latter was to prevent the establishment of a purely parliamentary regime and, moreover, to serve the selection of a new elite emerging from without the party hierarchies.[9] According to Meinecke, it was to amount to an "Ersatz-monarchy" *(Ersatzkaisertum).*[10] Thus the "elders" tried to save the "best of the old conservatism."[11]

In particular, Max Weber, serving on the staff of Hugo Preuss, the man who drafted the Weimar Constitution, was in a position to influence the definition of the powers of the president.[12] He was impressed by the popular basis of the American presidency, which commanded incomparably more authority than the French one, based as this was on parliamentary election. However, Weber may have neglected to see that the American executive was part of a democratic tradition and political balance which did not exist in Germany. It is ironical that Article 48 of the Constitution, which Weber helped to formulate, turned out to be one of the main factors which weakened the Republic. Surely, the extensive use of the Article in 1923-1924 and 1931-1932 did not reflect the ideas of Max Weber.

Altogether Prince Max von Baden, describing Weber's role as "the greatest political achievement of the post-revolution period"[13] clearly overrated it. The impact of Weber and his friends remained on paper. Some tried unsuccessfully to create new parties.[14] The somewhat academic nature of their idealism, which gave them measure and moderation, was at the same time the cause of their failure.

9 Cf. Max Weber, "Staatsform," *Schriften,* 361ff. and "Der Reichspräsident," *Schriften,* 390ff.; Meinecke, *Republik,* 21f. and "Verfassung und Verwaltung der deutschen Republik," *Die neue Rundschau,* xxx (1919), Vol. 1, 1ff.; Troeltsch, *Spektator-Briefe,* 59; Heuss, *Naumann,* 467.

10 Meinecke, *Erinnerungen,* 259.

11 Meinecke, *Republik,* 19.

12 Namely through Articles 41 and 48 of the Constitution.

13 *The Memoirs of Prince Max of Baden* (New York, 1928), I, 138.

14 Cf. Kessler, *Rathenau,* 249f.; Heuss, *Naumann,* 453f.

They remained incomprehensible to the people at large. They did not succeed in bridging the gap between the Republic and the people. The post-revolutionary Germany, Meinecke later conceded, "did not reflect the ideal for which we aimed during the war."[15]

The Post-War Youth Movement

Under these circumstance it is not surprising that the "elders" turned their hopes toward the post-war Youth Movement. Like its predecessor this was an element in German social and intellectual life carefully watched and furthered by serious-minded people. Eugen Diederichs, the editor of the *Tat* magazine, had been instrumental in getting together the 1917 meeting in Burg Lauenstein (Thuringia) which was dedicated to the affairs of the Youth Movement. It had an impressive list of participants.[16] Once more in 1919 Diederichs was the moving spirit of the meeting of the Freideutsche Jugend in Jena. For Max Weber the contacts with the Youth Movement were a source of encouragement in his feverish political activities during the days after the revolution, and the disappointment in the revolution made people like Troeltsch locate the "spiritual revolution" in the Youth Movement.[17] But this reliance on the Youth Movement meant building upon quicksand. After an initial phase of participation in the revolutionary excitement which spelled expectations of "spiritual and moral rejuvenation,"[18] the Freideutsche Jugend split into a Right and a Left. "Since 1919," Ernst Robert Curtius recorded, "the Youth Movement has stagnated in political

[15] Meinecke, *Erinnerungen*, 283.

[16] Included were Meinecke, Max Weber, Sombart, Tönnies, Heuss. Cf. Marianne Weber, *Max Weber. Ein Lebensbild* (Tübingen, 1926), 608.

[17] Cf. Georg Steinhausen, *Deutsche Geistes- und Kulturgeschichte von 1870 bis zur Gegenwart* (Halle, 1931), 485.

[18] Messer, *Freideutsche*, 69; cf. Otto Stählin, *Die deutsche Jugendbewegung. Ihre Geschichte, ihr Wesen, ihre Formen* (Leipzig, 1930), 44.

ties."[19] While the 1927 census showed that after the war the idea of youth organization had established itself, most of the registered groups[20] were connected with political parties, church organizations, labor unions, or sports clubs. The traditions of the Hohen Meissner meeting of 1913 were carried on by twenty-eight youth groups, so-called *Bünde* (brotherhoods),[21] which were known under the name of Bündische Jugend. But even these groups could not live up to the expectations of the "elders." With them the rebellion of youth degenerated into a quest for intangibles and into a "random revolutionary dynamism."[22]

Eugen Diederichs and the Tat

Among the neo-conservative groups the circle around the *Tat* had the longest history. Since its foundation in 1909 the magazine was part of the "cultural opposition" to the Second Reich. In particular, after the publisher Eugen Diederichs took over the *Tat* in 1912, it assumed an increasingly important place in German intellectual life. Among the great German publishers Diederichs was a rare idealist. He advertised his house, which went back to 1896, as the "leading publishing house of neo-romanticism."[23] An untiring disciple of Nietzsche and Lagarde, he proselytized actively and awkwardly for a new German *"Kulturpolitik."*[24]

Most of Diederichs' friends were members of the younger generation. Among his contemporaries he was close to few. Diederichs' ways, his insistent moralizing, his insatiable drive to organize congresses and new societies, must have been offensive to sober and mature people. His Ger-

[19] Ernst Robert Curtius, *Deutscher Geist in Gefahr* (Stuttgart, Berlin, 1932), 52f.

[20] Ninety-six groups controlling 4,338,850 members; Karl Otto Paetel, *Die Struktur der nationalen Jugend* (Flarchheim, 1930), 10.

[21] By the 1927 census the total membership amounted to 56,350.

[22] Rauschning, *The Revolution of Nihilism*, 64.

[23] Lulu von Strauss und Torney-Diederichs, ed., *Eugen Diederichs. Leben und Werk* (Jena, 1936), 52.

[24] *Ibid.*, 94.

man mysticism was more appealing to the younger generation—the generation of the Youth Movement—to whom he
came to devote most of his attention. After his active participation at the Hohen Meissner meeting, he became one
of its foremost supporters.

Under Diederichs the *Tat* became increasingly political.
Steering an independent course, it assumed a pronounced
critical attitude toward the kaiser[25] and took an outright
hostile stand against the Pan-Germans. The magazine became a forum primarily dedicated to a redefinition of conservative thought, and it occupied itself more and more
with the problems of a new aristocracy and a new socialism.
Indeed, in appreciation of the social developments during
the war, the *Tat* foresaw the "blending of conservative
spirit and socialism."[26] With the publication of a series of
booklets under the heading *Deutsche Gemeinwirtschaft*,[27]
the Diederichs house helped to carry the ideas of the new
socialism into post-revolutionary Germany.

With its strong socialistic accent and an intense awareness of the sociological impact of war and revolution upon
the middle classes[28] the *Tat* went through the process of at
first welcoming the revolution and soon after rejecting it.
However, throughout the 1920's the magazine maintained
an open-minded, flexible, experimental character. Diede-

[25] An interesting feature of the pre-war *Tat* was its September
issue of 1913, which, for the occasion of the kaiser's twenty-fifth ac-
cession jubilee, was devoted to a thorough criticism of the kaiser's
policies. Among the contributors to this issue we find Moeller van den
Bruck. He had already in an earlier year published the introduction
to his *Die italienische Schönheit* in the *Tat*. Cf. Moeller van den
Bruck, "Schönheit," *Die Tat*, III (1911-1912) , 138-142. In the *Tat*'s
jubilee edition he attacked the kaiser's city planning for Berlin because of its lack of style. This article is typical of Moeller's work, as
the architectural and political elements in it are perfectly interwoven. Cf. Moeller van den Bruck, "Der Kaiser und die architektonische Tradition," *Die Tat*, V (1913-1914), 595-601.

[26] "Rückblick," *Die Tat*, VI (1914-1915), 611.

[27] Between 1917 and 1920 eighteen booklets appeared in this series;
among the authors were Rathenau and Moellendorff.

[28] Eugen Diederichs, "Verproletarisierung," *Die Tat*, XI (1919-1920),
207f.

richs actually made a practice of farming out the *Tat* to various groups of writers, thus maintaining the independent nature of the *Tat* without affecting its main objectives. For a discussion of socialism he went to the Left, generally to the extreme Left, for inspiration.[29] In turn, for a discussion of the much-talked-about corporative state, Diederichs opened the *Tat* to a group of men closely connected with the June Club.[30]

One of the main functions of the *Tat*, emanating from Diederichs' connections with the Freideutsche Jugend, was the furthering of the Youth Movement. Diederichs thought of his journal as a "central organ for the Youth Movement."[31] During the war, a variety of articles on this subject had appeared with the tendency of encouraging an understanding among the many dissenting groups.[32] Toward the end of and after the war, when the Freideutsche Jugend virtually broke up, Eugen Diederichs wrote frantic articles admonishing the Youth Movement to abandon its aloofness and subjectivism and help construct the "folk state" (*Volksstaat*), which to Diederichs meant a federalized Germany.[33]

[29] Cf. the March 1925 and July 1926 issues, which included among the authors Ernst Toller, Ernst Niekisch (one of Germany's most persistent National Bolshevists, who during that time left the S.P.D. and shifted over to the extreme Right), and Hendrik de Man (the Belgian Social Democrat).

[30] Cf. the October 1925 issue, for which Heinz Brauweiler was responsible. Heinrich von Gleichen, Martin Spahn, and Heinrich Herrfahrdt were among the contributors. (For Gleichen's article see the November issue.)

[31] *Eugen Diederichs. Leben und Werk*, 279.

[32] Cf. M. H., "Freideutsche Jugend," *Die Tat*, VIII (1916-1917), 765-767; August Messer, "Zum Frieden in der freideutschen Bewegung," *Die Tat*, VIII (1916-1917), 187f.

[33] Eugen Diederichs, "Entwicklungsphasen der Freideutschen Jugend," *Die Tat*, X (1918-1919), 311ff., 314. Cf. also three other pieces by Diederichs: "Die Aufgabe der Freideutschen Jugend," *Die Tat*, XI (1919-1920), 313f.; "Mahnwort an die deutsche Jugend," *Die Tat*, XI (1919-1920), 569-571; "Zur Jugendbewegung," *Die Tat*, XII (1920-1921), 397f.

While the *Tat* stressed the socialistic mission of youth,[34] Diederichs warned against the plunge into proletarization which after the war had become a popular concept among the leadership of the Freideutsche Jugend. What was needed was not the destruction of the *Bürgertum* by a renegade generation but the formulation of a social theory which could justify the position of the *Bürgertum* as a ruling class. In stressing the "task of the *Bürgertum*" to win the revolution by establishing a true "community of the people (*Volksgemeinschaft*),"[35] Diederichs tried to guide the Youth Movement toward a new *noblesse oblige* and win it over to a concrete conservative position, that is, "a conservatism which is strongly social."[36] When finally in 1928 Diederichs handed over the direction of the *Tat* to the younger generation, the issue of whether the latter was to choose the way of pure revolutionism or of a sound conservatism was still in the balance.

Wilhelm Stapel and the Deutsches Volkstum

Like the circle around the *Tat* magazine, the men be-

[34] The whole *Tat* issue of July 1927 was dedicated to the so-called Hofgeismar Circle, a strongly nationalistic group emanating from the Young Socialist Movement, whose ideas about the "reorientation" of socialism fitted well into Diederichs' pattern of *rapprochement* between the proletarian and bourgeois socialisms. The Circle was named after Hofgeismar in Hessen, where in 1923 the Young Socialist Movement met. Under the impact of the Ruhr occupation, a majority pleaded a nationalistic course which came to be identified with the Hofgeismar Circle. Ernst Niekisch figured prominently in this group. While still a member of the S.P.D., Niekisch denounced the Policy of Fulfillment of the government and advocated a realistic foreign policy subordinating class consciousness to nation consciousness. Cf. Ernst Niekisch, *Grundfragen der deutschen Aussenpolitik* (Berlin, 1925). In 1925 the Hofgeismar Circle, pressed into the minority, left the Young Socialist Movement. It formed the nucleus for the Resistance Movement (Widerstandsbewegung) of Niekisch and Winnig, which took an important place in the reviving National Bolshevism of the early thirties.

[35] Eugen Diederichs, "Die Aufgabe des Bürgertums," *Die Tat*, xi (1919-1920), 267.

[36] *Eugen Diederichs. Leben und Werk*, 354.

hind the *Deutsches Volkstum* attempted to translate the experience of the war into conservative terms. The *Deutsches Volkstum,* formerly *Bühne und Welt,* received its new programmatic name in December 1918, when it was bought by the largest non-Marxian employees' union in Germany, the Deutschnationaler Handlungsgehilfen Verband (D.H.V.). The D.H.V. went back to Stöcker's Christian Social Movement of the late 1870's. Always strongly nationalistic, the D.H.V. early introduced the social question into German nationalism. From its wide membership[37] it excluded women, Jews, and Marxists. It controlled a well-defined and numerically large segment of the social group whose security was seriously challenged by the developments following the war.

The acquisition of the *Deutsches Volkstum* was in keeping with a policy on the part of the D.H.V. of an active cultural schooling and political indoctrination of its members. Wilhelm Stapel became the new editor. Stapel, who called himself a pupil of Friedrich Naumann and of the economist Lujo Brentano, was a prolific publicist. An ardent anti-Semite, a stiff-necked German Protestant à la Stöcker, and an insatiable phrase-monger, he started the new magazine on an editorial policy less intelligent and less broadminded than the *Tat*'s. But partly through its connections[38] the *Deutsches Volkstum* became more directly representative of the Rightist intelligentsia.[39] Also, the *Deutsches Volkstum* reflected clearly the unsettled condi-

[37] This was 409,009 by 1930; *Der Deutschnationale Handlungsgehilfen Verband im Jahre 1930, Rechenschaftsbericht erstattet von seiner Verwaltung* (Hamburg, 1931), 8.

[38] In 1920 all the publishing activities of the D.H.V. were taken over by the Hanseatische Verlagsanstalt, which became one of the most active nationalistic publishing houses in Germany, publishing works of Hans Blüher, Gerhard Günther, Ernst Jünger, Moellendorff, Stapel, and Winnig.

[39] Diederichs was a regular reader of the *Deutsches Volkstum* (*Eugen Diederichs. Leben und Werk*, 425) and Spengler was reported to have called it "the best German periodical" (Wilhelm Stapel, "Zwanzig Jahre Deutsches Volkstum," *Deutsches Volkstum,* XL [1938], 808).

tions among the Rightist intellectuals. It was, like the *Tat,* closely connected with the Youth Movement[40] and considered itself an arbiter of its affairs. Through Stapel the *Deutsches Volkstum* also had ties with a Hamburg Freikorps[41] and even with the National Bolshevist efforts in Hamburg in 1919.[42] Somewhat cryptically the magazine sought its bearing "to the left of the Left and to the right of the Right," because, as Stapel wrote in 1919, "the circle of the people closes itself only beyond the left and right wings of the official parties."[43]

The June Club

The most active center of neo-conservatism was the June Club in Berlin. As a predecessor of the famous Herrenklub (Gentlemen's Club), with which von Papen was connected, it has never yet been dealt with by historians on its own terms. Alongside the overrated but surely reactionary Herrenklub, it has been charged with being a conspiracy of Junkers furthering the cause of the Nazis.[44] The facts do not substantiate such theories. Political clubs are not necessarily made up of people with identical political opinions. The June Club, like the *Tat* Circle, consisted of men of all political camps. It was a meeting ground of minds and ideas above and beyond the party political horizon. It was an experiment.

The origins of the June Club must be explained in terms

40 Cf. Else Frobenius, *Mit uns zieht die neue Zeit. Eine Geschichte der deutschen Jugendbewegung* (Berlin, 1927), 201ff.

41 The Bahrenfelder Freikorps.

42 Cf. infra, 143.

43 Quoted in Wilhelm Stapel, "Zwanzig Jahre *Deutsches Volkstum,*" *Deutsches Volkstum,* XL (1938), 798.

44 Cf. Edmond Vermeil, *Germany's Three Reichs. Their History and Culture* (London, 1944) ; the author, not even distinguishing between the two clubs, claims that "the *Herrenklub* took into its hands the destinies of Hitler and Hitlerism" (p. 272), and "thus, between 1921 and 1923 Hitler was simply the manager for the ruling caste, which had definitely decided to lead the masses through his intermediary" (p. 274).

of the psychology of Germany in collapse and of the moment of confusion and indecision in the political scene
immediately following the war. The political *Burgfriede*
of 1914 was somehow reproduced after November 1918 by
a psychological vacuum. The men of the June Club who
had made so much of the "war experience" must have
been particularly sensitive to this oblique and ironical affinity between 1914 and 1918. They must have wondered
whether the "ideas of 1914" could be recaptured after 1918
in their original non-partisan connotation. Could the conservatism of the war be translated into revolutionary terms?
The June Club constituted an effort to force the general
confusion after November 1918 into a conservative pattern.

The origins of the June Club are connected with a number of short-lived organizations, all more or less interrelated through personal contact among their leaders, but
serving different purposes.[45] They were concerned with issues such as German propaganda and anti-Bolshevism,
which commanded the interest or support of the majority
of middle class Germans of whatever party affiliation.
Hence the June Club grew out of contacts with a variety
of groups which were backed by men of all political shades.

The leading members of the June Club were Heinrich
von Gleichen-Russwurm, the head of the Club, Moeller van
den Bruck, and Eduard Stadtler. Gleichen and Stadtler
were men of action, tireless organizers, whereas Moeller
was the man of ideas, retiring and sensitive. He, whose
written style was so challenging, was almost inarticulate in
conversation. He contributed the ideological orientation
for the June Club and thus became its saint and hero.

To Gleichen Moeller dedicated *Das dritte Reich*. A
nobleman from Thuringia and a direct descendent of Schiller, Gleichen moved to Berlin before the first World War
and played a role in politically interested circles. The key

[45] In connection with this network of organizations and personal
contacts the June Club has been often referred to by its members
as the Ring Movement (Ring Bewegung).

to his political activities was his interest in getting people together rather than his ideas. Thus he managed, during the war, to become head of the Association of German Scholars and Artists. The organization survived the end of the war until it was swallowed up by the June Club in 1919. Gleichen's functions in connection with the Association acquainted him with a great many men who later came to be close to the June Club.

Gleichen also headed another group which later merged with the June Club, the "Solidarity" (Vereinigung für nationale und soziale Solidarität). Founded in the October days of 1918 in the rooms of the Deutsche Gesellschaft 1914, it counted no more than twenty members, among whom were Moeller and Stadtler. The "Solidarians," as they called themselves, in their program of February 1919, claimed to be revolutionary though anti-Bolshevist, to be anti-liberal, and to be anti-parliamentarian. They called for the "realization of the genuine social folk state (*Volksstaat*) of the twentieth century."[46] Their concern with the social question led them to establish close relations with Adam Stegerwald, the leader of the Catholic trade unions and later oftentimes minister of the Republic.

Another parent organization of the June Club was Eduard Stadtler's Anti-Bolshevik Movement. Stadtler, an Alsatian by birth, came politically from the Center Party, whose youth movement he had headed before the war. The war saw him in front line duty on Germany's eastern front until 1917, when he was taken prisoner by the Russians. After Brest-Litovsk he stayed in Russia to direct the Press Bureau of the German Embassy in Moscow. Upon his return to Germany late in 1918 Stadtler—an ardent opponent of Matthias Erzberger, leader of the Center Party's left wing—left that party. In search for new contacts he joined the circle around Gleichen, with whom he remained closely connected politically through the middle of the

[46] Eduard Stadtler, *Weltrevolutionskrieg* (Düsseldorf, 1937), 186; cf. Eduard Stadtler, *Die Diktatur der sozialen Revolution* (Leipzig, 1920), 127ff.

1920's. Stadtler was a restless campaigner, a boasting demagogue rather than a politician, a scatterbrain and busybody rather than a man of competence. The witnessing of the Bolshevik Revolution had become the decisive experience in his life, and he managed to give himself out as an authority on Russia and became recognized as one of Germany's leading anti-Bolshevists.

Stadtler's Anti-Bolshevik Movement (Antibolschewistische Bewegung)[47] was a mass organization covering the whole of northern Germany.[48] It was founded late in November 1918, after a conference which took place in Friedrich Naumann's home. Naumann gave full support to the plan and even contributed 3,000 marks out of a political fund which was at his disposal. Another initial sum of 5,000 marks was obtained from the Deutsche Bank through the mediation of Karl Helfferich. A considerable fund was raised, according to Stadtler, in the form of an insurance policy amounting to 500,000,000 marks, by the German industry and bank world at a meeting in Berlin on January 10, 1919.[49] Subsequently, Stadtler had frequent opportunities to present his views to the leaders of industry and finance. Of these Hugo Stinnes became a most active patron of Stadtler.

The main core of collaborators to whom Stadtler turned were the "Solidarians." Under their influence the Move-

[47] Also known as Generalsekretariat zum Studium und zur Bekämpfung des Bolschewismus and as Antibolschewistische Liga.

[48] The southern anti-Bolshevik organization was the Orgesch (Organisation Escherich).

[49] Among the participants were Hugo Stinnes, Albert Vögler of the Vereinigte Stahlwerke, Ernst Borsig, Carl Friedrich von Siemens, Geheimrat Deutsch of the A.E.G., and Mankiewitz and Salomonsohn from the Deutsche Bank. After a talk by Stadtler on "Bolshevism as a Universal Danger," and after active intercession on the part of Stinnes, the fund was granted and earmarked for use by Stadtler's organization, by the Freikorps, and by various other organizations like the Orgesch. Cf. Eduard Stadtler, *Als Antibolschewist 1918-1919* (Düsseldorf, 1935), 46ff. Cf. also Hermann Müller, *Die November Revolution. Erinnerungen* (Berlin, 1928), 122; Ernst Niekisch, *Deutsche Daseinsverfehlung* (Berlin, 1946), 80.

ment was more and more diverted from its initial negative functions to serve their positive aims.[50] Stadtler frankly admitted in his memoirs the need of "camouflaging"[51] the ideas of the "Solidarians" behind anti-Bolshevism because of his financial dependence on industry.

An initial appeal of the League for the Protection of German Culture (as Stadtler's organization was now known), addressed "to all parties, to all classes, and to all branches (*Stämme*) of the German Reich," called for "a new spirit, a new national consciousness . . . , the spirit of German unity, of German liberty, and of German socialism (*Sozialgedankens*)."[52] Among the signers of this appeal were Count Bernstorff, former Imperial ambassador to Washington and Constantinople and cofounder in 1918 of the Democratic Party; Gleichen; Adolf Grabowsky, a leading publicist; Naumann; Stegerwald; and Troeltsch. By the end of January 1919 the organization of the League extended from Hamburg to Königsberg and from Düsseldorf to Breslau.[53] The publicistic activities were prolific.[54] A newsletter called *Antibolschewistische Korrespondenz* appeared three or four times weekly. In addition to its publicistic activities, the movement organized a great number

[50] Therefore, also, the change of name of the organization in January 1919 into the League for the Protection of German Culture (Liga zum Schutz der deutschen Kultur).

[51] Stadtler, *Als Antibolschewist*, 23.

[52] *Ibid.*, 76.

[53] According to the "Report for the Year 1920" it comprised 15 area headquarters (*Landesgruppen*) and 162 local groups. In want of available total membership figures, the figure for the area Hessen and Hessen-Nassau, namely 20,000, should be an indication of the size of the organization; cf. *Die Liga*, I (1921), 6, 42f.

[54] Within a few months after November 1918 the organization launched 8 different series of booklets containing about 70 titles written by close to 40 authors. Among the more widely known contributors were, besides Stadtler, Max Hildebert Boehm, the editor of *Die Grenzboten*; Max Cohen-Reuss from the *Sozialistische Monatshefte*; and Stegerwald. These data are assembled from a variety of sources, notably Stadtler's works, the available pamphlets themselves, and Helmut Tiedemann, *Sowjetrussland und die Revolutionierung Deutschlands, 1917-1919* (Berlin, 1936).

of mass meetings in the major cities of northern Germany, Eduard Stadtler being a seemingly tireless speaker in its behalf.

As the socialistic tendencies of the "Solidarians" became obvious, a conflict between them and the financial supporters became inevitable. Therefore, Stadtler, attacked by his financiers—with the exception of Stinnes and Vögler—saw himself forced to resign toward the end of March 1919 from the League.[55] With the exodus of the "Solidarians" the League ceased to play a part in the neo-conservative movement. And, in particular, after the stabilization of the Weimar Republic it was left without purpose and declined quickly to the role of an insignificant patriotic organization.[56]

A. THE MEMBERS OF THE JUNE CLUB

About the end of March the June Club got under way. It was officially founded in June 1919. Besides Gleichen,[57] Moeller, and Stadtler, its prominent members, largely "Solidarians," were Max Hildebert Boehm, who in 1920 became editor of *Die Grenzboten* and later became head of the Deutsches Auslandsinstitut in Stuttgart; Heinz Brauweiler, a publicist; Hans Schwarz, Moeller van den Bruck's editor; Paul Fechter, who became managing editor of the *Deutsche Allgemeine Zeitung;* Rudolf Pechel, who as editor of the *Deutsche Rundschau* was a leading figure in Berlin's intellectual life; Franz Röhr, the editor of a leading Catholic periodical *Deutsche Arbeit*; and Walther Schotte, who in 1920 became editor of the *Preussische Jahrbücher.*

Moellendorff and August Winnig,[58] who had been prom-

[55] Cf. Stadtler, *Als Antibolschewist*, 70f., 107, 115, 123f.

[56] Cf. *Die Liga*, I-V (1921-1925); the *Liga* itself ceased publication altogether in 1925.

[57] In whose home the Club at first held its meetings. Later the Club acquired headquarters in the middle class district of Berlin on the Motzstrasse.

[58] Winnig, since his break with Marxism during the war, started upon a political career which was nothing less than an Odyssey. He still had himself elected to the National Assembly in Weimar on the

inent advocates of the new socialism during the war, were connected with the June Club. Largely due to Gleichen's efforts, the circle of the June Club extended to men representing almost all political creeds. Among these men, however, the non-party-liners outnumbered the strict party-liners. Various noted university professors attended frequently—namely, Ernst Troeltsch, Otto Hoetzsch, Martin Spahn, and the economists Hermann Schumacher and Franz Oppenheimer. Among leading German Nationalists we find, in addition to Hoetzsch, Count Kuno Westarp and Oskar Hergt. Among leaders of the Center Party, besides Spahn, there were Heinrich Brüning and Adam Stegerwald. The Democrats were represented by Troeltsch and by Georg Bernhard from the *Vossische Zeitung*. Among Social Democrats we find August Müller, the former state secretary in the Reichswirtschaftsamt and superior to Moellendorff, and Otto Strasser, later leader of the Black Front (Schwarze Front). Even a young Communist attended the meetings.

The non-partisan character of the Club was not affected by the financial support which it got from German industrialists, including Alfred Hugenberg. The latter, interested in the Club's affairs through Spahn, contributed to its always needy treasury for about two years, after which he withdrew his support charging the June Club with having

Social Democratic ticket; however, he resigned his mandate after a few months of demonstrative absence from the proceedings. As the Reich's chief administrative official in East Prussia, he joined the Kapp Putsch, whereupon he was finally expelled from the Party and deprived of his office. An attempt toward political reorientation made him, together with Ernst Niekisch, support a secessionist movement from the S.P.D. in Saxony, called the Old Socialistic Party (Altsozialistische Partei). A further association of Winnig with Niekisch during the later twenties in the National-Bolshevik Resistance Movement (Widerstandsbewegung), followed by editorial writing for the Rightist *Berliner Börsen-Zeitung*, eventual submission to the Nazi creed, and, during the war, reversion against it, mark the remaining phases of an unsteady yet typical career of a German extremist.

been instrumental in the acceptance of the Dawes Plan.[59]

Max Hildebert Boehm recalled that the June Club saw its "richest and most stimulating period"[60] around 1919 and 1920. These were the years when the Club was, like the Weimar Republic itself, still an experiment, and when feelers were put out in all directions. Most of the Club's evenings were spent in discussions at which an average of 120 to 150 people appeared and to which special guests, like Oswald Spengler, were often invited.

In 1920 the Club launched a political academy of its own, the Politisches Kolleg. It was patterned after the Ecole Libre des Sciences Politiques in Paris, which had been founded in 1872 in answer to the French defeat in the Franco-Prussian War.[61] Headed by Martin Spahn, a professor of history in Cologne and within the Center Party one of the most outspoken enemies of Erzberger, it dedicated itself to the cause of "national politics."[62]

In the field of publicism, however, lay the main strength of the June Club. A weekly magazine, *Gewissen*, was founded in April 1919, serving as the organ of the Club and soon claiming 30,000 readers.[63] Indeed, in July 1920 Troeltsch recorded with alarm the fact that "the writers of the *Gewissen* are already in the process of taking over the newly bought Stinnes papers," and he attributed the political significance of the June Club chiefly to this fact.[64] In ef-

[59] Letter to the author from Heinrich von Gleichen, November 14, 1954.

[60] Max Hildebert Boehm, *Der Ruf der Jungen. Eine Stimme aus dem Kreise von Moeller van den Bruck* (3rd edn., Freiburg, 1933), 21, quoted in *Der Ring*, VI (November 10, 1933), 726.

[61] Cf. Martin Spahn, "Die Pariser Hochschule und Frankreichs Wiederaufstieg nach 1871," *Die Grenzboten*, LXXIX, 1/4 (1920), 28-30.

[62] For detailed information on the Politisches Kolleg see Paul Herre and Kurt Jagow, *Politisches Handwörterbuch* (Leipzig, 1923), II, 333; Heinrich von Gleichen, "Das Politische Kolleg," *Deutsche Rundschau*, CLXXXVII (1921), 104-109.

[63] *Gewissen*, IV (January 2, 1922). The circulation figure for 1923 was given as 10,000; Helmut Hüttig, *Die politischen Zeitschriften der Nachkriegszeit in Deutschland* (Magdeburg, 1928), 33.

[64] Troeltsch, *Spektator-Briefe*, 146. It is interesting that Troeltsch

fect Paul Fechter became managing editor of the Stinnes-owned *Deutsche Allgemeine Zeitung* and August Winnig wrote pro-Stinnes editorials in the *Berliner Börsen-Zeitung*. But it was in the world of the political periodical that the men of the June Club left their mark most clearly. In the early twenties they succeeded in determining the character of a number of leading publications. In 1919 Rudolf Pechel took over the editorship of the *Deutsche Rundschau,* one of the oldest and most recognized magazines in Germany. Already in November 1918 Moeller van den Bruck had published in its columns one of his first important political articles.[65] Between 1920 and 1924, however, neo-conservatism as interpreted by men like Moeller, Boehm, Brauweiler, Gleichen, and Stadtler became the predominant political note of the *Deutsche Rundschau.* For a shorter period *Die Grenzboten* adopted a similar policy. From the revolution until the year 1920 it modified its Pan-German point of view by opening itself to the neo-conservatives. For a short while in 1920 Max Hildebert Boehm functioned as editor of *Die Grenzboten.* In 1920 Walther Schotte, another member of the June Club, assumed the direction of the *Preussische Jahrbücher,* thus following in the footsteps of Rudolf Haym, Heinrich von Treitschke, and Hans Delbrück. Though the basic historical nature of this magazine was not altered, the political overtone of Schotte's editorials and of a number of political articles produced a noticeable emphasis on the ideas of neo-conservatism. Even the Pan-German *Süddeutsche Monatshefte,* through its editor, Paul Nikolas Cossmann,

---

in his fear of Stinnes as press lord followed a general and highly exaggerated rumor which circulated in 1920, and which attributed to Stinnes an empire of sixty to a hundred newspapers. In reality, Stinnes had bought no more than three papers, of which the *Deutsche Allgemeine Zeitung* was the most popular one. Cf. Gaston Raphaël, *Hugo Stinnes. Der Mensch, sein Werk, sein Wirken* (Berlin, 1925), 129.

[65] Moeller van den Bruck, "Das Recht der jungen Völker," *Deutsche Rundschau,* cxxvii (1919), 220-235.

began to pay attention to the June Club. "Among the daily arising new parties and fraternal organizations *(Bünden),*" Cossmann introduced it to his readers as the only one of "serious significance."[66] Through Franz Röhr, the editor of the *Deutsche Arbeit,* a mouthpiece of the Christian unions, another important connection was established. Winnig and Lensch joined together once more and published a bi-weekly, *Der Firn.* This periodical, by standing "for the achievements of the revolution, for a national consciousness, and against Communism,"[67] continued the same traditions which *Die Glocke* had established during the war. Various minor periodicals such as Hans Roeseler's *Die Hochschule* complete the picture of the publicistic activities of the circle around the June Club.

In the early 1920's a grand review of all neo-conservative forces appeared in the form of a collective work. Its title impressively suggested a "new front."[68] While it outlined the ideological, political, and social position of neo-conservatism, it represented, to be sure, a front of officers rather than soldiers, of intellectuals rather than the common man. As yet it had to stand the test of defining a clear political program acceptable to both the "elders" and the "young ones," and, indeed, of facing squarely up to the reality of the Weimar Republic.

[66] Editorial note in *Süddeutsche Monatshefte,* xviii, Vol. I (1920-1921), 8.

[67] Hüttig, *Die politischen Zeitschriften,* 67.

[68] Among the thirty-eight contributors there were a number of members of the Reichstag (including Walther Lambach from the D.H.V. and Reinhold Georg Quaatz), some independent nationalists (such as the poet Paul Ernst, the novelist Hans Grimm, and Georg Escherich from the Orgesch), and, otherwise, mostly men associated with the June Club and the *Deutsches Volkstum* (including, in addition to the editors, Martin Spahn, Rudolf Pechel, Wilhelm Stapel, Paul Fechter, Heinz Brauweiler, Walther Schotte, Hermann Ullmann, August Winnig, and Eduard Stadtler); Moeller van den Bruck, Heinrich von Gleichen, and Max Hildebert Boehm, eds., *Die neue Front* (Berlin, 1922).

*Neo-Conservatism at the Crossroads: The "Elders'"
Rejection of the Neo-Conservative Movement*

The early years of the Republic were the workshop of
the conservative dilemma. They saw neo-conservatism at
the crossroads. The split between the group of "elders"
and the "young ones" was an indication thereof. The main
difference between them was that the former took the
responsibilities of the intellectual seriously and were conscious of their nineteenth century heritage, while the latter
with more or less ease gave way to the irrational temper
of the times. While the June Club moved gradually
away from the premises of the Republic and thus turned
into a counter-revolutionary group, the "elders" preferred
to accept the "mediocrity and philistinism"[69] of the Republic.

The parting of the ways between the two groups of men
occurred clearly upon the initiative of the "elders." When
Stadtler sent the program of the "Solidarians" to Naumann with the comment that it reflected the opposition of
German youth to the "dead mechanism" of the old party
life and that, furthermore, it constituted a new edition of
Naumann's "oldest ideals of national socialism,"[70] he expected Naumann's full endorsement. Among the "elders"
Naumann was, perhaps due to his wide contacts, most
open-minded toward political experiments. After a further
communication from Stadtler[71] he sent his response, which,
however, amounted to a rejection of the anti-parliamentarianism of the "Solidarians." "The Führer-idea which
you emphasize can be realized on the basis of democratic
suffrage only through the formation of parties. Of course
this entails also for the leaders a certain check. But the
condition of a chaotic non-existence of parties precludes

[69] Troeltsch, *Spektator-Briefe*, 52.

[70] Letter of Stadtler to Naumann, March 9, 1919, quoted in Heuss,
Naumann, 500.

[71] Telegram of Stadtler to Naumann, March 12, 1919, quoted in
ibid., 500.

any political action whatsoever."[72] While assuring the "Solidarians" of his continued "good will and sympathy," he asked that his name be removed from the list of sponsors of the League. An overture by Gleichen to Rathenau to join the circle of the "young ones" was answered by a similar refusal.[73] Rathenau, less specific but all the more suggestive in his observations, stamped the mentality of the men of the June Club "dialectical and anarchic,"[74] and called instead for statesmanship and moderation. It was Troeltsch who since the early months of 1919 in his political column in *Der Kunstwart* took the "elders'" position to the public with sharp attacks against the men of the June Club. He complained about the destruction of the political center by extremism and he attacked the *Gewissen* for advocating dictatorship.

Indeed, in view of the threat of extremism, Troeltsch and Mann even saw fit to clarify their wartime stand on conservatism. Troeltsch stated his views in a lecture delivered to the Deutsche Hochschule für Politik in Berlin in 1922. At this time he made a point of developing conservatism from the classic, Christian and Western traditions. Using the Western democracies as the example he demonstrated the compatibility of democracy and conservatism. By contrast he suggested that the German romantic tradition amounted to a "mixture of mysticism and brutality" and represented the "counterpart to a conservative revolution."[75] In the following year Thomas Mann took the occasion to endorse Troeltsch's latest and, for once, clearcut statement.[76] He furthermore committed himself in support of the Republic in his often-remembered public

[72] Letter of Naumann to Stadtler, March 17, 1919, quoted in *ibid.*, 500f.

[73] Letter of Rathenau to Gleichen, May 23, 1919. Walther Rathenau, *Briefe* (2nd edn., Dresden, 1926), II, 148-153.

[74] *Ibid.*, 152.

[75] Troeltsch, "Naturrecht und Humanität in der Weltpolitik" (1922), *Deutscher Geist*, 5-7, 14.

[76] Thomas Mann, "Brief über die Schweiz" (1923), *Bemühungen*, 327.

address to the German students in Berlin where he introduced the notion that conservatism was a function of the
German Republic, indeed of democracy.[77] As Mann recalled much later, he had found that the Western-type democracy, though its institutions were outdated, was "after
all essentially aiming at human progress and at good will
toward the perfection of human society."[78]

We are faced here with the rejection of extremism by a
representative group of German men of letters, who originally had helped to define the ideas of neo-conservatism.
"What would Lagarde have said to all this insanity!"
Troeltsch exclaimed.[79] We cannot assume that any of these
men had fundamentally changed their views. Rathenau's
assertion to Gleichen that his faith in his cause had been
only strengthened by the war and the revolution can be
held representative of the whole group; as Mann expressed
it, the *"et nos mutamur in illis"*[80] did not apply. Nor can
we find an enthusiastic acceptance of the Weimar Republic on the part of the "elders." Their dissatisfaction with
the fruits of the November Revolution remained loud and
violent.

The "elders" found themselves in the position of apprentice magicians. Their conservatism had been an answer to
a crisis in which they saw life suppressed by reason. Their
nationalism and their socialism had been defined in defense
of life and in correction of an overly mechanized, indi-
vidualistic, and soulless age. However, they had never
thought of conservatism as meaning the destruction of
reason and denial of liberties; they had insisted on its
humanistic, "intellectualistic"[81] nature. But the events following war and revolution saw conservatism turning fiercely

[77] Thomas Mann, "Von deutscher Republik" (1923), *ibid.*, 141-190.
[78] Thomas Mann, *Doktor Faustus. Das Leben des deutschen Tonkünstlers Adrian Leverkühn, erzählt von einem Freunde* (Stockholm,
1947), 521.

[79] Troeltsch, *Spektator-Briefe*, 144.
[80] Mann, "Von deutscher Republik," *Bemühungen*, 163.
[81] Mann, *Betrachtungen*, 605.

anti-intellectual and upsetting the balance between reason and life in favor of the latter. It was, in Thomas Mann's terms, losing its capacity for "irony" and threatened to become the medium of political and social resentment. It became, therefore, obvious to any responsible thinker that a defense of life was no longer called for.

It seems tragic that so many of the "elders" died in the first years of the Weimar Republic. They were among its few outstanding intellectual leaders. But the question, to what extent their moderate conservative counsel might have strengthened the Republic, by making it more accept-able to the middle classes, must remain open. Undoubtedly, the influence of the "elders" with the Right rapidly waned. They were soon condescendingly put aside as "nineteenth century men." Moeller disposed of them as "eudaemonists," as those Germans "who do not deny their disappointment, but insist on trusting the reason in history. They are ration-alists and pacifists."[82] About Rathenau, Stadtler wrote in an illuminating review of the "innovating tendencies in Germany" that "he is read but rejected. Rathenau's spite against society has ended in resignation, but his ideas are marching forward. . . ."[83] Rathenau's final sacrifice under-scored the full tragedy of the "elders'" position. He died for a Republic of which he was not really representative. One of his assassins, Erwin Kern, admitted shortly before the actual attempt on his life that Rathenau "has written the most bitter criticism of men and the powers of his time." Nevertheless, "he is a man belonging to that very time and he is devoted to these powers. He is their last and ripest fruit, and he combines in himself whatever values and ideas, ethos and pathos, dignity and faith it contained. . . . I could not tolerate it if greatness grew once more out of this crumbling and despised time. . . . I could not tolerate it if this man gave to the people once more a new faith, if he once more swayed it in favor of a

[82] Moeller, *Das dritte Reich*, 7.
[83] Stadtler, *Die Diktatur der sozialen Revolution*, 123.

will and form which are the will and form of an age which died in the war, which is dead, three times dead. . . ."[84] As to Mann's and Troeltsch's position, it was considered a defection from the cause of conservatism and severely taken to task in the *Gewissen*.[85] Mann's address certainly constituted a swan song to the wartime conservatism and, in particular, to his *Betrachtungen*, the end of a phase which a decade afterward, and in retrospect, Mann described as "the last great retreat action, fought not without gallantry, of a romantic citizenry in face of the 'new.' "[86]

The "elders" were German Victorians at heart. They thought in terms of a world—a bourgeois world—which could be regenerated out of its own traditions. They met the first signs of catastrophe—war and revolution—with the courage of their spiritual reserves. Though they knew well that, so Meinecke recorded, "the old conservative world was bound to die," they hoped the "modern industrial population" would be the "heir of its better traditions."[87] Placed in a time when the dilemma of conservatism was inescapable, they threw in their lot with the Republic and refused to surrender to what Thomas Mann called the "new." They undoubtedly chose the way of greatness, and it turned out to be a lonely way for those few—like Meinecke and Thomas Mann—who survived the second war.

[84] Von Salomon, *Die Geächteten*, 302.

[85] Cf. Werner Otto, "Mann über Bord," *Gewissen*, iv (October 23, 1922); Erich Brock, "Thomas Mann's Manifest zum Schutze der Republik," *Gewissen*, v (July 23, 1923); Brock, "Thomas Mann als Prophet des Westens," *Gewissen*, vii (June 8, 1925), which article includes the attack against Troeltsch; Brock, "Die Brüder Mann auf der Wallfahrt nach Europa," *Gewissen*, viii (April 5, 1926).

[86] Mann, *A Sketch of My Life*, 49.

[87] Meinecke summarizing Naumann's thoughts; Meinecke, *Erinnerungen*, 126f.

CHAPTER III

THE LATER YEARS OF THE REPUBLIC

The Crisis and the Neo-Conservatives

THE formative years of the Republic were also the formative years of the neo-conservative movement. The latter, in particular since the parting of the ways with the "elders," had thrown away its opportunity to play a constructive role as a republican conservative movement. But while the neo-conservatives thought that they could condescendingly put the "elders" aside as "nineteenth century men," they were committed to explore new possibilities for a conservative policy. These explorations, however, took them far afield. One can only say that they stumbled into their dilemma. With the exception of some few thoughtful ones among them—such as Ernst Robert Curtius—they were unperturbed by the widening gap between what we have called the "logic" of conservatism and their own policies. We shall see that Moeller was blissfully unaware of the dilemma of conservatism. Spengler, the sober determinist, failed to face this one vital test case of historical inevitability, and Ernst Jünger boldly disregarded it. Vague, somnambulant, and irresponsible, they marked the degeneration of conservatism into a policy of extremism and nihilism in which eventually they found their master in the Nazi Party.

The above should not suggest that the neo-conservative groups had little or no impact upon the history of the Republic and of National Socialism. Indeed, in the later years of the Republic, the years of its final crisis, the neo-conservative movement, realigned in new groups, greatly stepped up its activities. The contemporary observer during the late twenties or early thirties, for a proper assessment of the temper of the country, had to pay increasing attention to the new type of "unpolitical" political formations.[1] If not their size, their number was impressive. Their role in these years is comparable to the one of the various Russian revolutionary groups around the turn of the century. They all played vital parts in an extremely complex situation. And if they turned out not to have been heroes on the stage, they were the chorus.

As in 1918, neo-conservatism in the later twenties was a product of crisis, except that now there was no "dreamland." Germany was no more in flux. "We have made all possible experiments and exercised patience; we have tried all methods without having had faith in them. But now we are in the depth of despair. . . . Germany is thoroughly shaken, and we have but *one* hope: things must improve because they cannot get worse anymore."[2] The crisis of the Republic was unmistakable. It was, as the *Tat* bragged under its new editorship, a "total"[3] crisis. It was quite clearly an economic and political crisis. Foreign loans had been largely responsible for German prosperity in the mid-twenties; now dependence on them was instrumental in precipitating the depression. The withdrawal of funds from abroad and the effect of the stock market crash in New York in 1929 had direct repercussions upon German industry as well as agriculture. The figures for the unemployed passed the two million margin for the first time in the winter of 1928-1929, and soared up to nearly six million at the end of 1931. Once more the middle class was hit along with the others. The middle class, it was now generally admitted, was "proletarianized." The radicalization

[1] Cf. Sigmund Neumann, *Die deutschen Parteien. Wesen und Wandel nach dem Kriege* (Berlin, 1932), 98ff. and 106ff.; Walter Gerhart (pseud. for Waldemar Gurian), *Um des Reiches Zukunft. Nationale Wiedergeburt oder politische Reaktion?* (Freiburg, 1932), passim; Eugen Diesel, *Die deutsche Wandlung. Das Bild eines Volkes* (Stuttgart, 1929), 345f.; Ernst Robert Curtius, *Deutscher Geist in Gefahr* (Stuttgart, Berlin, 1932), 33f.; Willy Hellpach, *Politische Prognose für Deutschland* (Berlin, 1928), 202.

[2] Curtius, *Deutscher Geist*, 7.

[3] "Wohin treiben wir?" *Die Tat*, xxiii (1931-1932), 343.

and "intellectualization"[4] of the *Bürgertum* was now a *fait accompli*. A number of studies published in the semi-monthly organ of the German National Association of Manufacturers (Vereinigung der deutschen Arbeitgeber-verbände), in acknowledging the alienation of the middle class from society as a result of the economic crisis, tried to indicate the resultant political implications.[5] They concurred in the trend registered since the middle twenties away from the old parties and in the direction of an outright anti-parliamentarianism. Indeed, in view of the social changes the old party structure appeared outmoded. The millions of disinherited were left out. For them the traditional nomenclature of "Right" and "Left" had no more meaning. They might have argued, along with the writer Edwin Erich Dwinger, "I cannot accept the Left because that is the side of Bolshevism, but the Right is the side of capitalism, which I hate as much as collectivism."[6] In the terms of Hans Zehrer, the new editor of the *Tat*, they stood "politically at the Right, economically at the Left."[7] It has also been said that they constituted a "homeless"[8] Right.

Clearly, the political fermentation since the year 1928 came from the Right. And, if one began to talk about the coming revolution from the Right[9] in Germany, it was as much due to the eloquent and spirited interpretations of the crisis which originated from the neo-conservative camp, as due to the noise and success of Nazi electioneering. These were the days when Moeller van den Bruck was read, reread, reedited in popular editions, and all but canonized, when Spengler was eagerly debated, and when

[4] Cf. supra, 78f.

[5] Dr. Joseph Winschuh, "Die Rolle der Sozialpolitik in den neueren politischen Strömungen," *Der Arbeitgeber*, xx (1930), 214-218; Georg Schröder, "Die Sozialismus der nationalen Jugend," *Der Arbeitgeber*, xx (1930), 218-221.

[6] Edwin Erich Dwinger, *Wir rufen Deutschland. Heimkehr und Vermächtnis* (Jena, 1932), 309.

[7] Hans Zehrer, "Der Fall Lambach," *Die Tat*, xx (1928-1929), 465.

[8] Rauschning, *Revolution of Nihilism*, 112.

[9] Cf. Hans Freyer, *Revolution von rechts* (Jena, 1931).

Ernst Jünger began to captivate the German youth. The neo-conservatives were the intellectuals of the Right who pointed toward the long-range spiritual roots of the crisis. And though until the very end in the fatal month of January 1933 the outcome of the crisis was still anybody's guess, the neo-conservatives were largely the ones to outline plans for possible solutions. There is no phase of the drama Brüning-Papen-Schleicher-Hitler which was not directly affected by them. Politically speaking, they may have wasted their imagination on a revolution, which, when it came off, was not of their making, but, historically speaking, they had a clear part in it and also they share, however tragically, the responsibility for it.

The Young Conservatives

Even in the later period there were those among the neo-conservatives who took a more or less tolerant attitude toward the Republic. They called themselves Young Conservatives. In part they grew out of the earlier neo-conservative groups, and in part they represented a secessional movement from the German Nationalists. They belonged no less than all the other neo-conservatives to the "homeless" Right. Their main center of activity was the Herrenklub, which was located in a stately building across from the Reichstag on the Friedrich Ebertstrasse. It had taken the place of the June Club some time in the year 1924 after the latter's funds had been withdrawn and the group had been left rocked by dissension.[10] The new organization

[10] Since the time of its dissolution the June Club had become a springboard for all sorts of political activities. Moeller himself withdrew because of differences with Gleichen and because he had ceased to believe in the effectiveness of the Club. Moeller already then showed signs of mental disturbance. Stadtler and Brauweiler moved close to the Stahlhelm, the latter of the two becoming its political adviser. Hans Schwarz later founded his own extremist journal, *Der Nahe Osten*. The tradition of the June Club was to some extent carried on by the insignificant Volksdeutscher Klub, which interested itself in work for Germans abroad. Most of its members eventually joined the Herrenklub.

was somewhat different in character. Headed jointly by Gleichen and Count Hans Bodo von Alvensleben, it became a meeting ground for the Junkers, heavy industry, and finance. Though its membership never much exceeded five thousand,[11] it exercised a penetrating influence on the intellectual life of the German Right. Its publication *Der Ring*,[12] which reflected the tenor of its weekly meetings, took the lead in the discussion of problems like the *Reichsreform*, the authoritarian state, corporatism versus parliamentarianism, and aristocracy. It was seconded by other independent magazines like the *Deutsche Rundschau*[13] and the *Deutsches Volkstum*.

The *Deutsche Rundschau*, still under Pechel's direction, opened its columns to the Munich lawyer Edgar J. Jung, who was one of the challenging young members of the Herrenklub. He had been a volunteer in the first World War and then active in the resistance against the French occupation and against separatism in the Palatinate. In 1928 his much-discussed work appeared, *Die Herrschaft der Minderwertigen*[14] (The Rule of the Inferiors), which added up to a violent criticism of democracy as representing the rule of the inferiors, that is, of money and the masses. He wrote about the "conservative revolution" as a Christian revival which would effect the "restoration of all those elementary laws and values without which man loses his ties with nature and God and without which he is incapable of building up a true order. In the

[11] Cf. Wilhelm von Schramm, "Was ist der Herrenklub?—Die Wirkung einer nationalen Gesellschaft," *Münchener Neueste Nachrichten*, No. 325 (November 29, 1932), as reprinted in *Der Ring*, v (December 9, 1932), 852f.

[12] Its edition was about one thousand.

[13] Rudolf Pechel emphasizes that, while there was a direct relationship between his magazine, the June Club, and the Volksdeutscher Klub, he was connected with the Herrenklub only through personal relations with some of its members; letter from Rudolf Pechel, October 10, 1954.

[14] Edgar J. Jung, *Die Herrschaft der Minderwertigen. Ihr Zerfall und ihre Ablösung durch ein Neues Reich* (3rd edn., Berlin, 1930).

place of equality there will be inherent standards, in the place of social consciousness a just integration into the hierarchical society, in the place of mechanical election an organic elite, in the place of bureaucratic leveling the inner responsibility of genuine self-government, in the place of mass prosperity the rights of a proud people."[15] Jung was not one of the most original thinkers among the neoconservatives. He, like most of his *confrères* who ventured into elaborate visions of the German past, present, and future,[16] owed a debt to Moeller. Also, Jung's work shows traces of Pareto, who had been his teacher while he had studied in Lausanne, and of the neo-romantic sociologist Othmar Spann. Spann, an Austrian, busied himself at the University of Vienna proselytizing from his lecture platform to captivated audiences for what he called the "true," "organic" or "corporative" state.[17] But among all the too theoretical conservatives Jung was primarily an ambitious man of action. He was a man of the world with excellent connections among politicians and businessmen, among the unions, and in the German intelligentsia. It was he who later, as secretary to von Papen and as author of Papen's famous Marburg address, was among those few who stood up for his conservative principles against the Nazis.

The *Deutsches Volkstum,* edited since 1926 by Albrecht Erich Günther in conjunction with Wilhelm Stapel, also served as a mouthpiece for the Young Conservatives. Through its connection with the D.H.V. the magazine carried the Young Conservatives' ideas to a broader public. The D.H.V. itself in the middle twenties acquired, through the Hanseatische Verlagsanstalt, the Ring Verlag and,

[15] Edgar J. Jung, *Deutsche über Deutschland* (Munich, 1932), 380.

[16] Cf. Hans Freyer, *Revolution von rechts* (Jena, 1931); Friedrich Hielscher, *Das Reich* (Berlin, 1938); Dr. Walther Schotte, *Der Neue Staat* (Berlin, 1932); Wilhelm von Schramm, *Radikale Politik* (Munich, 1932).

[17] Othmar Spann, *Der wahre Staat. Vorlesungen über Abbruch und Neubau der Gesellschaft* (Jena, 1921).

therewith, the rights for Moeller's *Das dritte Reich.* Along with the *Deutsches Volkstum* the D.H.V. was emphatic in its criticism of the capitalistic order, which it held responsible for what it called the "proletarization crisis." In its place it propagated a "healthy corporative order,"[18] and, in general terms, a "renewal" of the German people and state "out of a conservative-revolutionary spirit."[19] In an effort to formulate this policy the *Deutsches Volkstum* managed to rally as its contributors some of the leading German Rightist publicists, such as Othmar Spann, Ernst Krieck, Wilhelm von Schramm, Heinz Brauweiler, Hermann Ullmann, Theodor Böttiger, and, indeed, the shocking and paradoxical Ernst Jünger.

In spite of all the talk about the "conservative revolution" the men around the Herrenklub were hardly revolutionaries. They were not the prototypes of revolutionaries, these well-dressed aristocrats in their serene high-ceiling establishment. However, they found themselves in the midst of a situation—the crisis—which in itself was revolutionary by nature. Most of the Young Conservatives were monarchists at heart and disliked the Republic, which they identified with Germany's defeat. But they knew that there was no future for monarchism in Germany.[20] "Monarchy is a chapter of the past," Jung admitted, because "the question is not of returning to old loyalties, but of penetrating to new ones."[21] It was in this search for new loyalties that they got entangled with the Nazis. After all, both the Young Conservatives and the Nazis were heading for the magic Third Reich. And, in an at-

[18] *Der Deutschnationale Handlungsgehilfen Verband im Jahre 1930. Rechenschaftsbericht erstattet von seiner Verwaltung* (Hamburg, 1931), 8f.
[19] *Der Deutschnationale Handlungsgehilfen Verband im Jahre 1931* (Hamburg, 1932), 63.
[20] For a discussion of the attempts toward a restoration cf. Walter H. Kaufmann, *Monarchism in the Weimar Republic* (New York, 1953), passim.
[21] Jung, *Herrschaft der Minderwertigen,* 341, 76.

mosphere which was more conducive to vagueness and confusion than to precision of thought, the differences between Moeller's and Hitler's Third Reichs, between conservatism and National Socialism, were all too easily passed over. Many among the Young Conservatuals, such as Edgar J. Jung, felt uneasy about this situation and about the fact that the rising National Socialist Party pushed them increasingly into the background. Now and then voices were even heard among them advocating acceptance of the Republic. One of these was Theodor Böttiger, a lawyer from Breslau and member of the Herrenklub who, writing under the pseudonym of Georg Quabbe, dedicated his book on conservatism to Thomas Mann, alas, "the unpolitical observer."[22] All too late for the good of his friends Böttiger wrote, ". . . I think with sadness of Thomas Mann, but with equal regret we have to register that Troeltsch and Meinecke were and are against us. . . ."[23] Also, the Young Conservatives still kept up their connections with Ernst Robert Curtius, a distinguished scholar, who chose the *Deutsche Rundschau*[24] as a forum to warn the young German nationalists against the revolutionary myth which had essentially nihilistic features. "The new nationalism," he wrote, "wants to throw off not only the nowadays so-much-maligned nineteenth century, but all historical traditions."[25] And he concluded that Germany was the first country in which the nationalists formed a solid front against the spirit and against civilization. "And these anti-intellectuals are not mobs, but . . . intellectuals."[26] However, men like Böttiger and Curtius were lone voices pointing out one of the main evils, the *trahison des clercs,* which befell twentieth century conservatism in Germany.

[22] Georg Quabbe, *Tar a Ri. Variationen über ein konservatives Thema* (Berlin, 1927).

[23] *Ibid.,* 13.

[24] Ernst Robert Curtius, "Nationalismus und Kultur," *Deutsche Rundschau,* XLII (1931), 736-748. This article was incorporated subsequently into his book *Deutscher Geist in Gefahr* (Stuttgart, 1932).

[25] Curtius, *Deutscher Geist,* 40.

[26] *Ibid.,* 43.

It was the disintegration of the Deutschnationale Volks-partei which launched the Young Conservatives into political ventures. The D.N.V.P. had been split since the days of the Reichstag vote about the Dawes Plan into the irreconcilables and moderates, or, as one of its most influential members, Freytagh-Loringhoven, put it, the representatives of "nationalism" and those of "governmentalism."[27] The former, the right-wingers of the Party, were principally opposed to cooperation with the Republic. Prominent among them were men like Freytagh-Loringhoven himself and Alfred Hugenberg, the party leader since 1928. The latter were tending toward a constructive conservative policy within the Republican framework. They included mostly the Young Conservatives like Count Westarp, the party leader between 1924 and 1928, Gottfried Treviranus, Paul Lejeune-Jung, Hans Schlange-Schöningen, and Walther Lambach. There had been attempts on the part of the moderates in 1924 and again in 1926 to effect a conservative policy through a closer cooperation between the D.N. V.P. and the Deutsche Volkspartei, but in each case Gustav Stresemann had foiled their attempts. The actual crisis in the D.N.V.P. was precipitated as a result of the election of May 20, 1928, in which the Party suffered a spectacular defeat. The year 1928 was the last year of the prosperity which had marked the German economy since 1924, the last year before the start of the crisis. This fact may well explain the losses of the Nazis and of the German Nationalists, the latter dropping in the Reichstag from 103 to 78 deputies. Shortly after the elections the so-called "Lambach case" ("*Fall* Lambach") rocked the party from within. In the middle of the year Walther Lambach, the leader of the D.H.V. and member of the Reichstag for the D.N.V.P., published an article in the conservative weekly *Politische Wochenschrift,* in which he flatly stated that the German youth was staying away from the German Nationalists because the party had not kept up with the times.

[27] Freiherr von Freytagh-Loringhoven, *Deutschnationale Volkspartei* (Berlin, 1931), 40.

". . . The German youth has kept aloof from the German Nationalists because they do not care to restore the hereditary monarchy to their world of work and sport. . . .

". . . Kings and emperors are to our growing generation no longer sacrosanct and venerable persons or institutions. They have been degraded in the eyes of our youth to figures of the stage and of the screen. . . .

". . . This diagnosis must lead the present-day conservative to serious reflections regarding the necessities and possibilities of a truly conservative policy. He knows in his innermost soul that he no longer believes in a restoration of a true hereditary monarchy. . . . Nothing is left of his monarchism but the old *Kyffhäuser* dream; indeed, nothing else. . . .

". . . Youth wants action. Hopes for which one cannot fight will leave the more valuable part of our youth dissatisfied. We of the German National People's Party . . . must in the future appeal to the *entire* German electorate: Monarchists and Republicans, join our ranks! And with this change in our attitude, concerning the government, we must also change our program and our party leadership.

". . . Not as a one-sided monarchistic party, but as a new conservative party, the D.N.V.P. must start toward the future. If there is no leadership which is able to make this transition, then the party will lose its most promising elements."[28]

The political side of the dilemma of conservatism could not have been raised more clearly than by Lambach's article. But the Party organization not only went into instant action against Lambach;[29] adding insult to injury it elected as its leader in the fall of the same year, Hugenberg, the leading irreconcilable.

By 1928 the split in D.N.V.P. had become obvious and toward the end of the following year it came to a secession

[28] *Politische Wochenschrift*, iv, No. 24 (1928), quoted in Kaufmann, *Monarchism*, 182ff.

[29] Lambach's ouster from the Party was eventually revoked, though he was given a "reprimand."

on the part of the moderates over the issue of the Young Plan. In September 1929 Hugenberg and Hitler faced the German public with a "Law against the Enslavement of the German People," commonly called the "Freedom Law," which denounced the war-guilt clause of the Versailles Treaty and demanded the renunciation of all reparation obligations. Its most controversial paragraph, the fourth, demanded that the chancellor, the cabinet, and their plenipotentiaries be subjected to prosecution for treason if they agreed to any more financial commitments. The motion had to obtain support from 10 percent of the electorate, which its sponsors barely managed to get, in order to be brought before the Reichstag. At this point of the lengthy procedure a violent struggle originated between the Hugenberg faction of the D.N.V.P. and the moderates. While the Party Congress at Kassel on November 22-23 had voiced expectations that the Party would vote for the whole Freedom Law, a minority under the leadership of Treviranus refused to vote for Paragraph 4. The dissenting moderates, 23 out of the 78 German Nationalist deputies, were made up of Young Conservatives, agrarians, and Christian socialist trade unionists. The duel between Hugenberg and Treviranus led on December 3-4 to the resignation from the D.N.V.P. of twelve prominent Reichstag members, among them Treviranus, Lejeune-Jung, von Lindeiner-Wildau, Professor Hoetzsch, Schlange-Schöningen, and Lambach, and on January 28, 1930 to the foundation of the People's Conservative Association (Volkskonservative Vereinigung). In its initial convention, which appropriately was held in the old Herrenhaus building on the Leipzigerstrasse, the speakers—one of them was Lejeune-Jung—stressed the Association's non-partisan character and, as its aim, the return to Christian and enlightened conservative and social principles. Professor Hoetzsch concluded that Germany had at last found its form of "Tory democracy."[30]

[30] *Frankfurter Zeitung,* January 29, 1930. (*Zweites Morgenblatt.*)

On July 18, 1930 a second secession occurred from the D.N.V.P., over the Social Democratic motion in the Reichstag demanding the annulment of the emergency decrees of the new chancellor, Heinrich Brüning. Eighteen German Nationalist deputies under Count Westarp, who voted against Hugenberg's instructions and for the Brüning government,[31] left the party. They joined the group around Treviranus to form the Conservative People's Party (Konservative Volkspartei), thus making the final step into politics. But, living up to the traditional pattern of sectarianism, the agrarians and the Christian socialists founded their own parties, the Christian Socialist People's Service (Christlichsozialer Volksdienst) and the Christian National Peasant's Party, commonly called the Deutsches Landvolk.

Neither of these parties could assert itself with the people. Their poor showing in the election following their formation in September 1930[32] seemed to seal their fate as well as cast a dark shadow over the future of the Republic. The victors in the election were the Nazis and the Communists. It has been rightly stated that the real importance of the secessionists from the D.N.V.P. lay not so much in their parliamentary showing as in their connections outside parliament,[33] through men like Treviranus and von Westarp. In particular, Treviranus was a protégé of President Hindenburg. But in the last analysis precisely a man like Treviranus epitomizes the failure of his movement. He was but another Papen. His naval background—he liked to refer to himself as Kapitänleutnant a.D.—of which a great deal was made, gave him an air of promise. In the cramped political situation of these days he seemed to emerge from the outworn parliamentary machinery as one of the "new"-type men. Along with his friends he was characterized by Stapel as being "young" and as giving a "new" meaning to

[31] Which at the time included Treviranus as minister for occupied territories.

[32] The Conservative People's Party emerged with four deputies, the Christian Socialists with fourteen, and the Landvolk with nineteen.

[33] Neumann, *Die deutschen Parteien*, 69.

conservative, national, and Christian policies.[34] But somehow Treviranus could not sustain his drive. He remained
the man of promise. It may be that he had only one ounce
of charisma, not enough to reach the common man. His
shortcomings were the shortcomings of the whole group of
the Young Conservatives and, ultimately, of their conservatism. Without the "elders" they were, as Böttiger implied,
morally orphaned. And though they loyally supported
the Brüning and Papen governments, they did not really
support the Republic. They expected of each of these two
governments that it would establish an authoritarian state
by liquidating party rule. They had too many reservations
about the Republic. A republic cannot live on being condescendingly, and grudgingly, tolerated. And, on the other
hand, the Young Conservatives never really appealed to the
masses. Their ideas, however, were taken over and distorted to serve the purpose of the National Socialist movement.

The Conservatives of the Tat Circle

Elsewhere in Berlin, on the Rankestrasse, where the *Tat*
Circle met in the early thirties, the atmosphere was mark-
edly different from that of the Herrenklub. It was less
gentlemanly and more what one used to call in Germany
"jugendbewegt" (dedicated to the ways of the Youth
Movement). In fact, the *Tat* Circle was one of those centers
of the revolution from the right in which the concept of
the "gentleman" tended to be scoffed at as a symbol of the
nineteenth century past; it was, after all, part of those
Western traditions which seemed to be crumbling right
and left. The friends of Hans Zehrer had never quite outlived their "experiences" in the Youth Movement; they
were still hiking and singing in spirit. There was no use
being dignified and reserved—one might as well be forthright. "There once was a *Bürgertum* . . . ,"[35] and in what

34 Wilhelm Stapel, "Geht die Rechte in Bruch?" *Deutsches Volkstum*, XXXII (1930), 76f.

35 Hans Zehrer, "Bürgerliche Mitte: Kompromiss oder Synthese?"
Die Tat, XX (1928-1929), 280.

they saw as the struggle between generations, the field, they argued, was open to the young generation.[36]

Actually, the new *Tat* was fulfilling the legacy of Eugen Diederichs. In the spring of 1928 he had handed over the editorship of his magazine to the young poet Adam Kuckhoff in hopes of having the magazine "participate more actively in life,"[37] so the editorial notice ran. Kuckhoff, in turn, proceeded to announce that the new generation had taken over. "We long for dogma and for certainty *(Eindeutigkeit)*." And he stated the *Tat's* readiness for a "most radical solution" in the "relentless controversy with the powers of the times."[38] During these days appeared the first articles in the *Tat* by Hans Zehrer, who, soon after Diederichs' death in September 1930, assumed the all-over editorship of the magazine. For a long time Zehrer, a highly gifted but somewhat unstable publicist, had been riding the fence. While contributing actively to the *Tat,* he held the position of editor of the democratic, middle-of-the-road Ullstein paper *Vossische Zeitung.* Only in October 1931 did it occur to Zehrer that he had outlived his usefulness to this very "bourgeois" paper, from which, at last, he resigned. It was under Zehrer that *Tat* rose to the commonly recognized position as "the leading political magazine in the country."[39] He attracted prominent publicists like Adolf Grabowsky, concerned with a definition of the new conservatism; Giselher Wirsing, who emerged with an uninhibitedly offensive version of Naumann's Central Europe concept;[40] and Friedrich Zimmermann, who under the well-known pseudonym Ferdinand Fried propagated his idea of "autarchy." Before long the *Tat* reflected a

[36] Cf. Hans Zehrer, "Um die politische Jugend," *Die Tat*, xx (1928-1929), 228.

[37] *Die Tat*, xix (1927-1928), 966.

[38] *Die Tat*, xx (1928-1929), 78f.

[39] Edgar Ansel Mowrer, *Germany Puts the Clock Back* (Penguin edn., Harmondsworth, Middlesex, England, 1939) , 118.

[40] In contrast to Naumann's *Mitteleuropa,* he called his own version *Zwischeneuropa.*

well-defined and dynamic political program[41] which made it one of the main centers of the younger intelligentsia of the Right.[42] Between 1929 and 1932 its subscriptions rose from 1,000 to more than 20,000. Furthermore, in August 1932 Zehrer, urged by General Kurt von Schleicher, acquired the *Tägliche Rundschau,* a daily newspaper which had served as mouthpiece for the Christian Social People's Service. Within a few months Zehrer managed to put it on the map as one of the politically best-informed Berlin newspapers.

There was nothing defensive about the *Tat.* It turned as relentlessly against the Republic as against what it called "restoration."[43] The efforts of the Young Conservatives were derided and compared with the "Metternich era."[44] They had compromised themselves in particular by joining the Brüning government. But the *Tat* was no less aggressive against the Nazis. Like the Communists they were but a product of chaos. They were specifically exposed for their poverty of ideas. The *Tat* men turned on the Nazis for reasons of snobbism rather than principle. While the Nazis were the mob, they were the intellectuals. But in terms of Curtius's analysis of German anti-intellectualism, can we say which one of the two was worse? Surely the *Tat* had done a thorough job in undermining the Weimar Republic. As Chancellor Brüning put it, it cost him "enormous difficulties."[45] "Attention, young front, stay out!"[46] was one of its powerful slogans.

Furthermore, the *Tat's* position gained some immediate

[41] "The world economy to be ended, the authoritarian state, planned economy, autarchy, a Southeast policy, and the need for a blending of nationalism and socialism and of Right and Left in a people's community *(Volksgemeinschaft)* ." "Der Weg der Tat," *Die Tat,* xxiv (1932-1933), 517.

[42] Cf. Curtius, *Deutscher Geist in Gefahr,* 36.

[43] Cf. "Das Jahr der Entscheidung," *Die Tat,* xxii (1930-1931), 841.

[44] "Metternich-Ära," *Die Tat,* xxii (1930-1931), 299f.

[45] Interview with Brüning, May 12, 1948.

[46] Hans Zehrer, "Achtung, junge Front! Draussenbleiben!" *Die Tat,* xxi (1929-1930), 25ff.

political significance by the fact that Zehrer established close ties with some army generals,[47] notably Schleicher. He was one of the chief "political" generals of the Reichswehr. His views and maneuvers found their expression in Zehrer's clamor for a "revolution from above"[48] based upon the presidency and the army. When Schleicher finally became chancellor, the *Tat* became a semi-official publication. "With this cabinet we have now arrived at a turning point."[49] proclaimed the *Tägliche Rundschau*. The *Tat* had for some time prepared the ground for the last-minute negotiations of Schleicher with Gregor Strasser and the trade union leaders Stegerwald and Leipart by its feverish call for a "Third Front."[50] A variation of Moeller's "Third Reich," it alluded to an alleged popular movement cutting across party lines. Schleicher's overtures to Gregor Strasser, who headed within the National Socialist German Workers' Party (N.S.D.A.P.) the National Socialist Labor Organization (N.S.B.O.), were designed to win over the strong labor element from the Party. Equally the detaching of the other unions from their party affiliations would have led toward a corporative front of unions and an elimination of party influence. This would have meant a strike against political democracy as well as against the Nazi Party, which at that time was committed to an assumption of power through legal—that is, parliamentary—means. Even after Schleicher's policy had obviously failed in March 1933, the *Tat,* in an anonymous editorial questioning the finality of the Hitler-Papen combination, advo-

[47] Brüning's contention that General Walter von Reichenau inspired articles hostile to his government has been contradicted by Hans Zehrer, who maintains that Reichenau, having established a close connection with Hitler, was hostile to the *Tat* Circle; interview with Brüning, May 12, 1948; letter from Zehrer, August 10, 1954.

[48] Hans Zehrer, "Die Etappe Papen," *Die Tat*, xxiv (1932-1933), 626.

[49] *Tägliche Rundschau* (December 3, 1932) , quoted in *Das deutsche Reich von 1918 bis heute* (ed. Cuno Horkenbach, Berlin, 1932), 409.

[50] Hans Zehrer, "Die dritte Front," *Die Tat*, xxiv (1932-1933), 97ff. and "An der Wende!" *Die Tat*, xxiv (1932-1933), 433ff.

cated the union between the army and the workers as represented by the "social general" and the "socialistic exponent of the N.S.D.A.P."[51] However, the *Tat*'s daydreams evaporated in view of the nightmare which had started in January 1933.

The Radical Conservatives

Beyond the Young Conservatives and the *Tat* Circle, *in extremis*, operated several radical conservative groups which grew up under the shadow of the crisis. Associated with names like Hans Schwarz (one of those who had left the June Club under protest), Otto Strasser (who left the Nazi Party with much fanfare in 1930), and the National Bolshevist Ernst Niekisch, they reflected uninhibitedly the violent temper of the years before 1933. They were extreme Rightists or extreme Leftists or, indeed, both.[52] They joined the Young Conservatives and the *Tat* Circle in the front against liberalism and democracy. Like them they swore by the name of Moeller van den Bruck, but did so in their own way. Actually Moeller became an object of dispute. While the *Tat* discussed the "danger of the misunderstood Moeller,"[53] Hans Schwarz, as trustee of the so-called Moeller Archives, objected to the reprint of Moeller's dedication to Gleichen in the third edition of *Das dritte Reich*.[54] He even managed to enlist Moeller's second wife, Lucy, to declare that, in her opinion, the circle around Gleichen had taken a course contrary to the spirit of Moeller and had "liberalized" him instead of "revolutionizing" him.[55] Niekisch flatly charged that the

[51] "Schleicher und Strasser," *Die Tat*, xxiv (1932-1933), 1068.

[52] Even their designations as "national revolutionaries," "social revolutionary nationalists," or "National Bolsheviks" reflected the realm where "*les extrèmes se touchent.*"

[53] Wolfgang Herrmann, "Moeller van den Bruck," *Die Tat*, xxv (1933-1934), 273.

[54] Wilhelm Wunderlich, "Die Spinne," *Die Tat*, xxiii (1931-1932), 843.

[55] She added that she considered National Socialism the only movement which had succeeded in "revolutionizing" Moeller; L. Moeller

"Herrenklub cabinet of Herr von Papen" had "abused" the name of the prophet.[56] Nor did he have a kindly comment left for the *Tat*. The radical conservatives had little of the aristocratic bearing of the Herrenklub group or of the intellectualism—however anti-intellectual—of the *Tat* Circle. They were, whether or not they admitted it, proletarian conservatives. For Hans Schwarz's periodical *Der Nahe Osten* the revolution from the right was mainly an agrarian affair. From the beginnings of the Conservative Party in Prussia to the *Nahe Osten,* conservatism had come full circle. It had started as an agrarian movement and as such it appeared again in the columns of the *Nahe Osten*. However, if, as the men of the *Nahe Osten* claimed,[57] Prussian conservatism had been coupled with a socialism from above, their own conservatism tended to be socialism from below. They telescoped the needs of agriculture and the needs of Germany into one. Both made them reject the West as "bourgeois," "capitalistic," "old," and made them look eastward for new horizons. "The *dritte Reich* and the *nahe Osten* are words of apocalyptic force."[58] What would Naumann have said to these expansive Central Europe designs—once more supported by Giselher Wirsing—which extended the German sphere of influence all the way to the Russian borders? And what was left of German conservatism in an attitude which had no resources other than a vague, adolescent longing for the far away and unknown? "Things are not quite so simple," Curtius wrote, "that the history of the Western mind could be revised. . . . from geopolitical points of view."[59] However simple-minded and, indeed, lunatic the notions of the men of the *Nahe Osten* were, they cannot really be

van den Bruck, "Moeller van den Bruck's drittes Reich," *Der Nahe Osten,* IV (1931) , 1.

[56] "Preussen," *Das dritte Reich,* IX (1932), 223.
[57] Cf. Friedrich Schinkel, *Preussischer Sozialismus* (Breslau, 1934), passim.
[58] Hans Schwarz, "Der nahe Osten," *Der Nahe Osten,* I (1928), 29.
[59] Curtius, *Deutscher Geist in Gefahr,* 42.

dismissed as belonging to the "lunatic fringe." In a situation of crisis they constituted more closely the lunatic center. Though their Eastern orientation was not in conformity with the position of National Socialism, they could safely call themselves part of the Nazi movement—though not of the Party. In fact, the year 1933 brought a complete self-obliteration on the part of the *Nahe Osten,* which became "part of the great stream of the German revolution."[60]

Among the many radical conservative groups Otto Strasser's Black Front (Schwarze Front) gained the most notoriety, and that largely through its spectacular secession from the N.S.D.A.P. Otto Strasser, the younger brother of Gregor, had a checkered political career. In the early years of the Republic, while a Social Democrat, he had been close to the June Club and had actively contributed to the *Gewissen.* When in the middle twenties he joined the N.S.D.A.P. it was he who claimed to have introduced Moeller's notion of the "Third Reich" to the Party.[61] The Strasser brothers were responsible for transplanting National Socialism, originally a South German movement, to the North. But though they nominally acknowledged the over-all leadership of Hitler, they actually established—at first in cooperation with Goebbels—a party within the Party. Not only did they control a following very different from that of the Munich Party—and, for that matter, different from those of the most of the other neo-conservative groups—by agitating among the industrial proletariat of northern Germany, but they also developed a definite program which was at variance with the policies of the Party. No doubt the Strasser brothers were too theoretical for the expedient Hitler. Otto Strasser, in particular, outlined elaborate schemes for a neo-feudal conservative-socialistic order which involved Germany's withdrawal from the world market, abolishment of private property, decentrali-

[60] "An unsere Leser," *Der Nahe Osten,* vi (1933), 298.
[61] Richard Schapke, *Die Schwarze Front* (Leipzig, 1932), 41.

zation of Germany's economic and political structure, and, in foreign affairs, an alliance with Russia. Moreover, Hitler, who was dependent upon large money grants for the Party, could not accept the Strassers' violent anti-capitalism and their fanatic revolutionary course. Over one issue in particular, the popular referendum in 1926 concerning the disposition of the properties belonging to the former German ruling houses, did the Strassers and Hitler come to blows. In keeping with their socialistic views the former pressed for the Party's support of the expropriation referendum. They did not prevail. In fact, Hitler succeeded in 1926 in an all-out attack against the Strasser brothers to break their hold over the North by the appointment of the repentant Goebbels as *Gauleiter* of Berlin and by having his less and less meaningful twenty-five-point Party program reaffirmed as against the Strassers' program. However, while Hitler outwardly maintained Party unity on his own terms, the N.S.D.A.P. remained divided within itself between the larger group of moderate "petty-bourgeois" pro-capitalists and the revolutionary anti-capitalists.

An important landmark in the struggle between these two groups was the secession of Otto Strasser, with Gregor continuing the struggle in the Party until he was executed in the famous "night of St. Bartholomew," June 30, 1934. After two heated and unsuccessful interviews with Hitler in May 1930, Otto Strasser finally left the Party. With the slogan "the socialists leave the N.S.D.A.P.," he founded his own "Fighting Association of Revolutionary National Socialists" (Kampfgemeinschaft Revolutionärer Nationalsozialisten), popularly called the "Black Front."[62] The exodus of Otto Strasser did not halt the N.S.D.A.P. in its sweep toward victory. In fact, Otto Strasser's group, in

[62] Black, standing for resistance against poverty and national humiliation, has been generally accepted among the radical conservatives as a symbol. The immediate inspiration came, as usual, from Moeller; Moeller, *Das dritte Reich*, 229. The black flag has its origins in the times of the peasant risings in 1525.

spite of frantic attempts to appeal for a union to other groups—such as the *Tat* Circle, the rebellious Storm Troopers under the former police captain Walter Stennes, the Resistance Movement of Ernst Niekisch and elements of the Bündische Jugend as well as of the former Freikorps[63]—never succeeded in building an effective counterbalance to the N.S.D.A.P.

The emblem of the Black Front, a hammer and a sword crossed at the crux of a swastika,[64] was indicative of a good deal of ideological crossbreeding, if not confusion, in Strasser. It reflects his political peregrinations, if we allow the hammer to stand for his Leftist phase, the swastika for National Socialism, and the sword for a militant kind of conservatism. While Hitler in one disputation with Strasser denounced him as a Marxist[65] and again as a "parlor Bolshevik,"[66] a modern critic called him the "Trotzky of the Nazi Party."[67] Strasser certainly was no materialist in the Marxian sense of the word, even though his violent anti-capitalism often came close to the position of the extreme Left. And if Strasser was a Nazi, he was so in a very personal way, with his own hopes and reservations. He had the same kind of loyalty to his principles as Trotsky had, though he did not have Trotsky's originality. Indeed, he was a muddy, mystical thinker. Ideologically his place was with the tradition of the Youth Movement and with neo-conservatism. In his own terms, his world was the world which turned its back on liberalism; it was the world of "allegiances," of the "we-idea," of "conservatism."[68] And his socialism was a conservative socialism or a "solidarism" calling for "harmony between capital and

---

[63] Schapke, *Die Schwarze Front*, 75f.

[64] The swastika was omitted after Strasser's break with Hitler.

[65] "What you call socialism is pure Marxism"; Otto Strasser, *Aufbau des deutschen Sozialismus* (2nd edn. Prague, 1936), 130.

[66] Konrad Heiden, *Der Führer* (New York, 1944) , 349.

[67] Alfred Werner, "Trotzky of the Nazi Party," *Journal of Central European Affairs*, xi (January-April 1951), 38ff.

[68] Strasser, *Aufbau*, 11f.

labour and between the individual and the community."[69] Throughout, Otto Strasser remained one of Moeller's diversified fold. He was the magician's apprentice, a conservative most definitely, but a conservative gone mad, vulgar, proletarian. Though the so-called "Strasser Program,"[70] which had been defined in 1925 in Hanover, excluded any idea of dictatorship and opposed the uniformity of National Socialism, the rowdy members of the Black Front would have been the least qualified to administer a moderate program. We are led to believe that, in practice, Strasser's conservatism would have incorporated the worst features of the both Rightist and Leftist extremism.

[69] Otto Strasser, *Hitler and I* (Boston, 1940), 83. "Solidarism" has become the slogan of the League for German Revival (Bund für Deutschlands Erneuerung), the organization of Strasser adherents in post-World War II Germany; Werner, "Trotzky of the Nazi Party," *Journal*, 42.

[70] Strasser, *Hitler and I*, 81ff.

CHAPTER IV

NATIONAL BOLSHEVISM AND THE
NEO-CONSERVATIVES

THERE remains to be discussed National Bolshevism, a current of opinion which manifested itself among the neo-conservatives and became rampant in the crucial years before 1933. National Bolshevism, which stands for a *rapprochement* between German nationalism and Russian Communism, appears strangely paradoxical and unsavory. It is the story of strange bedfellows. It was the most imaginative and abstruse child of anti-Versailles and anti-Weimar Germany, and it became during the crisis the most extreme and desperate refuge of the "homeless" Right.

The origins of National Bolshevism take us back to the immediate post-war period. It was fully anticipated in Brockdorff-Rantzau's warnings at Versailles that the policy of the Western powers might give rise in Germany to an ideology which would combine nationalism with socialism or communism. To his keen political sense a German anti-Versailles movement and Russian anti-capitalism and anti-imperialism were closely akin. Although one thought in terms of nations and the other in terms of classes, both were have-not movements. For both, the West was bound to appear as the common oppressor, the common enemy; both were bound to discover their mutual affinity in terms of anti-Westernism and anti-cosmopolitanism.

Indeed, National Bolshevism was based on a psychology of resentment toward the West and an intense love-hate relationship toward the East. Whereas resentment against the West in the first years after Versailles was more or less widespread among Germans of all classes and denominations, concern with the East became the unique feature of National Bolshevism and distinguished it from the other brands of German nationalism. In a way, the attitude of

National Bolshevism in the post-Versailles world was much more consistent than, for example, the policy of the old-type nationalists of the D.N.V.P. The latter did not share that sweeping equation: anti-West equals anti-capitalism equals pro-East equals pro-Bolshevism. National Bolshevism approximated it. In this, National Bolshevism is a typical twentieth century movement. It seeks an emotional outlet through simplification of issues at the expense of sound reasoning. Indeed the National Bolshevik fascination with the East is pure irrationalism.

The metamorphosis of the psychology of National Bolshevism is particularly evident among the Freikorps troops in the Baltic under General von der Goltz in 1919. The Baltic Freikorps defy definition. To label them as violently anti-Bolshevik would constitute a gross oversimplification. Their units fought neither for the Western powers nor for the German government, whose authority they did not recognize. They were soldiers of fortune; they were no man's soldiers. Their Russian adventure was the escapism of a young generation of desperados who could not face the facts of Weimar and Versailles. Russia was their escape. In fact, they hoped to acquire Russian citizenship and rights to settle on Russian soil. As long as they fought the Reds, they did, whether they wanted to or not, serve the Western powers. But by doing so, were they not really, as Karl Radek suggested later at a crucial moment, "hirelings of the Entente against the Russian people"? Were they not all "wanderers into the void"[1] like the often-singled-out Albert Leo Schlageter, who fought with the Freikorps Medem and became a martyr of German nationalism during the Ruhr struggle? The position of the Freikorps was most ambiguous. Some of their leading spokesman, like Ernst von Salomon, Ernst Jünger, and others, finally admitted openly that the Freikorps had been exploited, that

[1] Moeller van den Bruck, *Das Recht der jungen Völker* (ed. Hans Schwarz, Berlin, 1932), 75-79.

they had fought "on the wrong front."[2] The Freikorps, then, were neither Whites or Reds; they were, as one of the popular interpreters of their fate, the novelist Edwin Erich Dwinger, suggested, "between White and Red."[3] They were political irresponsibles. In fact, the reasons which made them fight on the side of the Whites—adventuring, and freeing Germany from the yoke of Versailles—could have been satisfied equally well or equally little by teaming up with the Reds.

This strange mixture of feelings and attitudes in the Baltic was the seeding ground for National Bolshevism. Bolshevik Russia, which in the course of the civil war became more and more a political reality, began to attract the imagination of the young Freikorps fighter. Ernst von Salomon, while engaged in fighting the Bolsheviks in Riga, thus became fascinated by the "tremendous new force in the making" in the East. "Beyond the border," he admitted, "arises an amorphous but growing power, standing in our way, which we half admire and half hate."[4] Bolshevik Russia gradually emerged as a potential ally in the war against the West.

The same self-contradictory pattern of thought in relation to Russia can also be found in Germany proper in the early twenties among the younger generation of the German nationalistic intelligentsia, notably in the various neo-conservative circles. Even Stadtler's Anti-Bolshevik Movement was anti-Bolshevik and pro-Bolshevik at once. Though Stadtler set out to fight Bolshevism, he could not

[2] Ernst Jünger, "Die Geburt des Nationalismus aus dem Kriege," *Deutsches Volkstum*, xxxi (1929), 578. Cf. also Friedrich Wilhelm Heinz, *Die Nation greift an. Geschichte und Kritik des soldatischen Nationalismus* (Berlin, 1933), 113; Ernst von Salomon, *Nahe Geschichte. Ein Überblick* (Berlin, 1936), 24.

[3] Cf. Edwin Erich Dwinger, *Zwischen Weiss und Rot. Die Russische Tragödie* (Jena, 1930).

[4] Salomon, *Die Geächteten*, 66, quoted in Ruth Fischer, *Stalin and German Communism. A Study in the Origins of the State Party* (Cambridge, Mass., 1948), 284.

help being impressed by the "new phenomenon" in Russia.[5] He advocated a "German Bolshevism" or "German social- ism" "to safeguard for the twentieth century the anti- nineteenth century tendency of Bolshevism."[6] In this con- nection, also, there is significance in a survey made in 1920 by Heinrich von Gleichen among the members of the As- sociation of German Scholars and Artists concerning their attitude toward Bolshevism. The poll showed the same strange indecision about Russia. Though no one consulted would have called himself a "communist," many recog- nized the religious content of Bolshevism and saw in its socialistic message the wave of the future.[7]

It should be stressed here that National Bolshevism ac- quired a political reality of some sort only on Communist initiative. As a political movement, however ill defined, it was the work of Karl Radek.[8] And though National Bol- shevism never became an official policy of the Comintern,[9]

[5] Stadtler, *Als Antibolschewist*, 19.

[6] Heinrich von Gleichen and Anneliese Schmidt, *Der Bolschewismus und die deutschen Intellektuellen. Äusserungen auf eine Umfrage des Bundes deutscher Gelehrter und Künstler* (Leipzig, 1920), 75f.

[7] Cf. *ibid.*

[8] Radek was one of the main wirepullers of the Comintern. He had been together with Lenin on that crucial trip in the "sealed train" through Germany in April 1917; he had been a member of the Russian delegation to the Brest Litovsk negotiations. He was thor- oughly familiar with Central European affairs. A cofounder in De- cember 1918 of the Spartacus League, he was soon after arrested by the German police and was confined until January 1920 in the Moabit prison. This jail became, due to Radek's status as a privileged prisoner, a "political salon" in which he freely received visitors. While thus "imprisoned" he saw, besides his fellow Communists and various Social Democrats, representatives of the Reichswehr, Walther Ra- thenau and his business associate in the A.E.G. Felix Deutsch, and Professor Hoetzsch, who was a persistent advocate of an Eastern orientation up to his death in 1946. Through these connections Radek laid the ground for a cooperation between Germany and Russia on various levels, including National Bolshevism. Cf. E. H. Carr, "Radek's 'Political Salon' in Berlin 1919," *Soviet Studies*, III. (1951- 1952), 411ff.; Fischer, *Stalin*, 192, 207.

[9] Though it was backed by Bukharin and by the Soviet economist Eugen Varga, it was consistently rejected by Lenin, who blasted its

there runs through the history of the German Communist Party (K.P.D.) a persistent trend of National Bolshevism. Three times during the life span of the Weimar Republic was National Bolshevism launched in Germany—in 1919, 1923, and again in 1930; we can be certain that the last two attempts were backed by the K.P.D. It is clear, therefore, that this "crying absurdity," even though it was not considered to fit into the plan of Leninist strategy, played a definite role at least in the framework of Communist tactics. It was a "grandiose diversion."[10]

The 1919 phase of National Bolshevism was initiated by the leaders of the Communist Party in Hamburg, Dr. Heinrich Lauffenberg and Fritz Wolffheim. In October 1919 they made a pilgrimage to the Moabit prison in order to win Radek's backing for a policy which was to concentrate on the liberation of Germany from the Treaty of Versailles. The two Hamburg Communists failed in their efforts and were expelled from the Party. And yet they were not deterred from continuing their project. They founded a party of their own, the Communist Workers' Party of Germany (K.A.P.D.), and various affiliated organizations, none of which was long lived.

In southern Germany, also, National Bolshevism flared up. The threat of the Red General Budenny to consolidate his advance through Poland into a "front from the Rhine to Vladivostok" was echoed in Munich by the Bavarian Soviet Republic with a demand for a "Red front on the

---

"crying absurdities" (Nicolai Lenin, *"Left" Communism. An Infantile Disorder* [no loc., 1920?], 56). Lenin maintained that the signing of the Treaty of Versailles and the ensuing disorder would be much to the advantage of the revolution and that the Germans should accept Versailles the way the Bolsheviks had accepted Brest Litovsk. But Radek, who had disagreed with Lenin on Brest Litovsk, also disagreed on Versailles. His National Bolshevism was always a deviation from Marxist-Leninist orthodoxy. In theory at least, Marxism was incompatible with nationalism. And still in the days of Lenin the support of National Bolshevism was as adventurous and paradoxical for the Marxist as this policy was for the German nationalist.

10 Fischer, *Stalin*, 96.

Rhine." This slogan was devised by Ernst Niekisch, then a Social Democrat still and a minister of the short-lived Soviet Republic.[11] But the retreat of Budenny put an end to this dream.

No doubt the first phase of National Bolshevism was uneventful; it surely was passed over by the main currents of German history. It was marked by mutual suspicion on the part of the two protagonists, the Communists and the nationalists. Even Karl Radek found it expedient to come out with a warning against the Hamburg National Bolsheviks, whose ventures he branded as opportunism endangering the future of Communism itself.[12] This move of Radek's was undoubtedly a concession to the Leninist point of view. On the nationalistic side the response was not much different. Count Ernst Reventlow, who showed a most active interest in National Bolshevism, exposed in his newly founded periodical *Der Reichswart* the "delusion of the so-called National Bolsheviks that Communism could turn toward nationalism."[13] Had the experiment been tried, he argued one year later, it would have become obvious that "Bolshevism would have swallowed the national element whole."[14]

If the immediate impact of Versailles produced such extremist political speculations among only a few nationalists, the following years were to carry the issue of National Bolshevism to a broader circle of intellectuals. The conclusion of the Rapallo Treaty, obviously encouraged this trend; it represented after all the first real achievement of of German foreign policy. And on the whole the new Republic continued to be identified with Versailles and also with the failure of the then popular socialization program. As Ernst Troeltsch commented, the struggle of the

[11] Cf. Erich Müller, "Zur Geschichte des Nationalbolschewismus," *Deutsches Volkstum*, xxxiv (1932) , 785.

[12] Cf. Karl Radek, *Die auswärtige Politik des deutschen Kommunismus und der Hamburger nationale Bolschewismus* (Vienna, 1919?), 8.

[13] "Nationalbolschewismus," *Der Reichswart*, i, No. 6 (1920), 8.

[14] "Wir und Russland," *Der Reichswart*, ii, No. 44 (1921), 4.

government to reestablish law and order was viewed unsympathetically by an "alliance between the Independents, Bolshevists, men of letters [*Literaten*], ideologists, and Conservatives."[15] The resurgent wave of National Bolshevism appealed to these people. This time, however, it was a well-schemed Russian importation. There was the theory of Eugen Varga, elaborated in the early twenties, that Germany was being transformed into an "industrial colony" by British and French imperialism.[16] This theory became the basis for an elaborate campaign on the part of Radek, Nikolai Bukharin, and others, who appealed to the German workers and also to the middle class—here the "grandiose diversion" comes in—to offer national resistance to this exploitation by the West. Radek, who had been released from prison in January 1920, divided most of his time in the following years between Moscow and Berlin.

The Ruhr invasion of 1923 finally presented the welcome occasion for the Soviet agitators to launch their offensive. In June 1923, at the meeting of the Enlarged Executive Committee of the Comintern, Radek delivered his now famous "Schlageter oration,"[17] in which he sought to exploit for Communism the martyrdom of Schlageter. Did Schlageter, facing the French firing squad, die as a stooge of German capitalism? Did he die in vain? Was he a "wanderer into the void"? Schlageter's prior Freikorps affiliations were subjected to a similar scrutiny. Appealing to the "nationalistic lower bourgeois masses" and to the "patriotic circles" in Germany, Radek called for a common "front against the capital of the Entente and of Germany."[18] The so-called "Schlageter policy" of the K.P.D. produced mass meetings attended by Fascists as well as by Communists, political broadsides carrying both the swastika and

[15] Troeltsch, *Spektator-Briefe*, 50.
[16] Cf. Fischer, *Stalin*, 196ff.
[17] " 'Leo Schlageter, der Wanderer ins Nichts,' Eine Rede Karl Radeks," Moeller, *Das Recht der jungen Völker* (1932), 75-79.
[18] *Ibid.*, 77f.

the Soviet star. Even Ruth Fischer took it ungracefully upon herself to incite the students of the University of Berlin against both "Jew-capitalism" and "French imperialism."[19]

The response in the nationalistic camp to the Communist campaign was spectacular, sympathetic, but in the last analysis negative. A direct answer to Radek by Count Reventlow appeared, to everyone's surprise, not only in *Der Reichswart* but also in the columns of the Communist mouthpiece *Rote Fahne*.[20] Reventlow on the whole reiterated his earlier stand on the question, as he thought the middle classes not yet ready for the experiment. To the offer of the Communists to go together "part of the way" *(ein Stück Wegs)*, Reventlow answered in the negative.

For the June Club Moeller van den Bruck took up the argument of National Bolshevism in the *Gewissen*.[21] It was Moeller to whom Troeltsch referred as "the best counter-revolutionary writer in Germany,"[22] who had conferences with Radek. Moeller was one of Germany's most enthusiastic Easterners. Germany and Russia were to him "young peoples" as against the "old peoples" of the West.[23] He recognized Russia as the pivot of an active German foreign policy and even in the "labyrinth of Marxian theories and dogmas" he would seek "affinities with German ideas."[24] The chief purpose of a German-Russian alliance was the

[19] Ossip K. Flechtheim, *Die Kommunistiche Partei Deutschlands in der Weimarer Republik* (Offenbach a.M., 1948), 89; Ruth Fischer's attempts in her own work (Fischer, *Stalin*, 283) to explain away this episode are unsubstantiated and unconvincing.

[20] Reventlow later explained that he chose to publish his own point of view in the *Rote Fahne* because the edition of his own weekly was not large enough; Reventlow, "Ein Stück Wegs?" *Die Tat*, xxiii (1931-1932) , 989ff.

[21] His three answers to Karl Radek—"Der Wanderer ins Nichts," *Gewissen*, v (July 2, 1923); "Der dritte Standpunkt," *Gewissen*, v (July 16, 1923); "Wirklichkeit," *Gewissen*, v (July 30, 1923)—are reprinted in Moeller, *Das Recht der jungen Völker* (1932), 81ff.

[22] Troeltsch, *Spektator-Briefe*, 269.

[23] Cf. infra, 158f.

[24] Moeller, *Das dritte Reich*, 26; cf. also *ibid.*, 162.

fight against the "Entente capitalism."[25] On the whole, however, Moeller's answer to Radek, like Reventlow's, amounted to a rebuff. At the same time that General Hans von Seeckt presumably was able to implement his Eastern policy in secret negotiations with Radek held in Schleicher's home,[26] the public disputations among the intellectuals remained inconclusive.

By 1930, however, National Bolshevism became the prevailing mood among the Rightist intelligentsia. For many German nationalists and particularly for those affected by the economic crisis, even National Socialism came to mean a compromise. National Bolshevism with its rigorous anti-capitalism became very meaningful to the new proletarians. Also, since Stalinist Russia had embarked upon its "socialism-in-one-country" course, Moeller's original assumption that "each people has its own socialism" and that socialist Germany and socialist Russia could live peacefully side by side came closer to realization. One speculated that now Russia was on the verge of becoming a "national socialistic Russia"[27] and that Bolshevism had been purged of its international aspects;[28] given these premises, even the ultra-Leftist, pacifistic *Weltbühne* would admit the importance of National Bolshevism.[29]

The K.P.D. exploited the situation in its "Program for the National and Social Liberation of the German People" of August 1930. This new platform for the September elections, drawn up by Heinz Neumann, was introduced by a sharp attack on the Versailles "Peace Treaty,"[30] the

[25] Moeller, *Das Recht der jungen Völker* (1932), 84.
[26] Cf. *Seeckt. Aus seinem Leben, 1918-1936* (ed. General Dr. Friedrich von Rabenau, Leipzig, 1940), 309, 319.
[27] Hans Schwarz, "Von deutscher Revolution," *Der Nahe Osten*, VI (1933), 246.
[28] Cf. Adolf Ehrt, *Totale Krise—totale Revolution? Die "Schwarze Front" des völkischen Nationalismus* (Berlin, 1933), 41.
[29] Cf. Kurt Hiller, "Linke Leute von Rechts," *Weltbühne*, XXVIII, 2 (1932), 154.
[30] Quotation marks in the original; cf. Flechtheim, *Die K.P.D.*, 281ff.

reparations settlement, and the Young Plan. In the spring of 1931 this document was followed by a Communist program appealing to the German peasants (*Bauernhilfsprogramm*).

The *cause célèbre* of National Bolshevism during the early thirties involved Richard Scheringer, a young Reichswehr lieutenant who with two other junior officers in his regiment was arrested in February 1930, on charges of spreading Nazi ideology in the army. The trial which began late in September gained so much importance and publicity because it was on this occasion that Hitler appeared as a defense witness and swore his famous legality oath. But Scheringer, once tried and imprisoned, forsook the N.S.D.A.P. and joined the K.P.D.[31] Scheringer's "conversion," as spectacular an event as the trial had been, was not unique.[32] After all, the chief of the army command, General von Hammerstein-Equord, found it necessary to repudiate officially National Bolshevism while admitting that it had at one time made serious inroads into the army.[33] And the prominent Leftist publicist Leopold Schwarzschild wrote somewhat hysterically that "in all probability up to 90 percent of the German youth consists of Scheringers of the Right and the Left."[34] They had to be taken seriously at least; they were a vital expression of the German crisis and they might conceivably have be-

[31] For a formulation of Scheringer's views see the article written by him while in captivity: Lieutenant Scheringer, "Revolutionäre Wehrpolitik," *Die Sozialistische Nation*, I (1931), 69-72.

[32] Lieutenant Wendt, one of Scheringer's codefendants, left the Nazi Party for Otto Strasser's Black Front. Among the deserters of the N.S.D.A.P. for the K.P.D. we find Ernst von Salomon's brother Bruno, who became prominent in the Communist movement directed at the peasants.

[33] *Berliner Tageblatt*, August 30, 1930, referred to in Ernst Fraenkel, "German-Russian Relations since 1918," *Review of Politics*, II (1940), 45.

[34] Leopold Schwarzschild, "Jugend in Chaos," *Montag Morgen*, August 30, 1930, reprinted in *Die Sozialistiche Nation*, I, 9/10 (1931), 2-4.

come those "forces of the future," as a French journal dedicated to German affairs described them.[35]

The Schlageters of 1930 were no more "wanderers in the void"; the "so-called West,"[36] as Hans Zehrer put it, had been exposed, and the ground was prepared for the National Bolshevik venture. While Ernst Jünger talked about Russia as a "destination" (*Reiseziel*),[37] there were innumerable "fellow travelers" to Russia. Even among the Young Conservatives the *Deutsches Volkstum,* whose A. E. Günther had been involved in the early Wolffheim-Lauffenberg affair, insisted on the "readiness of radical youth for the National Bolshevik decision."[38] On this score the *Deutsches Volkstum* was not far behind the *Tat,* the *Nahe Osten,* and Otto Strasser's Black Front. Then there were the sundry groups of the post-war Youth Movement[39] and the organizations dedicated to Freikorps tradition such as the Wehrwolf and Oberland,[40] with all of whom the Eastern orientation and also the acceptance of Communism became a matter of course. In these days at long last an inveterate National Bolshevik, Ernst Niekisch, came into his own. His political career had been, like those of his friends August Winnig and Otto Strasser, unsteady. It was the career of an outsider, an extremist at all cost, to whom National Bolshevism became the one and only point of orientation. Niekisch also had negotiations with Radek; it is even recorded that he was sent by Seeckt on a mission to

[35] Alex M. Lipiansky, "Pour un Communisme national," *Revue d'Allemagne,* VI (1932), 849.

[36] Hans Zehrer, "Die Frühjahrsoffensive," *Die Tat,* XXIV (1932-1933), 13.

[37] Cf. infra, 188.

[38] A. E. Günther, "Zwischen Weiss und Rot," *Deutsches Volkstum,* XXXIII (1931), 942.

[39] Cf. in particular, Alfred Ehrentreich, "Bündische Jugend gegen den westlichen Imperialismus," *Die Tat,* XXI (1929-1930), 382ff.

[40] The founder of the original Freikorps Oberland, Joseph Römer (called Beppo Römer), a colorful World War I captain, joined the Communists, was repeatedly imprisoned after the Nazi seizure of power, and was finally executed in September 1944 on the charge of having plotted the assassination of Hitler.

Moscow.[41] Throughout his life, as a Social Democrat and after leaving the Party in the middle twenties, he advocated a militant anti-Western variety of socialism. His violent opposition to the Fulfillment Policy of the Republic induced him to sponsor various minor political movements, until in the late twenties he created his influential National Bolshevik Resistance Movement (Widerstandsbewegung). He chose for it the nightmarish slogan "Sparta-Potsdam-Moscow" and an emblem consisting of a Prussian eagle, a sword, a hammer, and a sickle. Partly through its aggressively edited periodicals[42] the Resistance Movement influenced the increasingly radical temper of the neo-conservative groups. We ought not to minimize the seriousness and integrity of people like Niekisch. The National Bolshevists were more honest, more thorough, more penetrating in their criticism of our society than the Nazis. However, by talking in terms of the "curse of liberty"[43] and boastfully chiding the "idea of humanity" while praising "barbarism,"[44] they on one hand took conservatism to the point of no return, while on the other hand their rigid doctrinaire position was easily outmaneuvered by the National Socialist Party.

[41] Fabian von Schlabrendorff, *Offiziere gegen Hitler* (Zurich, 1946), 15.

[42] *Widerstand; Entscheidung; Das dritte Reich.*

[43] Ferdinand Fried (pseud. for Friedrich Zimmermann), *Autarkie* (Jena, 1932), 9f.

[44] Ehrt, *Totale Krise—totale Revolution?*, 54.

PART III

THREE MAJOR EXPRESSIONS OF
NEO-CONSERVATISM

CHAPTER I

THE THIRD REICH OF MOELLER
VAN DEN BRUCK

IT IS NOW TIME to throw light on the course which the new
conservatism took after the war by a study of the doctrines
of its three main exponents: Moeller van den Bruck, Oswald Spengler, and Ernest Jünger. "Tough Nietzscheans"
all, they complained of the insufficiencies of the bourgeois
values and formulated a conservatism which was, to say
the least, revolutionary. They appealed to the imagination
of the defeated nation's returning soldiers and promised
them hope for a better future. Their style was pseudo-
Nietzschean: aphoristic and impatient. Lacking the sharp-
ness of Nietzsche's, it was well suited to the demi-genre
of the political pamphlet. But it tended to obscure more
often than to enlighten, and to act as a drug rather than as
medicine. While Moeller revived the suggestive medieval
concept of a Third Reich—which Hitler later took over—
and while Spengler impressed his German public with the
neo-Spartan idea of a Prussian socialism, Ernst Jünger became the frantic protagonist of a German nihilism. In one
way or another, they made their pact with the devil. They
were less conscientious than the "elders," but ultimately
no less tragic. They thought they could base their conservatism on visions and myths rather than on traditions.
They killed the conservatism in themselves.

Arthur Moeller van den Bruck[1] was born in 1876 in
Solingen in the Rhineland. The Moellers, his father's
family, were descended from a line of Protestant ministers
from central Germany; his father himself had moved to
western Germany in the capacity of a government archi-

[1] He usually omitted his first name from his signature; until well
into his thirties he used the name Moeller-Bruck.

tect. Moeller's mother, whose maiden name was van den Bruck, was half Spanish and half Dutch by origin. Moeller, the very man who was to declare war against the spirit of the West, was himself very much a son of that West.

The Nietzschean influence affected the young Moeller's attitude toward the Second Reich of Bismarck. Moeller's own pre-war works became part of the tradition of the "cultural opposition" against the Second Reich. "In no society," Moeller summed up later, "so much as in Germany were the eminent, the original, the outstanding men left outsiders or indeed isolated against their will."[2] Hence he called Lagarde, Langbehn, and even Nietzsche "outsiders of conservatism,"[3] whose conservatism was not recognized by the official conservatism. Like them Moeller criticized the delusion of grandeur which Germany displayed during its so-called *Gründerjahre* ("founders' years"). "We have not understood the meaning of our unification,"[4] Moeller complained. The solution of 1871 was authoritarian and strictly political. It made for a "forced patriotism."[5] Like Nietzsche's, Moeller's thoughts therefore became "thoughts out of season." While dedicating himself to what he called the eventual "politicization"[6] of Germany, Moeller kept emphasizing her "unpolitical" past. Indeed, the "unpolitical" and the "political" constitute a basic contrapuntal pattern with Moeller. The former is a necessary ground for the later. "Woe to the people," Moeller once wrote, "which holds no mystery for itself."[7] While Thomas Mann defended Germany's "poor boundaries,"[8] Moeller romanticized the German "dualisms." "We must have the strength to live with our dual-

[2] Moeller, *Der politische Mensch*, 67.

[3] Moeller, *Das dritte Reich*, 202.

[4] Moeller van den Bruck, *Sozialismus und Aussenpolitik* (ed. Hans Schwarz, Breslau, 1933), 53.

[5] Moeller, *Der politische Mensch*, 29.

[6] Moeller van den Bruck, *Das Recht der jungen Völker* (1932), 125.

[7] Moeller, *Sozialismus*, 59.

[8] Mann, *Betrachtungen*, xxxxi.

isms."[9] The German indistinctions and disunities became a dynamic force with Moeller. This force, which he called "myth," was his version of Nietzsche's concept of life, an assertion of the elementary forces of German culture transcending the mediocrity of the Bismarckian and Wilhelmian solution.

Moeller's early career was wholly "unpolitical"; he did not merely ignore politics, he fled from politics. His journey to Paris in 1902 was nothing more than an escape from German conditions. Like many *fin de siècle* German intellectuals Moeller was influenced by Burckhardt's thesis that a people could not have a great culture and political significance at the same time. In Paris Moeller was a pessimist, an escapist. There he found a world of *l'art pour l'art;* he familiarized himself with the French theatre and with modern literature. In Paris he also began a voluminous historical work, consisting of a series of German biographies.[10] Here German history for once was not forced into the preordained pattern which the Prussian school of historians had imposed on a Prussianized Germany, but was, nevertheless, overdramatized and distorted. The work in question was neither history nor, strictly speaking, poetry, but a German mythology, in which Moeller was laying the foundations of his irrationalism.

Moeller's tendency toward irrationalism was strengthened by his preoccupation with Dostoevsky. While still in Paris he set out, together with his wife, his sister-in-law, and the Russian mystic Dmitri Merezhkovsky, to prepare a German translation of the great Russian, which appeared in 1913 in Munich. Germans like the young Moeller and the young Thomas Mann were excited by Dostoevsky's attack against Western rationalism and by his sharp distinction between the spirit of the East and that of the

9 Moeller, *Das dritte Reich*, 235.
10 Moeller van den Bruck, *Die Deutschen. Unsere Menschheitsgeschichte* (8 vols., Minden, n.d.), reprinted in part as Moeller van den Bruck, *Das ewige Reich* (ed. Hans Schwarz, 3 vols., Breslau, 1933-1935).

West. They made a mental pilgrimage to the country which owed its cultural consciousness to their own countrymen Herder and Hegel. While Mann in his *Betrachungen* flirted with Dostoevsky's thesis of "Germany as the protesting Reich,"[11] Moeller called Dostoevsky both a conservative and a revolutionary because he projected the "new man," the "new word" from Russia to Europe.[12] Dostoevsky gave a certain "meta-geographical" direction to Moeller's thought; in other words, he awoke in him a fascination with the East.

More traveling took Moeller to Italy, where he wrote a book on Italian art,[13] much in the same style as his earlier historical work, inspired but all too subjective. Disagreeing with the so-called "Renaissancism" which prevailed at the time, he searched for German influence as a decisive factor in the Italian civilization. In 1912 Moeller went to Russia and in 1914 to Scandinavia. The role of the expatriate had so far taken him across most German borders. His early experiences had been the ones of a thoroughly European German.

The first World War focused Moeller's thought on Germany. In his exciting book on Prussian architecture he discovered what he called the "Prussian style,"[14] a term which he endowed with political connotations and which reflected his growing awareness of the German political realities. "Prussianism is the will to the state, and the interpretation of historical life as political life in which we must act as political men."[15] This concept of the "Prussian style" became a corrective for Moeller's initially unpolitical concept of myth.

But Moeller's new nationalism was qualified. He con-

[11] Mann, *Betrachtungen*, 1ff.
[12] Moeller, *Das Recht der jungen Völker* (1932), 69.
[13] Moeller van den Bruck, *Die Italienische Schönheit* (Munich, 1913).
[14] Moeller van den Bruck, *Der preussische Stil* (Munich, 1916).
[15] *Ibid.*, 202.

tinued to object to the "intellectual isolation"[16] of a Germany which for him was, as it had been in the early days of German nationalism, a European problem. To be sure, Moeller never quite explained whether his Germany was to be Europeanized or his Europe was to be Germanized. He was less representative of his country than of the temper of a new generation, a generation highly critical of the so-called bourgeois values of the nineteenth century, an irrational and iconoclastic generation. There was a close link, then, between the "unpolitical" Moeller and the "political" Moeller; his politics were inspired by a search for the daemonic, for the myth. They were unscientific and unorthodox, but also dynamic and suggestive. It was both the weakness and the strength of Moeller's politics, as it was of the politics of all neo-conservatives, that, compared with traditional Bismarckian standards, they remained basically "unpolitical."

Under the influence of war and revolution, Moeller turned altogether into a political writer. Between 1918 and 1925, the year of his death, he published and edited an enormous amount of political literature.[17] It was a literature of crisis. Just as Karl Marx had issued his *Manifesto* in the face of the workers' defeat in 1848, so Moeller wrote in the face of Germany's defeat in 1918. The parallel between Marx and Moeller is not incidental. In spite of all

[16] Moeller, *Der politische Mensch*, 29.

[17] His most publicized books were: Moeller van den Bruck, *Das Recht der jungen Völker* (Munich, 1919) and *Das dritte Reich* (Berlin, 1923). Furthermore, Moeller wrote a vast number of articles which generally appeared in the *Gewissen*, Some few articles appeared in the *Deutsche Rundschau* and *Die Grenzboten* and in the Rightist press, namely, in *Der Tag* and the *Norddeutsche Allgemeine Zeitung* (the later *Deutsche Allgemeine Zeitung*). Many of Moeller's articles were reedited and posthumously published by Moeller's friend Hans Schwarz in a series of volumes as follows: Moeller van den Bruck, *Das Recht der jungen Völker. Sammlung Politischer Aufsätze* (Berlin, 1932); *Rechenschaft über Russland* (Berlin, 1933); *Der politische Mensch* (Breslau, 1933); *Sozialismus und Aussenpolitik* (Breslau, 1933).

the obvious differences between the two, and though Moeller—whose critical knowledge of Marx is a matter of conjecture—had only scorn for Marx's "materialism," he was not far from Marx when he criticized a bourgeois world in which man had been alienated from society. Like Marx he aimed at superimposing his logic, a fundamentally existential logic, over the unwanted reality. Like Marx, moreover, Moeller came into the limelight as the prophet of a wave of the future.

"The ideas of 1914 . . . are in reality the problems which point beyond 1914,"[18] Moeller wrote. Victory and defeat alike are only ephemeral decisions in the larger context of the war between liberalism and socialism, between the nineteenth century and the twentieth century, and between the "old" and the "young" peoples. The "contrast between the old and the young peoples" became for Moeller "the key to the World War."[19] Moeller's "young peoples" were Marx's working class, but it was a much weaker generalization. Though Moeller boasted that the "young peoples" have "Darwin and Nietzsche on their side,"[20] his concept rested on no scientific criterion, but only on the emotions of a young generation. The cult of youth which the Youth Movement had launched before the war was merely translated into terms of peoples, and the wartime anti-Western bias in Germany was blown up into a strange geographic mysticism. We are not surprised to find the English, the French, and the Italians among the "old peoples." But it is interesting that the line-up does not correspond to that of the war. Along with Prussia-Germany, Russia and America were declared "young." Russia and America fought the war on the wrong side. While the war served as a purgatory for Russia and made it emerge once more as a truly Eastern nation, it put the United States into a unique position to sway the balance between the "old" and "young" peoples. Indeed, it seems

[18] Moeller, *Das Recht der jungen Völker* (1919), 60.
[19] *Ibid.*, 18.   [20] *Ibid.*, 24f.

that the primary purpose of Moeller's publication was to persuade President Wilson to represent the interests of the "young peoples" during the Paris Peace Conference.[21]

Surprising as the line-up of Germany-Russia-America may appear at first sight, it had a certain momentary reality. The Wilsonian "open diplomacy" was particularly appealing to the powers which emerged from the war defeated. There seemed at first to be an outright correspondence between Wilson's policies and the Leninist formula of "no annexations and indemnities." Both, however different their basic premises, suggested the substitution of a new fair deal among peoples for the old era of power politics. Moeller's thesis fitted well into this context. It attacked the Pan-German imperialism as sharply as it did the West and its balance-of-power theories.[22] Moeller's "Right of the Young Peoples" was, like Leninism, an anti-imperialistic theory. But, while it helped bridge the gap between German nationalists and the Bolsheviks, it did not even reach the ears of Woodrow Wilson.

Moeller's appeal to Wilson was a typical expression of the mentality which prevailed in Germany during the short-lived "dreamland of the armistice period." Had Wilson's Fourteen Points been accepted in Paris and become the basis of the Peace Treaty, Moeller's interest in Wilson's ideas might have proved to be more than idle speculation. In that case Moeller might not have fathered the modern German "Third Reich" concept. But it was the fate of the Fourteen Points which partly accounts for Moeller's bitterness and his determination to carry the war further into the time of peace. In other words, Moeller's ideas, as they were brought into final form in the early twenties, owed much to the disappointment over the failure of the Fourteen Points.

21 This is the usual interpretation given by the friends of Moeller, in particular, Hans Schwarz; a short version of the book appeared under the same title in the fall of 1918 in *Deutsche Rundschau,* CLXXVII (1918).

22 Cf. Moeller, *Das Recht der jungen Völker* (1919), 86.

Moeller emerged from the war with two rationalizations about the defeat. According to one he maintained that the Western powers had achieved only a Pyrrhic victory. *"A people is never lost, if it understands the meaning of its defeat."*[23] For a conservative this was an extremely interesting position. It suggested that while victory had once more blinded the West to the urgency of the cultural crisis, defeat turned out to be a blessing to Germany for it brought the Germans closer to an understanding of their times. Moeller's other line on the German defeat conformed with the so-called "stab-in-the-back" theory. The German armies of the field were never defeated, "but the home front (Heimat) failed, and this dearest word . . . got now its foulest sound. The people of this home front did not understand as yet the issues of this war."[24] In using this argument without being wholly convinced by it, Moeller surrendered reason and truth to the passions of the defeated nation.[25]

Elaborating on the view that a war can be lost with profit, Moeller proposed that "a revolution must be won."[26] The revolution was to survive defeat, and in it the war was to find its proper continuation. Moeller thus reversed Clausewitz's doctrine that war is a mere continuation of politics by other means, by implying that politics is a mere continuation of war by other means.

[23] Moeller, *Der politische Mensch*, 43. Italics in the original.
[24] Moeller, *Sozialismus*, 55.
[25] This fact becomes evident from a letter of Moeller to the writer Hans Grimm of January 20, 1919 and quoted in Paul Fechter, *Moeller van den Bruck. Ein politisches Schicksal* (Berlin, 1934), 63-65. Moeller wrote, "The Germans are able to consider themselves the victorious nation though they have been defeated" (pp. 64f). And he continued, "Nevertheless, there is a certain truth in the claim that we are undefeated. And I believe that we must exploit this truth politically. The first step is the necessity for us to adjust ourselves to the new conditions. We are already in that phase now. The necessity under these new conditions for reconstruction will be the second step." The third step, Moeller suggested, was to be the claim that the Germans have "in fact 'won' [quotation marks in the original] the war" (p. 65).
[26] Moeller, *Das dritte Reich*, 15.

A typical neo-conservative, Moeller formed his political vocabulary under the impact of his disappointment in the November Revolution. "The revolution has disappointed many expectations, socialistic expectations and others."[27] The men of the revolution failed to "stir up an enormous wave of excitement among the disappointed people"[28] against the "fraud" of Versailles. In retrospect the German November Revolution was "not even a revolutionary interlude."[29] Hence Moeller's phrase, "the political revenge of the conservative-revolutionary idea."[30] Moeller became a counter-revolutionary. He decided that it was up to "conservative man" to take over the revolution, in other words, that the "second phase" of the revolution would be conservative.[31]

Moeller made the concept of the "Third Reich" his central theme and slogan. The term goes back to medieval mysticism (Joachim of Floris) and to medieval imperial traditions. In the German popular tradition it has been preserved as a vague myth of promise and future, and it has always been an escape into a nationalistic eschatology. Thus, right after the war, as has usually been the case in times of political instability, the perennial demand for the "Third Reich" was renewed. Eugen Diederichs' *Tat* magazine played with "the coming of the Third Reich," the "Reich of the future."[32] To Oswald Spengler the "Third Reich" meant *the Germanic ideal,* an eternal tomorrow, on which all great men from Joachim of Floris to Nietzsche and Ibsen . . . have oriented their lives."[33] Moeller gave new life and meaning to this concept of a "Third Reich." Whereas the First Reich had been "too unpolitical" and the Second Reich was but an "interreg-

[27] *Ibid.,* 23.　　[28] *Ibid.,* 25.　　[29] *Ibid.,* 192.
[30] *Ibid.,* 177.　　[31] *Ibid.,* 221.
[32] *Die Tat,* x (1918-1919), 642-646, 953.
[33] Oswald Spengler, *Der Untergang des Abendlandes. Umrisse einer Morphologie der Weltgeschichte* (33rd-47th edn., Munich, 1923), I, 467. Italics in the original.

num,"[34] the "Third Reich" would be Germany's "Third Rome." It was final. For once, Moeller postulated, the idea should be "removed from the realm of illusions and translated into political reality." Ironically, however, he also warned that "the idea of the Third Reich could well become the greatest of all illusions" and that the German people "might perish by it."[35]

We are told by Max Hildebert Boehm, one of Moeller's closest friends and associates, that in considering the title for his main work, which came to be called *Das dritte Reich,* Moeller had alternative titles in mind, such as the "third point of view" or the "third party."[36] These, like the term "Third Reich," recur throughout Moeller's late work, and being variations on a single theme, each in turn throws light on the full meaning of Moeller's political credo.

The "third point of view" reflects Moeller's basic conservatism: his recognition of the German "dualisms." They were concrete realities which could not be ignored. They were the secret of German strength and had to be "accepted." But while Moeller insisted that the Germans should be strong enough to live with their "dualisms," the "Third Reich" which he foresaw was to be a "Reich of synthesis,"[37] which would assure unity within diversity.

The "third party" was an expression of Moeller's ideas on political strategy. In the dedicatory letter addressed to Heinrich von Gleichen which accompanied his book *Das dritte Reich,* Moeller made it clear that his political activity was based on the conviction that "all the misery of German politics is derived from the parties." The book was, therefore, meant as a "critique of the parties."[38] But, however vulnerable German parliamentarism was, Moel-

---

[34] Moeller, *Das dritte Reich,* 232, 242.

[35] *Ibid.,* 7.

[36] Max Hildebert Boehm, "Moeller van den Bruck im Kreise seiner politischen Freunde," *Deutsches Volkstum,* xxxiv (1932), 695.

[37] "*Reich der Zusammenfassung*"; Moeller, *Das dritte Reich,* 7.

[38] *Ibid.,* 5, 6.

ler's "non-partisan point of view" was not the best safeguard of political freedoms. He was thinking in terms of a
"movement from the right"[39] implemented through the
masses. The "third party" concept implied a challenge to
the traditional give and take of a multi-party system and
contained the seeds of the twentieth century monolithic
"movement."

Moeller's view of liberalism shows little of the moderation of a Ranke or a Mill. To Moeller, liberalism was
"the terrifying power of the nineteenth century,"[40] readily
equated with materialism, relativism, individualism, nihilism, and frequently with freemasonry. Liberalism, as Moeller saw it, was "sectarian liberalism,"[41] to use Professor
Carlton J. Hayes's term: a business philosophy rather than
an ideological concept. And if during the war Moeller
still voiced his faith in the regenerative force of liberalism,[42] and if even after Weimar and Versailles he based his
violent attacks on liberalism on the theory that it no longer meant freedom, these subtleties were lost on Moeller's
readers. The "generation of 1919,"[43] for which Moeller
wrote, was, in effect, taught to distrust its own freedoms.

Moeller's style was marked by a cavalier ambiguity
which he used to cover up the predicament of his position, of his wanting to be a Burke, a Disraeli, in twentieth
century Germany. Instead of making things explicit, Moeller hid behind the mantle of an oracular style. His chief
shortcoming lay in his failure to see that the dilemma of
conservatism could not be solved by a virtuosity of style.
Moeller's revolutionary conservatism was an exciting and,
indeed, imaginative concept, but in the last analysis all
too ineffective in assuring a minimum of conservatism

[39] Moeller, *Das Recht der jungen Völker* (1932), 140.
[40] Moeller, *Das dritte Reich*, 68.
[41] Carlton J. Hayes, *A Generation of Materialism, 1871-1900* (New York, 1941), 46ff.
[42] "We shall have to rededicate the word liberalism as meaning freedom"; Moeller, *Das Recht der jungen Völker* (1919), 59.
[43] Cf. Moeller, "Die drei Generationen," *Der politische Mensch*, 23ff.

against a maximum of revolutionism. The function of conservatism was, for Moeller, to replace "reason by faith, the individual by the community, disintegration by allegiance *(Bindung)*, 'progress' by evolution."[44] The old nineteenth century conservatism, Moeller claimed, had failed to fulfill those requirements, and he therefore, submitted it to rigorous criticism. He called Friedrich Julius Stahl, the nineteenth century Prussian conservative, a "liberal." From Stahl to the kaiser, he argued, conservatism in Germany had experienced an inglorious history: it had developed into "party conservatism" and had become infected with the malady of the century, namely, liberalism.

Moeller further focused his definition of conservatism by emphasizing the dichotomy between the "reactionary" and the "conservative" man, which, largely through his writings, became part of the generally accepted political vocabulary during the Republic. "The reactionary man is a degenerated species of the conservative man."[45] While the former is concerned with the past for its own sake, the latter looks to the past for its enduring values. While prewar conservatism had belonged to a class, post-war conservatism belonged to the whole people. Moeller's refusal to go along with the German Nationalists, who came closest to his definition of "reactionary," thus set him and his friends off on an independent course toward a new conservatism.

Among the various elements of Moeller's conservatism, nationalism was the basic one. "The conservative counter-movement . . . puts the idea of the nation above all other ideas, even above the monarchic idea."[46] Moeller's nationalism was closely dependent on his historical perspective. For him the nation remained an essentially unpolitical, dynamic concept. Concretely speaking, it seemed best embodied in a federal structure "more organically built than the Germany of Bismarck" and "organized by geographic districts and economic areas" which would "maintain their

[44] Moeller, *Das dritte Reich*, 94.
[45] *Ibid.*, 167. [46] *Ibid.*, 175.

autonomy."[47] Moeller assumed that only the idea of the nation could hold the Germans together after the fall of the monarchy. In his scheme it replaced monarchism as the main pillar of conservative thought.

Socialism was the most challenging element of Moeller's conservatism. All the vague socialistic hopes which were raised on the Right in connection with the revolution found expression in his work. To all the experiments in defining a new socialism, of which we find so many in the neo-conservative movement, Moeller's definition was a common denominator. This definition of socialism gives us the best indication of how deeply and how concretely socialistic thinking had penetrated into the Right, and, consequently, how sincere and well founded the complaint over the failure of Weimar was. It is likely that all the Diederichses and Stapels and Stadtlers really did not mean much by their socialistic demands, and, if asked to substantiate them and to solve the "socialistic problem," would have been at a loss. We must not preclude the possibility that their socialism was more a tribute to a temporary fashion than it was a constructive program.

Was Moeller's socialism truly socialism? It has become too customary in our times, which are so preoccupied in one way or other with Marxism, to apply the Marxian yardstick to all forms of socialism. But the history of socialism goes further back than Karl Marx. During the war years, moreover, we have followed the growth of a socialistic tradition which was clearly independent of Marxist thought—which was, if anything, anti-Marxist. Moeller's idea of socialism likewise proceeded from a lengthy critique of Marxism. While rejecting, along with Marx and Engels, the values of the bourgeois society, he attacked their materialistic philosophy. In trying to solve the "prob-

[47] Moeller, *Der preussische Stil*, 201. This passage is taken from the last chapter of the book. The chapter was included first in the second edition, which appeared in 1922. Cf. also Moeller, *Das Recht der jungen Völker* (1932), 142.

lem of the masses"[48] by economic formulae, they ignored the need of the masses for a spiritual regeneration. Both Marxism and liberalism—between which Moeller saw a close connection—appeared as expressions of an Age of Materialism. And in Germany socialism had become since the nineteenth century the monopoly of a party, the Social Democrats, for which Moeller had little use. "The German Social Democracy dropped from among its two elements the socialistic one and maintained only the democratic one."[49] Moeller had little respect for a party which he held responsible for the failure of the 1918 Revolution and of the socialization.

Moeller's socialism was a "German socialism" which he defined as "a corporative theory of the state and the economy, which might have to be achieved by revolutionary means, but which will be carried out in a conservative spirit."[50] He sought its roots in the medieval guilds and particularly in the leader of the sixteenth century German peasant revolt, Thomas Münzer. Münzer became the Spartacus of the conservative socialists. *In concreto* Moeller identified himself with Moellendorff's *Gemeinwirtschaft*.[51] He accepted the *Arbeitsgemeinschaften* as representing the solidarity between employer and worker within the framework of the national economy. Like Winnig and Stadtler, Moeller was an admirer of Stinnes,[52] possibly because he appeared in the early years of the Republic as one of the strongest public figures and leaders; indeed, Moeller acknowledged the "natural distance between two groups of men, the employers and the workers."[53] We feel that this socialism, had it been put into practice, would have left the Stinneses and Krupps in undisturbed charge of their empires.

Even though Moeller was evasive about this rather vital

[48] Moeller, *Das dritte Reich*, 123ff.
[49] *Ibid.*, 135.   [50] *Ibid.*, 67.   [51] *Ibid.*, 67.
[52] Max Hildebert Boehm, "Moeller im Kreise seiner politischen Freunde," *Deutsches Volkstum*, xxxiv (1932), 696.
[53] Moeller, *Das dritte Reich*, 132.

point, he offered, at least a formula for a society based on the principle of solidarity of opposed interests rather than on class struggle. He replaced the Marxian scientific structure of socialism with his own metaphysics. His socialism has been labeled rightly a "socialism of sentiment" rather than a "socialism of reason";[54] with him socialism as an idea had a more central function than socialism as a reality. Moeller always remained the artist in politics, an inspirer as much as a mystifier. Furthermore, though Moeller's own position was inspired by the plight of the impoverished middle classes who tried to withstand proletarization, he did not speak for this group only. His socialism was in the purest sense a national socialism. He overcame class consciousness by nation consciousness. He thus—and here lies the significance of his socialism— provided a pattern of socialism which was acceptable to the German conservative, and which affected the orientation of the Right during the following years.

Moeller's thoughts on foreign affairs were in keeping with his revolutionary conservatism. Impatient with the spade work which the Republic had to do in order to get Germany back into the position of a European power, and with the almost entirely negative foreign policy approach of the German Nationalists, Moeller developed his own grand scheme. It was pure ideology. Like geopolitics, it was one of the numerous lofty constructions of the time which offered a rationale for a German revival. In particular, Moeller was instrumental in building up the German claim for *Lebensraum*. He pointed to the population problem (*Bevölkerungsproblem*) which was shared by all defeated peoples. "The population problem is a universal socialistic problem."[55] Moeller, therefore, talked in terms of a "socialistic foreign policy." It took a slight twisting of Marxian materialism and a mere watering down of Lenin's theory of imperialism to shift the basis of socialism from

[54] Kolnai, *The War against the West*, 326.
[55] Moeller, *Das dritte Reich*, 61.

the "oppressed classes" to the "oppressed nations."[56] The difference between the exploiters and the exploited, Moeller claimed, "will after the Treaty of Versailles be transferred from the level of the individual man to the level of whole nations. The only alternative for socialism is to transform itself from a socialism of classes to a socialism of nations."[57] The oppression of individuals and classes existed only insofar as they were part of nations which were themselves oppressed.

Moeller's definition of a "socialistic foreign policy" established the basis for an orientation toward Russia and Italy. The Russian case appears at first sight especially paradoxical. Besides the fact that neither Russia nor Italy was in the strict sense a defeated power after the first World War, Russia was not an overpopulated country. Moreover, was Russia not a Marxist country? It was clear to Moeller, however, that Russia was the only power which after 1918 had taken up the fight against the West. Moeller and his friends of the June Club celebrated the "victory of Lenin" against the Allied interventionists, which meant, as they put it, a "victory of the Russian people over our enemies."[58] Moeller saw in the red flag the symbol of Russia's independence,[59] and he showed no mean insight into the Russian situation when he recognized Mother Russia behind the cloak of Bolshevism. But whatever Moeller's rationalizations about the character of Bolshevism, his theories constitute an early instance of the now very familiar pattern of a rising nationalism turning toward Russia.

As for Italy, it was, if not a defeated nation, a revisionist power.[60] Italy, after turning Fascist in 1922, Moeller argued, had shown that nationalism and socialism were one

[56] *Ibid.*, 147; for a discussion of Lenin and the "population problem" see Moeller, *Sozialismus*, 85ff.

[57] Moeller, *Sozialismus*, 81.

[58] Eduard Stadtler, "Der Sieg Lenins," *Gewissen*, III, No. 13 (March 30, 1921).

[59] Moeller, *Das dritte Reich*, 162.

[60] In 1919 Moeller still labeled Italy an "old people."

and the same, and that the population problem was of utmost importance in international relations. *"Italia docet,"* Moeller boasted in November 1922. All too readily did he venture the opinion that "fascism is part of the conservative counter-movement which is sweeping Europe."[61]

Moeller's political theories make up an organic whole, the cultural, historical, and political aspects of which are clearly interdependent. All his speculations led back to the idea of the Third Reich, his central theme. The Third Reich was an architectural structure, but it was founded on the infirm ground of despair and fanaticism. It was a myth as powerful and appealing as the classless society of Karl Marx and the general strike of Georges Sorel. Indeed, Moeller's scheme has been called a "political religion."[62] At least, it presented the rudiments of faith, a new faith, and it transcended reason. Moeller for once made German conservatism exciting. But, as we have seen, his ambiguities led him often into suggesting positions which were hardly conservative any more. The vagueness of both his style and his thought invited basic misunderstandings. He must have noticed this after his unsuccessful meeting with Hitler in 1922.[63] He may also have been aware of it when, after having suffered a nervous breakdown, he took his life in May 1925.

[61] Moeller, *Das Recht der jungen Völker* (1932), 123-125.
[62] Professor Tazerout, "La Pensée Politique de Moeller van den Bruck," *Revue Internationale de Sociologie*, XLIV (1936), 65.
[63] Cf. infra, 193f.

CHAPTER II

THE PESSIMISM OF OSWALD SPENGLER

SPENGLER, like Moeller, belonged to the generation[1] which had one foot in the nineteenth century and the other in the twentieth, a generation which not only saw Germany collapse, but also perceived the fragility of all Western civilization. It was a generation divided between those whom Moeller liked to call "eudaemonists" and the prophets of doom, between optimists and pessimists, between the "nineteenth century men" and the "twentieth century men." As we have seen, this division ran through the entire neo-conservative movement of the twentieth century. The "elders," though by no means unaware of the impending crisis, believed in the regenerative power of nineteenth century values. In comparison Moeller and Spengler sounded like apostates. But even Moeller's rejection of the past was, in essence, no more than a grand gesture, for he was divided against himself and found no way out of his dilemma. Spengler went further than Moeller, being less sensitive to the complexities of the world in which he lived, and carried along by the force of his own ferocious prophecies.

Spengler's view of the world was a matter of intuition rather than observation. He came from Central Germany, the birthplace of many outstanding German mystics and romantics, and was himself possibly the greatest mystic of modern Germany. He did not require Moeller's European experience to formulate his views, nor did he test his theories by discussing them with other scholars. After his retirement from schoolteaching in 1911, he led an austere and isolated life in Munich, as lonely as his great idol Nietzsche after the latter had withdrawn from his professorship in Basle. In this isolation Spengler created his great historical interpretations of the world.

[1] He was born in 1880.

The kind of abstractions in which Spengler was interested—the rise and decline of cultures—had to be approached intuitively. His thesis that cultures were living organisms and passed from youth through maturity to old age was an audacious one. It was as audacious as Burckhardt's and Nietzsche's dire predictions had been. And even though Spengler may have been second-rate, secondhand Burckhardt and Nietzsche—Thomas Mann called him Nietzsche's "clever ape"[2]—his "philosophy of the future" was part of the world of Burckhardt's and Nietzsche's intuitions and premonitions. The significance of Spengler is that he penetrated beyond the obvious and apparent and wrestled with ultimate questions.

Spengler's detractors have been legion.[3] He has been attacked for charlatanism and dilettantism, for his predictions as well as, specifically, for his pessimism. But these attacks have generally failed to acknowledge what Spengler's Eckermann, August Albers, called the "rhythm"[4] of his mind. They have altogether misfired. Rather than censoring *what* Spengler said they might more profitably have criticized *the way* he said it. For on this latter score Spengler was most vulnerable. He deserved criticism above all for his utter lack of humor. Spengler was too dogmatic and pedantic. What Stefan George once said in his poem about Nietzsche, that he should have sung, was even more applicable to Spengler. His ideas were better suited to poetry than to systematic exposition. Unfortunately, he had too much Ph.D in his stomach. This was his Germanic vice, of which both his great predecessors Burckhardt and Nietzsche and his successor Toynbee were free. In this respect Spengler was akin to Hegel and Marx. Indeed, he did to the thought of Burckhardt and Nietzsche what Marx had done

[2] Thomas Mann, "Nietzsches Philosophie im Lichte unserer Erfahrung," *Die Neue Rundschau* (Herbst, 1947), 382.

[3] For the controversy about Spengler see Manfred Schroeter, *Der Streit um Spengler, Kritik seiner Kritiker* (Munich, 1922).

[4] August Albers, "Oswald Spengler," *Preussische Jahrbücher*, CLXXXXII (1923), 129.

to that of the early socialists: he forced it into a strait jacket by making it into a historical law. European pessimism had found its systematizer. What Marx had been for the optimists, Spengler was for the pessimists.

Like most pessimists, Spengler stood for a philosophy of acceptance. His was not, however, the position taken by the early nineteenth century conservatives who had accepted the realities of this world within the context of a divinely created order. Whereas they had been Christian conservatives, Spengler was a heathen conservative. "Destiny" was the key concept of his thinking and the object of his "acceptance."[5] Ernst Robert Curtius remarked that "we Germans seek recourse too easily in destiny and tragedy."[6] Moeller, too, had taken refuge in "destiny." It was a favorite notion of the German neo-conservatives. It served them as a means of retreat into a world of vagueness, as refuge from a reality with which they could not cope. Spengler, however, elevated destiny to a superior form of experience. Far from being vague it was the "word for an inner certainty that is *not* describable."[7] Destiny, so Spengler claimed, transcended reality. It stood for "organic logic" as against the "logic of the inorganic."[8] It constituted, in particular, an attack against the professional historians' "causality principle." With Spengler it became a sort of watchword for the "counter-movement" against the modern spirit of rationalism. From it followed the fullness of "life experience" as against the insufficiencies of "scientific experience," the power of "seeing" as against the power of "calculating," "depth" as against "intellect."

Mr. Hughes talks about Spengler's "rather romantic" position.[9] It was romantic, indeed, in its exploration of a realm of experience beyond reason, beyond clarity and

[5] For a spirited discussion of Spengler's theories see H. Stuart Hughes, *Oswald Spengler. A Critical Estimate* (New York, 1952).

[6] Curtius, *Deutscher Geist in Gefahr*, 45.

[7] Oswald Spengler, *The Decline of the West* (New York, 1947), I, 118. Italics in the original.

[8] *Ibid.*, 117.   [9] Hughes, *Spengler*, 70.

language. Upon closer examination, however, this Spenglerian destiny turned out to be far from romantic. It committed man to a rigorous naturalistic law of rise and decline. " 'Mankind' is a zoological expression, or an empty word,"[10] he proclaimed. "Everything depends on our seeing our own position, our *destiny*, clearly, on our realizing that though we may lie to ourselves about it we cannot evade it. He who does not acknowledge this in his heart, ceases to be counted among the men of his generation, and remains either a simpleton, a charlatan, or a pedant."[11] Spengler was scientific, though in a way different from the positivists. Let us say that he was pseudo-scientific. He approached science through mysticism, and the latter led him to hard and fast facts. It was not a mysticism of love but a tough, cold-blooded one. Troeltsch's metaphor about the German combination of "mysticism and brutality"[12] was best borne out in the thinking of Spengler.

In Spengler's scheme the nineteenth century was a late phase in the history of the Western, or "Faustian," civilization, a phase in which self-consciousness took the place of "style" and creativity. It was a self-deceptive age with its "sentimental" optimism, its faith in the power of ideas, its always negative concept of freedom. And it was a mere transition period between the noon of the Faustian culture and the new Caesarism of the twentieth century. Spengler's twentieth century is a dreadful one. It is an era of Caesars struggling for domination, of atomized life in the big city—the "megalopolis" of drifting masses. But it has "style" again, one of "facts" rather than "ideals" and "truths"[13] whose very bleakness shatters the deceptions of the nineteenth century. It is the "style" of the *amor fati*.

Spengler's *Decline of the West* was not intended as a commentary on defeat. Indeed, the first volume, which appeared in the summer of 1918, was written with a German

10 Spengler, *Decline*, i, 21.
11 *Ibid.*, 44. Italics in the original.
12 Cf. supra, 113.   13 Spengler, *Decline*, ii, 368.

victory in mind. Spengler had expected post-war Germany to assume a role analogous to that of Rome after the Punic Wars.[14] But this fact was lost on most of Spengler's readers. To some of them the book was a timely justification of defeat, and it helped make pessimism a subject of thought and conversation as fashionable as existentialism after the second World War. To others, Spengler's pessimism seemed ill timed, ill advised, and unjustified. As a result, Spengler soon found himself forced to clarify his position and to restate it in more concrete terms. He continued to stress that "decline" was not identical with "catastrophe," and that he had been thinking in terms of "fulfillment." Indeed, he vigorously refused the label of "pessimist."[15] A pessimist, he stated, sees no tasks ahead, while he, Spengler, saw all too many yet to be performed.

It was in defending his position that Spengler staged his entry into German politics. Early in 1920 he came down from his Olympian retreat with a political pamphlet, *Preussentum und Sozialismus* (Munich, 1920), the first of a series which appeared between 1920 and 1924. It antedated by two years the appearance of the second volume of the *Decline*. Early in 1920, moreover, Spengler accepted the June Club's invitation to discuss his work with Moeller.[16] At the June Club he must have found himself in a friendly setting, for the few favorable reviews which his *Decline* had received so far had come from some of the neo-conservatives.[17] As for his debate with Moeller, it is evident that there were disagreements between the two. It cannot have been a brilliant meeting. Both Moeller and Spen-

[14] Cf. Schroeter, *Spengler*, 5.

[15] Cf. Oswald Spengler, "Pessimismus: *Preussische Jahrbücher*, CLXXXIV (1921), 73-84.

[16] Cf. Otto Strasser, *History in My Time* (London, 1941), 200. Though no exact date is given by Strasser for the meeting, it must have taken place shortly before Moeller's elaborate discussion of Spengler's work in the July 1920 issue of the *Deutsche Rundschau*; Moeller, *Das Recht der jungen Völker* (1932), 9-39.

[17] Cf. Schroeter, *Spengler*, 7.

gler lacked the ease and wit which make for good discussion. Indeed, neither was made for discussion; for that, Moeller had been too sheltered by the cult-like atmosphere in his club, and Spengler by his isolated life as *Stubengelehrter*. From Moeller's article on Spengler we get the impression of a head-on clash between two winds, a storm of abstract verbiage. Nevertheless, our one informant tells us that Moeller's and Spengler's positions were "complementary," and he records that the audience "moved by this moment solemnly swore" to devote their lives "to the realization of these visions."[18]

While Moeller was little known outside neo-conservative circles until after his death, Oswald Spengler quickly became one of the most influential German publicists of the immediate post-war period. The year 1924 saw him actively lecturing to groups such as the Hochschulring deutscher Art—a student organization which was closely connected with the D.H.V. and the *Deutsches Volkstum*— to the Hamburg "Overseas Club," and to the 1924 meeting of the German aristocracy in Breslau.[19] Spengler's initial impact, however, was due to his *Preussentum und Sozialismus*. It had an electrifying effect on the public.[20] Moeller called it a "necessary book,"[21] and it was no doubt Spengler's most significant political tract.

Spengler's political message was socialism. In socialism he saw the product of a declining civilization, a way of life suited to an age of masses and big cities. And yet *Preussentum und Sozialismus* was a criticism of Marxism. Like Marx, Spengler was a determinist, and like Marx he saw in socialism an "end-phenomenon."[22] Spengler was, in ef-

[18] Strasser, *History in My Time*, 200.

[19] Oswald Spengler, "Politische Pflichten der Jugend," "Neue Formen der Weltpolitik," *Politische Schriften* (Munich, 1933), 127ff., 157ff.; "Aufgaben des Adels," *Reden und Aufsätze* (3rd edn., Munich, 1951), 89ff.

[20] By 1924 the edition ran to 65,000; Oswald Spengler, *Neubau des deutschen Reiches* (Munich, 1924), appendix.

[21] Moeller, *Sozialismus*, 13.   [22] Spengler, *Decline*, I, 356.

fect, a pseudo-Marx. But he regarded Marx as the mere "stepfather"[23] of socialism. For Spengler, as for Moeller, Marx was simply part of the world of liberalism. But whereas Marxism was too materialistic for Moeller, it was too idealistic for Spengler. It was characterized, so the latter charged by "ideals" and "truths"; indeed it was mere "literature."[24] Spengler's Marx, we are led to believe, was the Marx of the *Manifesto* rather than of *Capital*, the willful and passionate Jewish moralist rather than the German political scientist. In any case, Spengler dismissed as purely arbitrary Marx's class theories. He rejected the distinction between bourgeois and workers as unreal and ultimately pointless. All modern men were workers. In our ageing civilization the worker was not part of a class but a representative "type."[25]

Preussentum und Sozialismus was an appeal to the Germans to live up to this type, a domineering, strong type —Spengler in the *Decline* wrote about a last "race"[26]— which was to end the interregnum of liberalism and democracy. It fitted in well with the German "hero" as opposed to the English "trader," to use terminology popularized by wartime Germans. As a matter of fact, Spengler, though he was by no means an Anglophobe,[27] used the *Los von England* slogan to sharpen his argument. The difference between the Englishman and the Prussian—the "Prussian" stood for the ideal German—corresponded to the difference between the capitalist and the socialist. With acid irony Spengler dismissed English ethics as the ethics of "fine society" and of "ladies and gentlemen." On the other hand, he equated Prussian traditions with socialism, inasmuch as "the German, more specifically the Prussian,

[23] Spengler, *Preussentum*, 3. [24] *Ibid.*, 3, 80.
[25] *Ibid.*, 68.
[26] Spengler, *Decline*, ɪɪ, 431.
[27] In his later tract "Neubau des deutschen Reiches," *Politische Schriften*, 185ff., he gave full vent to his respect for English traditions. Cf. p. 201 on conservatism in England, p. 238 on Eton, p. 244f. on English law.

instinct was such that the power was in the hands of the whole. The individual *serves* the whole. The king is the first servant of his state (Frederick the Great). . . . Such has been *since the eighteenth century* authoritarian socialism, which is essentially illiberal and anti-democratic as against English liberalism and French democracy. . . ."[28] Prussian socialism was "instinctive socialism";[29] Prussia's traditions—notably the army, the civil service, the workers of the type of August Bebel[30] had anticipated the ethical and political pattern of our society. *"In this sense,"* Spengler bragged, *"Frederick William I, and not Marx, was the first conscious socialist."*[31]

Spengler, pseudo-Marx, had a dialectic of his own which led to a clash between the two rival systems, capitalism and socialism. In the fashion of a Russian dictator he emphasized that "there is no coexistence between the two."[32] In the end, his dialectic culminated in Prussianism. In a way he thus brought dialectics back to the point from which it had developed in the nineteenth century. The powerful Hegel had originally set the goal of world history in the Prussian state. Marx, his defiant student, had turned Hegel upside down, postulated the stateless and classless society as the end of history. Spengler gave Prussia back her "rights" and made *"travailler pour le roi de Prusse"* the motto of his modern man.[33]

Disillusionment with the November Revolution and a general rejection of defeat established the rapport between the politician Spengler and his readers. He adopted the stab-in-the-back theory and called the revolution the "revolution of stupidity."[34] Spengler wrote *Preussentum und Sozialismus* during the "dreamland" period, and he did not share the early optimism of the other neo-conserv-

---

[28] Spengler, *Preussentum*, 15. Italics in the original.

[29] *Ibid.*, 81.

[30] Spengler had great admiration for the veteran German socialist, whom he contrasted to Marx.

[31] *Ibid.*, 42. Italics in the original.

[32] *Ibid.*, 50.   [33] *Ibid.*, 46.   [34] *Ibid.*, 9.

atives. He was more realistic than was Moeller with his Wilsonian dreams. But, like Moeller, he expected the revolution to result in socialism. Although a monarchist by temperament, he reminded the conservatives that their alternative was "socialism or destruction."[35] At the same time he appealed to the anti-liberal traditions of the Social Democrats. Had not Bebel once said in the Reichstag that Social Democracy was "a sort of preparatory school of militarism"? In fact, according to Spengler, the traditions of both conservatives and socialists were "specifically Prussian." "Both are in a higher sense socialistic," he said. The political implications of this lofty interpretation are obvious: the two socialistic parties in Germany must find each other against the common enemy, against the "inner England," the Trojan horse in Germany. Both had "national instinct,"[36] and their differences were merely on the surface.

Spengler brought his criticism of the nineteenth century to bear upon the new Republic: it, too, was a mere interregnum. And who can squarely refute Spengler's verdict that it had "no stature," "no passions," "no audacity," "no lasting message," and that is produced "no great men"?[37] The German Republic, Spengler subsequently declared, was not a form of government but a "business enterprise"[38]—another echo of Marx, who had identified a parliamentary republic as a bourgeois "joint stock" government.[39]

Compared with his hard-hitting critique of the Republic, the positive side of Spengler's argument was scarcely convincing. At best he contributed fragments toward a conservative policy. From Pareto he borrowed the concept of the elite, as has been pointed out by Mr. Hughes. His other notions are largely derived from Plenge and Lensch. He talked in terms of a "General Labor Service"; a "corporative structure"; and a "Workers' Council" which would

[35] *Ibid.*, 98.   [36] *Ibid.*, 63, 65.   [37] *Ibid.*, 11.
[38] Spengler, "Neubau," *Schriften*, 194.
[39] Karl Marx, "The Civil War in France," *Handbook of Marxism*, 142.

include military officers, civil servants, peasants, and miners, and take the place of parliament.[40] The problem of private property was to be "solved" by "transformation of property into a sort of hereditary fief . . . which . . . involves rights and duties." Socialization, Spengler maintained, involved a process extending over decades and leading toward the "state of civil servants."[41] In 1924 he strongly declared himself against egalitarianism.[42]

Spengler left no mark on the Social Democrats. As yet the party was committed to at least a nominal acceptance of Marxism, and, moreover, it became, to Spengler's disappointment, one of the pillars of democracy in Republican Germany. Spengler's impact on the conservatives is harder to assess. In a way, he helped loosen their political thinking, for, like Moeller, he gave expression to the socialistic temper of the Right. His blending of "Prussianism and Socialism" by a sort of alchemy made for an exciting and dynamic concept, one of many during the early post-war period to point the way toward a new conservatism. But Spengler failed to face the dilemma of conservatism. Even though in the early twenties Hitler had not yet become the nucleus of a Rightist mass movement, Spengler's premonitions of the coming age of the masses should have led him to a more guarded and responsible statement of conservatism. As it was, Spengler encouraged resentment rather than steering it. He made himself the master of ambiguity, as when he boasted that Germany would not produce another Goethe, but, indeed, a "Caesar."[43] Who was this Caesar to be? Was nihilism to be the essence of the new conservatism? Spengler was confused and he spread confusion. In effect, he lent himself to prepare the ground for National Socialism in Germany. Spengler was but a living example of the fact that the German spirit, as well as German society, was in danger.

[40] Spengler, *Preussentum*, 66.   [41] *Ibid.*, 90.

[42] Spengler, "Neubau," *Schriften*.

[43] Spengler, "Pessimismus?" *Preussische Jahrbücher*, CLXXXIV (1921), 84.

CHAPTER III

THE NIHILISM OF THE EARLY
ERNST JÜNGER

ERNST JÜNGER gave another distinct note to neo-conservatism. Born in 1895, he was considerably younger than Moeller and Spengler. The latter were trying to cope with the ills of our civilization by a thought process designed to reopen the realm of the irrational. Jünger, however, protested against thinking per se. For him Moeller and Spengler were "literature": his rejection of the bourgeois world took the form of praise of pure action. He was an activist. In view of the stifling effect of society and the futility of its values and aims, there was left for Jünger, as an expression of revolt only, the grand gesture. Moeller's *l'art pour l'art* phase in Paris, in itself a protest against a wrong bourgeois purposefulness, was outdone by Jünger's "action for action's sake." The key to Jünger's revolt was a direct plunge into adventure, into daring, or into "pure existence."[1] It started with his early flight from home and school into the exciting world of Africa; it found its climax in the first war, which became his greatest adventure. Africa and war gained a deep significance for Jünger. They represented a foot-loose generation's exploration of new values and quest for a new religiousness. Like Adrian Leverkühn, the hero of Thomas Mann's *Doktor Faustus*,[2] Jünger ventured into the realm of the barbaric and daemonic and struck his pact with the devil in order to rejuvenate our civilization. Barbarism became for him, in Mann's terms, a—however "slightly compromising"—form of conservatism,[3]

[1] Ernst Jünger, *Der Arbeiter. Herrschaft und Gestalt* (Hamburg, 1932), 134.

[2] Thomas Mann, *Doktor Faustus. Das Leben des Deutschen Tonkünstlers Adrian Leverkühn, erzählt von einem Freunde* (Stockholm, 1947).

[3] *Ibid.*, 431.

180

and the devil a source of religiousness.[4] Jünger's world was a strange, desperate, thoroughly paradoxical one, and in the last analysis the problem of Ernst Jünger was whether the barbaric and the daemonic, were stations of our rejuvenation or self-destruction.

Undoubtedly the early troublesome Ernst Jünger was as much a figure of European significance as is the mature Ernst Jünger of our days. He belonged in the line of thinkers whom we now call "existentialists." His concentration on the German situation was his way of experiencing the European crisis. For him, as for Marx and Nietzsche, Germany was simply the country par excellence of crisis. For, like Marx and Nietzsche, Jünger was a European, though perhaps he did not live up to the claim of being a "good" one. Among the European existentialists he stood at a vital point during the first war when, according to Paul Tillich, "the Existentialist revolt ceased to be revolt," and became "the mirror of an experienced reality."[5]

Ernst Jünger was not, then, an isolated phenomenon. He was part of a restless generation and he thought that restlessness was a good thing. He became a spokesman for those driven by dissatisfaction with our civilization to search for the grand gesture. He stood for what has been called "adventurism."[6] He may, therefore, be called a German T. E. Lawrence. Lawrence exchanged the Western world for the cause of the Arabs, and, finally, after his disillusionment with the British policy toward the Arabs, joined the Royal Air Force as an anonymous soldier. The desert and the air were his refuge. Jünger also resembles Saint-Exupéry, who sought liberation in flying, and Mal-

---

[4] The devil in *Doktor Faustus*: "The religious sphere pertains to me as clearly as it does not pertain to bourgeois culture." *Ibid.*, 377.

[5] Paul Tillich, *The Courage to Be* (New Haven, 1952), 137.

[6] Cf. Roger Stéphane, *Portrait de l'Aventurier. T. E. Lawrence, Malraux, von Salomon* (Paris, 1950). Also, Alfred von Martin, *Der heroische Nihilismus und seine Überwindung. Ernst Jüngers Weg durch die Krise* (Krefeld, 1948), 14, who talks in terms of the "*Weltanschauung* of the adventurer."

raux, who, like Sartre himself, escaped from the everyday world into political extremism of one sort or another.

But there is also something particularly German about the case of Ernst Jünger. It has been suggested that Jünger's quest for the daemonic was basically part of "a recurring German destiny."[7] In this connection it might be remembered that Jünger, like Goethe, was an amateur naturalist and that the study of organisms served him as an avenue to mystification rather than enlightenment. Jünger, after all, was Doctor Faustus—whether Goethe's or Thomas Mann's—and German in his rejection of moderation, in his inability to come to terms with life, and in his quest for fulfillment through fullness of experience. Particularly German, however, was Jünger's fascination with war. There is no country in modern history in which the "divine majesty of war," as Treitschke once put it, has been as consistently celebrated. The Germans have always been more fascinated by the idea of war, by war as a romantic and metaphysical principle of creativity, than horrified by war as a brutal reality. Hegel was their modern Heraclitus: he saw in war the "father of all things." Jünger, of course, belonged to the generation of those who volunteered for the war, and who were the real heroes of 1914. For most of the neo-conservatives whom we have so far encountered, the "ideas of 1914" remained a relatively intellectual concept. The war service of most of the "elders" consisted of speech making. Rathenau and Moellendorff saw the war from the desks of the War Raw Materials Division; Thomas Mann considered his *Betrachtungen* and Spengler his *Decline of the West* their contributions to the Fatherland. And not even Moeller, a member of the Landsturm and eventually engaged in propaganda work at the Eastern front, ever saw action. For Jünger, however, war was more than a political and intellectual phenomenon: it was an adventure. The sight of an outgoing regiment gave him the "impression of blood, roses, and splendid

<hr/>

[7] Von Martin, *Nihilismus*, 8.

tears."⁸ Battle, alas, as recorded in Jünger's war books, is a magic delight. It is a "magnificent" "show of destruction"⁹ and a splendid miracle: a transformation of the bourgeois into the adventurer. It is the birth-hour of a new "type"— the "warrior," who overcomes the meaninglessness of yesterday by a rediscovery of cosmic values and is the resurrected man of the twentieth century.

Jünger's warrior fought neither for the kaiser nor for victory; he fought for fighting's sake. Indeed, Sartre has pointed out that for the adventurer victory would be equivalent to failure; it would bring "disillusionment."¹⁰ The adventurer, like Jünger's warrior, was a new type of soldier who refused the victory which he once wanted. Like the soldier of Walter Flex, one of Germany's most beloved war authors, who himself died in battle in 1917, he was a "wanderer between the two worlds,"¹¹ between life and death, who sought out battle as a way of penetrating into the realm of magic. The logic of his daring led him to further daring and eventually to—defeat.

Just as Spengler's "decline" became a symbolic situation after the war in Germany, Jünger's "warrior" became a symbolic type. Defeat was his situation par excellence. There is no emphasis on the "stab-in-the-back" theory in Jünger's argument as there had been in Moeller's and Spengler's. Nothing done in German history should be undone—not the war, not defeat. Jünger's warrior, after all, was a fighter "against the eternal Utopia of peace, the pursuit of happiness, and perfection."¹² The defeat was, Jünger explained, merely part of a pattern of "heroic realism."¹³

If Ernst Jünger became so much more representative a writer in Germany than T. E. Lawrence in England, it

8 Müller, *Ernst Jünger*, 19.

9 Ernst Jünger, ed., *Krieg und Krieger* (Berlin, 1930), 59.

10 Cf. Stéphane, *L'Aventurier*, 24f.

11 Walter Flex, *Der Wanderer zwischen beiden Welten* (Munich, 1917).

12 Ernst Jünger, "Der heroische Realismus," *Literarische Welt*, VI, No. 13 (1930), 3.

13 *Ibid.*, 3f.

was partly because of the German defeat. In a society which did not yet feel darkened by the shadows of decline, Lawrence was considered an eccentric. Jünger seemed more meaningful to a society which was itself eccentric—that is, which was clearly sick. He fascinated his own generation and the younger one: his war books launched a wave of others of the same kind that swamped the German book market in the late twenties with glorifications of the war experience. He became an inspiration to those members of the German Freikorps who continued fighting a war in defiance of the peace, a war with changed and confused fronts, a war with no purpose save that of refusing to return home and of fighting on. It was thanks largely to this inspiration that Ernst von Salomon (born in 1902), one of the most colorful members of the Freikorps and one of the plotters of Rathenau's murder, gained his questionable stature. He was thus able to talk himself into justifying murder. For him the alternative to the bourgeois life was no longer the vitality and creativity of the artist as it had been for Thomas Mann, but the boldness of the murderer. Or take a member of a definitely younger generation, Bismarck's great-grandson, Count Heinrich Einsiedel (born in 1921), whose restlessness led him from the Youth Movement to the Luftwaffe—flying "from eternity to eternity"[14]—and who after being shot down over Stalingrad went through a communist phase. All the positions which he took make sense only through their senselessness, through their extremism. The drifting and shifting Count was less a child of his great ancestor than he was of Ernst Jünger. The latter became an avowed spokesman for all "conspirators," "prisoners," "saboteurs," "adventurers," and "soldiers of fortune."[15]

In the history of Western thought the early Ernst Jünger stands at the point where existentialism and nihilism

[14] Heinrich von Einsiedel, *I Joined the Russians* (New Haven, 1953), 3.

[15] Ernst Jünger, "Die Geburt des Nationalismus aus dem Kriege," *Deutsches Volkstum*, XXXI (1929), 580.

meet. As we have seen, he stood for a peculiarly activist brand of existentialism. He also represented a particular brand of nihilism. He has little in common with Bazarov, the protoype of the nineteenth century nihilists. Bazarov, Turgenev's hero in *Fathers and Sons,* was a child of the seventeenth and eighteenth century rationalism. Politically a liberal, he carried liberalism *ad absurdum.* He was, if you wish, a "tough" Cartesian. His world was one of progress which was scientifically predetermined and which required no mind, no culture, and, of course, no religion. Ernst Jünger was an anti-rationalist. He was, we might assume, a "tough Nietzschean." His world was one of Spenglerian recurrence, of violent catastrophes, which reestablishes an existential relation between man and the elementary powers, rather than a world of progress, which alienates man from them. Politically his world was the extreme opposite of "the three-times spit-out phrases of the French Revolution."[16] Politically he might have been called a "conservative" had he not carried conservatism *ad absurdum.*

Jünger's war books were followed by a theoretical work, *Der Arbeiter,*[17] which appeared in 1932. This represented a further step in his development. The "warrior" was succeeded by a new type, the "worker." Mark that Jünger's worker had no class consciousness, strictly speaking, in the Marxian sense, or nation consciousness in Moeller's sense.[18] He was the new "type" destined to take over after the bourgeois order had destroyed itself. We recognize in this determinism the influence of Spengler, the pseudo-Marxist. Indeed, the *Arbeiter* was clearly affected by Spengler's reasonings: Spengler's *amor fati* was also Jünger's.[19] The

16 *Ibid.,* 580.
17 Ernst Jünger, *Der Arbeiter, Herrschaft und Gestalt* (Hamburg, 1932).
18 *Ibid.,* 151.
19 Jünger did not acknowledge his debt to Spengler. In fact, he attacked the "comparative mythology as it is being observed these days" as an "archaic affair" and as an occupation for "collectors" and "romanticists." *Ibid.,* 80.

worker was anti-bourgeois not by choice but because of historical necessity.

Der Arbeiter offered the vast panorama of a "landscape of ice and fire."[20] Jünger, like Spengler, was no nice sociologist. He saw that the "pedestrian"—that is, the individual—represented a "dying species"[21] in an age of technology. The worker was the soldier in the work uniform, the Prussian in the factory. For we are still in Prussia: *"Travail pour le roi de Prusse"* was also the worker's motto.[22] He came to terms with his society through anonymity, finding new allegiances in the fascinating world of masses and machines.

Surely, Ernst Jünger's work was sociology without ethos. He was undisturbed by the fact that in an age of attacks against civilian populations war had lost the glamour which it may have had in earlier times. Jünger did not plead for chivalry but for a stoic conditioning to the new situation. Everything short of this he labeled "romantic." Like the modern sociologists, Jünger faced the creeping encroachment of the laws of modern technology upon the individual's freedom of action. If planning was needed in our age, Jünger did not ask the question which Karl Mannheim asked: "planning for what?"[23] He preferred the escape into the "methods of coercion, command, pressure, genocide,"[24] as they spelled the end of the bourgeois era.

Jünger realized as clearly as did the "elders" the dilemma of conservatism in the twentieth century. But he took the opposite way out. He was as deeply involved as Rathenau and Moellendorff in the problems of mechanization. But he outbid their complex position by a streamlined formula. While rejecting individual freedom as "suspect,"[25] he seized upon "total mobilization"[26] as an ideal situation in which freedom would survive only insofar as

[20] *Ibid.,* 91.   [21] *Ibid.,* 112.   [22] Cf. *ibid.,* 107.
[23] Karl Mannheim, *Freedom, Power and Democratic Planning* (New York, 1950), 8.
[24] *Ibid.,* 23.
[25] Jünger, *Krieg und Krieger,* 15.   [26] *Ibid.,* passim.

it spelled total participation in society. In other words, Jünger admitted a Hegelian identity between freedom and obedience.[27] He shifted the basis of freedom from ethics to a pure esthetics which amounted to an obliteration of the individual for the sake of the full experience of the whole. He sacrificed principle to *élan*. Among all the neo-conservatives he illustrated most clearly the point at which conservatism lost its identity to nihilism. The *Deutsches Volkstum*, with which Jünger had close ties, had every reason to state at this point that "for the conservative man the way of Ernst Jünger would mean a major upset."[28]

Some of Jünger's conclusions certainly deserve our consideration: he emphasized the weakness of the old world of which conservatism was a part. Whereas Moeller and Spengler aimed at a revival of conservatism, Jünger ultimately discarded this possibility as hopeless. He thought a mere political reform inadequate for the graveness of our crisis. Whether we call Jünger an existentialist or a nihilist, he was one of those modern men of letters who do not stop short of aiming at a basic regeneration of man. Ernst Jünger was in stature an almost religious thinker who struggled with what Thomas Mann called the "religious paradox" of deriving hope from the depth of despair.[29]

And if, as Arthur Koestler said in a recent speech, the basic issue of our time has been no longer capitalism and socialism but freedom and slavery,[30] on what side did Jünger stand in this struggle? Has Jünger, the adventurer, freed men from the bourgeois yoke? Did Jünger's revolutionism not equate extreme liberation with a new extreme bondage? No easy answer can satisfy us here. Ernst Jünger never was a Nazi. But he stood in the anatomy of the

27 Cf. Jünger, *Der Arbeiter*, 145.
28 A. E. Günther, "Die Gestalt des Arbeiters," *Deutsches Volkstum*, xxxiv (1932), 781.
29 Mann, *Doktor Faustus*, 745.
30 Arthur Koestler, "Das falsche Dilemma," *Der Monat*, ii (July, August, 1950) , 436ff.

Nietzschean revolution—if this term be allowed here—at a point corresponding to the one where Lenin and Stalin stood in the anatomy of the Marxian revolution. In less than one century Marxism had been translated by the Russians into a collectivist system. Analogously Jünger wanted "service" and "sacrifice" as much as he wanted freedom. This was the contradiction in his thinking. And his new "types"—"warrior" and "worker"—and his new "landscape" carried the stamp of "service" and "sacrifice." These, Jünger suggested, were the twentieth century "wave of the future." In fact, he looked with greatest fascination toward Russia, that is, Stalin's Russia: Russia was the "land of planned economy" that belonged to the "great destinations *(Reiseziele)* of our times."[31] In the struggle between freedom and slavery, therefore, Jünger adopted the wrong side: a system of enslavement more terrible than the bourgeois oppression had ever been. In other words, the "worker" could not serve as a doctor in the crisis; at best he was its index. In a study of Ernst Jünger the much-maligned bourgeois comes back into its own, and the "philistine" landscape of the nineteenth century gains a quiet grandeur. We like to rest our eyes on it again. It has its wasteland in its midst indeed, but altogether it is more human, and, through its complexity, heroic. In revolting against it, we might hesitate to go beyond the point of no return. Jünger went beyond it, and this was his tragedy. However unwillingly on his part, he was used by the Nazis: however unwittingly, his thought led into the German catastrophe. And when during the second war Jünger saw the light, when through the bent steel of destruction he looked back nostalgically to the world where people lived their lives in "small communities under a peaceful roof, with good talks,"[32] all was lost. Admittedly, Jünger's change of heart came too late.

[31] Ernst Jünger, "Ein neuer Bericht aus dem Lande der Planwirtschaft," *Widerstand*, VIII (1933), 280.
[32] Ernst Jünger, *Auf den Marmor-Klippen* (Hamburg, 1941), 5f.

PART IV

NEO-CONSERVATISM AND NATIONAL SOCIALISM

CHAPTER I

THE FAILURE OF THE FINAL TEST: THE CONVERGING OF THE TWO MOVEMENTS

As WE HAVE SEEN, there were variations in outlook within the neo-conservative camp. While the sons of the always respectable but troubled middle classes might safely have taken home Moeller and, of course, Spengler for reading, indeed thought-provoking and challenging reading, a concern on their part with Jünger—with his *Arbeiter*, specifically—might well have been considered by their families as suspect and objectionable. Among the neo-conservatives one was more or less anti-bourgeois, more or less against the Republic, against parliamentarism, and for some sort of corporative order or socialism. One was more or less suspicious of the West, nationalistic, and, indeed, dreaming of salvation in the East. One was tolerant of Russia and even of Karl Marx. One was more or less tired of freedom. For the younger generations, surely humanitarianism or Christianity became more or less hollow concepts. Whether they clamored for a new medieval age, for a Third Reich, for a magic Third Front, or a new Caesarism, they were in a more or less apocalyptic mood. And while some early neo-conservatives in expectation of a new *Zwingherr zur Deutschheit* had put their hopes in Stinnes, while later some banked on the shallow "authoritarian" Papen, and others on the mysterious Schleicher, it was Adolf Hitler whom even the neo-conservatives came increasingly to look to as a messiah.

All these gradations in outlook merely represent varying ways of coping, more unconsciously than not, with the dilemma of conservatism. All the elaborate schemes and proposals went back to some of the basic premises of conservatism, but, at the same time, they outdid each other in extremism. They sacrificed in one way or another the logic of conservatism to hopeful-sounding but devastating visions, and, in effect, they lost the purity of purpose and conviction which was needed to stand up against the Nazis. One can maintain neither the position that the neo-conservatives were apologists for National Socialism nor the position that the neo-conservatives lost out against the Nazi Party in an all-out struggle for leadership in the German Revolution. There were basic disagreements between the two groups, but it never came to a clear-cut conflict between them. In their stand against National Socialism the neo-conservatives became more and more like their opposites, and, indeed, the radical conservatives and Ernst Jünger outdid them. In the last analysis, the neo-conservatives themselves beclouded the issue and defeated themselves. They were irresponsibles all, and they were confused and spread confusion. And the advent of National Socialism heightened and sharpened the dilemma of the conservatives. It represented the final test which the conservatives did not pass.

If any occasion is to mark the start of the intricate relations between the two movements—the neo-conservatives and the National Socialists—it was appropriately the meeting between Moeller van den Bruck and Adolf Hitler, between the prophet of the Third Reich and its architect, in the spring of 1922. Hitler had just emerged as undisputed head of his Munich Party. Admittedly, he was a *homo novus* of obscure background, not even a German himself, and he surrounded himself with a gang of unpredictable rowdies, his newly created Sturmabteilung (S.A. or Storm Troopers). He was an irritating rabble rouser. But in these days in troublesome Bavaria, which had been through the Räterepublik experience, one was willing to overlook a good deal in a nationalist. After all, the Reichswehr had found Hitler useful as instruction officer in an effort to indoctrinate the troops against the new revolutionary ideas, and, be it through his magnetic oratory or his ruth-lessness, Hitler had made himself the spokesman for the Bavarian counter-revolutionary elements. While in Bavaria the authorities, like the new minister president, Knilling, and minister of justice, Gürtner, were hoping to harness the young Nazi movement for their own ends, in the North one was starting to be merely curious about Hitler. He had been in the North in the summer of 1921 establish-ing contacts with various nationalistic groups. In the spring of the following year Rudolf Pechel met Hitler through the initiative of the geopolitician Karl Haushofer and his devotee Rudolf Hess, and through Pechel, in turn, a visit of Hitler to the June Club was arranged. This occurred some time in 1922. As things turned out, Hitler spoke to an unusually small gathering of about thirty men. After what turned out to be one of Hitler's usual tirades, Moeller, Hitler, Pechel, and Lejeune-Jung[1] with-drew and continued in discussion until well into the morning hours of the next day. Hitler had come to ask for support: "You have everything that I lack," he is quot-ed as having said to his three opposites. "You produce the intellectual tools for a renascence of Germany. I am nothing but a drummer and demagogue."[2] But Hitler's plea for cooperation was not accepted. He was merely promised copies of the *Gewissen* and other publications of the June Club. Moeller, after Hitler had taken leave, is said to have remarked that "this fellow will never under-stand"[3] and, more drastically, that if Hitler were to abuse the Third Reich concept for purposes of power, he (Moel-

[1] A Catholic politician, a close friend of Chancellor Heinrich Brüning, and one of the secessionists from the D.N.V.P. in 1930 who founded the Conservative People's Party. Later he was involved in the preparations for the plot against Hitler (July 20, 1944). He was scheduled to become minister of economics in the provisional gov-ernment that was to follow. He was executed by the Nazis.

[2] Rudolf Pechel, *Deutsche Widerstand* (Zurich, 1947), 279; *"Ich bin nichts als ein Trommler und Sammler."*

[3] *Ibid.*, 279.

ler) would commit suicide.[4] The meeting was a failure. And yet, it is interesting that this outcome was never publicly revealed until after the final *débâcle,* through Pechel's account. The other reports about the event which appeared in the early thirties[5] were cryptic and evasive about the disagreements, as if in order not to interfere with the commonly held notion of the union between Moeller and Hitler. Hitler, so it seems, had his way after all.

Up through the first months of the Nazi regime Moeller was indiscriminately celebrated as the "prophet of the Third Reich."[6] This was the impression one got from the special issue which the *Deutsches Volkstum* devoted to Moeller, from the many books and articles which appeared about Moeller after 1930.[7] Ironically, Moeller's own publisher advertised him as a precursor of Hitler and as the "anti-Spengler."

It is interesting that the Nazis themselves merely tolerated this Moeller cult. In general, their publications, including the *Nationalsozialistische Monatshefte,* edited by Alfred Rosenberg and dedicated to "intellectual" matters, paid only scant attention to the theoretical foundation of National Socialism. An occasional reference praised Moel-

[4] This statement has been obtained indirectly through Chancellor Brüning, who got it from Lejeune-Jung.

[5] Max Hildebert Boehm, "Moeller van den Bruck im Kreise seiner politischen Freunde," *Deutsches Volkstum,* xxxiv (1932), 696; Paul Fechter, *Moeller van den Bruck. Ein politisches Schicksal* (Berlin, 1934), 78; Paul Fechter, "Das Leben Moellers van den Bruck," *Deutsche Rundschau,* ccxxxix (1934) , 20.

[6] So advertised in a pamphlet issued by the Wilh. Gottl. Korn publishing house in Breslau, May 1935.

[7] The Moeller issue of the *Deutsches Volkstum* appeared in September 1932. Books and articles connecting Moeller with National Socialism are: Reinhard Adam, *Moeller van den Bruck* (Königsberg, 1933); Paul Fechter, *Moeller van den Bruck. Ein politisches Schicksal* (Berlin, 1934); Herbert Schack, *Denker und Deuter. Männer von der deutschen Wende* (Stuttgart, 1938); Eugen Schmahl, *Der Aufstieg der nationalen Idee* (Stuttgart, 1933); Wolfgang Herrmann, "Moeller van den Bruck," *Die Tat,* xxv (1933-1934), 273ff.; Paul Fechter, "Das Leben Moellers van den Bruck," *Deutsche Rundschau,* ccxxxix (1934), 20.

ler as "a Greater German patriot"[8] and his work as a prophecy of a national-revolutionary future" and as an "anti-liberal heroic inspiration of the national youth."[9]

Neither Spengler[10] nor Jünger fared much better in clarifying their respective positions toward National Socialism. Spengler's record of criticizing the Nazis goes back to 1924 when he delivered his address concerning the Political Duties of the German Youth to the Hochschulring deutscher Art, which was followed in the same year by his pamphlet *Reconstruction of the German Reich*.[11] The year 1924 was the year following the unsuccessful Hitler Putsch. While lashing out violently against the Weimar regime—a "business enterprise"—and the Versailles settlement—which made out of Germany a "reparation colony"[12]—Spengler also turned against the *"Völkischen."*[13] They thought to replace competence in politics by enthusiasm and feeling. In particular, Spengler argued, race feelings cannot form the basis for "great politics." The *"Völkischen,"* he charged, "are the *jeunesse dorée* of today," "determined young men" who were making history "with fists and clubs, unconcerned about the difficult questions of politics, administration, and the public economy."[14] In the name not of humanitarianism but of *Realpolitik* Spengler attacked the foundations of the Nazi *Weltanschauung*.

Jünger, on the other hand, never took public stand against the Nazis, until his veiled attack in his *Auf den Marmor-Klippen* (Hamburg, 1939). Who but the few initiated and the subtlest of his readers could have guessed that the "adventurer" looked down upon the Party—which

[8] "Das Recht der jungen Völker," *Nationalsozialistische Monatshefte*, III (June 1932), 267.

[9] *Völkischer Beobachter*, quoted in Wilh. Gottl. Korn pamphlet, May 1935.

[10] For a discussion of Spengler and National Socialism see Hughes, *Spengler*, 120ff.

[11] Cf. supra, 175.   [12] Spengler, "Neubau," *Schriften*, 194, 200.

[13] The term, derived from the German *"Volk"* (folk), refers to the German racists in general and the National Socialists in specific.

[14] *Ibid.*, 203.

he never joined—as a megalomaniac petty-bourgeois organization, far removed from the realm of the "elementary"? Who would have known that when Jünger despisingly talked about the *"Demos"* he meant the Nazis themselves? But Jünger's public in those days was hardly adult and little disposed to discriminate—much unlike his present-day highly sophisticated clientele. Like Moeller, Spengler and Jünger also emerged, much in spite of themselves, to be regarded as intellectual fathers of National Socialism.[15] And, alas, it was in the *Völkischer Beobachter* that Jünger was praised as a "poet . . . who recognizes clearly and honestly the needs of our times."[16]

Revolutionary times are not discriminating intellectually; in fact, they are not intellectual at all. They have an affinity for the lowest common denominator, an affinity for —the "drummers." On the basis of this lowest common denominator the two movements, the neo-conservatives and the National Socialists, converged. This was the level which mattered historically. It mattered little that the neo-conservatives traced their lineage back to Burckhardt and Nietzsche and not to Joseph Arthur Gobineau and Houston Stewart Chamberlain.[17] It mattered little that the neo-conservatives had at least set out to redress some of the

[15] All three are included, for example, in Schmahl, *Der Aufstieg der nationalen Idee.* A semi-official bibliography of National Socialism (Erich Unger, *Das Schrifttum des Nationalsozialismus von 1919 bis zum 1. Januar 1934* [Berlin, 1934]) listed the works of Edgar J. Jung, Ernst Jünger, Moellendorff, Moeller van den Bruck, Spann, Stapel; not, however, of Spengler. The omission of Spengler may be due to the fact that Rosenberg had taken issue with Spengler in his *Der Mythus des 20. Jahrhunderts* (Munich, 1930), 403f., 551, 673, 696, and in "Oswald Spengler," *Nationalsozialistische Monatshefte*, I (July 1930), 180ff. Unger's bibliography was referred to in the *Nationalsozialistische Monatshefte*, v (June 1934), 554 as "*the* bibliography of National Socialism." Italics in the original.

[16] *Völkischer Beobachter*, quoted in a pamphlet issued by the Hanseatische Verlagsanstalt in 1936.

[17] All three, Moeller, Spengler, and Jünger, rejected the strictly biological race theories: Moeller, *Das Recht der jungen Völker* (1932), 191ff.; Spengler, *Untergang*, II, 146ff.; Jünger, *Arbeiter*, 145.

basic failings of the liberal era and to give a new-old meaning to freedom in the form of be it federalism, corporatism, or socialism. It mattered little that, whatever their particular emphasis, they had firm convictions. It only mattered in these days that both movements were counter-revolutionary agents in the Republic and appealed to the worst instincts of the population. The vicious charges of the neo-conservatives against the political parties, the Weimar "system," or the Western powers, their mere use (with whatever mental reservations) of the new glittering vocabulary—words like "myth," "totality," and "race"—were but grist for the Nazi propaganda mill. That is why the initial alienation of the neo-conservative forces from the Republic was so fatal an event. It paved the way for the Rightist intelligentsia to serve the aims of the Nazi revolution.

In particular, after the Hitler Putsch in November 1923 Hitler's claim for the leadership within the ranks of the extreme Right was close to established. Stapel, however annoyed by the excess of Hitlerian "agitation,"[18] conceded that the Munich events had "brought all national hopes into focus."[19] In other words, the Burckhardtians, however grudgingly, had to put up with the *"terrible simplificateur."* Moeller's principles notwithstanding and, literally, over Moeller's dead body, the neo-conservatives furnished the "intellectual superstructure"[20] for a movement which was without ideas, principles, and, indeed, without a binding program.

Meanwhile the Nazi Party played the two ends against the middle. While usurping the ideas of Moeller, Spengler, and Jünger, it profited from lacking a basic theory and binding program of its own. Up to the year 1934 National

[18] Wilhelm Stapel, "Die Zukunft der nationalen Bewegung," *Deutsches Volkstum*, xxvi (1924), 6f.

[19] Wilhelm Stapel, "Zwiesprache," *Deutsches Volkstum*, xxvi (1924), 45.

[20] The application of the term in this connection is borrowed from Joseph Peter Stern, *Ernst Jünger* (New Haven, 1953), 11.

Socialism was "action pure and simple, dynamics *in vacuo,* revolution at a variable tempo, ready to be changed at any moment."[21] It has been pointed out before that absence of a basic theory is one of the important differences between National Socialism and Bolshevism.[22] While Lenin long before 1917 had committed himself to a definite program, Hitler remained a sphinx even after 1933. His "program," the famous "Twenty-five Points," going back to the year 1920, contained a hodgepodge of ferocious and pious "demands" which were designed to woo the most diverse elements in society.[23] It might be suggested that this particular difference between National Socialism and Bolshevism accounts for the different pattern in the relationships between these parties and the other revolutionary groups in their respective countries. Whereas in Russia the "competition for revolution" remained a factor through the days of the Civil War, in Germany the neo-

[21] Rauschning, *Revolution of Nihilism,* 23.

[22] Franz Neumann, *Behemoth,* 39.

[23] There were the "socialistic" Points (11, 13, 17), which were to appeal to the anti-capitalistic mood of the masses. But they turned out to be a farce. While on May 22, 1926 Hitler still declared the Twenty-five Points "unalterable," he soon retracted. On April 13, 1928 he redefined the controversial Point 17 in an official statement "to clear up false interpretations": "In view of the fact that the N.S.D.A.P. believes in the principle of private property, it is self-evident that the phrase 'expropriation without indemnities' refers only to the creation of legal means whereby land which was acquired in illegal ways or which is not being administered to the best interests of the nation might be expropriated if necessary. This is directed primarily against Jewish land-speculation." Quoted in S. William Halperin, *Germany Tried Democracy* (New York, 1946), 221.

Another example of the indistinctness of the Twenty-five Points is Point 24, which committed the Party to "positive Christianity," a vague and deceptive concept which later proved to mean Christianity without the Old Testament, the Judaic tradition, and without the "negative" aspects of Christ's passion—a he-man's Christianity.

Finally, Point 25, dealing with the political organization of the state, called for a "centralized Parliament" and the "formation of Chambers for classes and occupations." While on one hand disguising its anti-parliamentary, anti-democratic tendencies, the Party left the door open to—never substantiated—corporative experiments.

conservative groups more and more abdicated their own revolutionary role. The ideological weakness of the Nazi Party turned out, after all, to be its political strength.

In effect, the neo-conservative and the Nazi movements got thoroughly intertwined. "The two last years of the Weimar Republic represented one of the most fertile phases of our history," reminisced Hans Zehrer. "Never before has there been so much thinking and planning in Germany. The ice was suddenly broken when the old powers, the ones of the Weimar system, at last started to abdicate. All the minds suddenly seemed to have overcome the vagueness of jargon and began to communicate in a new way. Suddenly the old and meaningless concepts disappeared, the crazy categories of Left and Right. . . . It was like a trance. Everything seemed possible if only tackled in the right way, and everywhere there were forces about to get going. None of the old wisdoms which had been preached for years seemed to apply any more, and everything assumed a new meaning. But then it occurred at every discussion that there was a silent guest who mostly was not even visible but who nevertheless dominated the discussion, because he raised the issues, dictated the method, and determined the objective. And this silent guest was Adolf Hitler."[24] As time went on the political expectations of the neo-conservatives became more and more coupled with the Nazi Party. In one way or other the neo-conservatives rationalized themselves out of their own position. In 1932 a book appeared with the challenging title *What We Expect of National Socialism*.[25] The editor, Albrecht Erich Günther, had canvassed a number of Rightist intellectuals, mostly non-Nazis and several of them Young

[24] Quoted in Ernst von Salomon, *Der Fragebogen* (Hamburg, 1953), 216f.

[25] *Was wir von Nationalsozialismus erwarten. Zwanzig Antworten* (ed. Albrecht Erich Günther, Heilbronn, 1932). Cf. also Rauschning, *The Conservative Revolution*, Chap. XII ("What We Expected from National Socialism").

Conservatives,[26] about their attitude toward National
Socialism. The book contains the usual invectives against
the "party state." The German people, Günther stated,
needed "genuine authority" and was looking toward the
"front of national resistance which we have seen growing
under various names and at different occasions" and which
"today finds in the National Socialist movement its greatest rallying point, even though perhaps not in its final
form."[27] A subtle hint, a rapid postscript, but one which,
so it seems, the author himself likes to have overlooked.
To Winnig the "National Socialist movement as represented by the N.S.D.A.P." had become a "German
necessity" standing for the "German will as against foreign
power, the elite conception [*Auslese*] as against the rule
of the masses[!]." Indeed, any possible criticism of the
admittedly vague social program of the Party, Winnig
urged, should defer to the Party's "the Common Interest
before Self."[28] Leafing further through the book, we
wonder what reason a Roman Catholic author had to expect the coming Reich to be a *"sacrum imperium,"*[29]
and a Protestant one to be confident that National Socialism would not "transgress the limits of the political" and
that it would not "claim for itself the whole man?"[30] And
how could the Nazi concept of "positive Christianity" be
construed as an assurance that Christianity would not be
transformed into a "German religion"?[31] What tragic deceptions this volume reveals. It surely shows that by 1932
Hitler had come close to becoming "all things to all men."

It is interesting that all the various neo-conservative
groups saw themselves, in one way or other, related to
National Socialism. Most of them liked to think in terms
of their being part of a popular "movement" of which the

[26] A. E. Günther from the *Deutsches Volkstum*; August Winnig;
Albert Mirgeler, a Catholic; Heinrich Forsthoff, a Protestant clergy-
man; Hans Bogner; Georg Steinbömer; Wilhelm Stapel.
[27] *Was wir vom Nationalsozialismus erwarten*, 7, 10.
[28] *Ibid.*, 14, 19f.   [29] *Ibid.*, 22ff.
[30] *Ibid.*, 39.   [31] *Ibid.*, 40.

Nazi "Party" was but one expression. While for Edgar J. Jung the "German revolution" had two roots, one nationalistic and one conservative, and while the radical conservatives, as well as some *Tat* people, tended to see in Hitler the Girondist and in themselves the Jacobins, and fancied the notion that the Nazi Party was but a "popish" Southern party,[32] almost all of them—with the notable exception of Niekisch[33]—sooner or later were reduced to pious hopes for the "second phase" of the revolution.[34] Little was left to them but the argument that the Nazis could be "harnessed." Finally, no more explanation could hide the ignominious defeat. It became clear that the neo-conservatives had "slipped into a political association destructive of every political virtue"; they had become "spiritual victims."[35]

[32] Edgar J. Jung, *Sinndeutung der deutschen Revolution* (Oldenburg, 1933), 10; Carl Dyrssen, *Die Botschaft des Ostens* (Breslau, 1933), 132; Weigand von Miltenberg (pseud. for Herbert Blank), *Adolf Hitler Wilhelm III* (Berlin, 1931), 93; Ernst Niekisch, *Hitler—ein deutsches Verhängnis* (Berlin, 1932), 8f.; "Girondist Hitler—Betrachtungen zum Nürnberger Parteitag," *Die deutsche Revolution*, XI. (September 16, 1934); Rolf Boelcke, "Die Spaltung der Nationalsozialisten," *Die Tat*, XXII (1930-1931), 357ff.; Hans Zehrer, "Rechts oder Links?" *Die Tat*, XXIII (1931-1932), 550.

[33] Cf. Niekisch, *Hitler*.

[34] Jung, *Sinndeutung*, passim; Strasser, *Aufbau des deutschen Sozialismus*, passim; Hans Thomas (pseud. for Hans Zehrer), "Der Weg der deutschen Revolution," *Die Tat*, XXV (1933-1934), 121ff.; slogan in *Die deutsche Revolution*, XI (September 16, 1934).

[35] Rauschning, *Revolution of Nihilism*, 113.

CHAPTER II

THE "GOD THAT FAILED"

WHAT follows is the history no longer of a movement but of individuals. As a political movement neo-conservatism had failed the German people. The neo-Burckhardtians had themselves become simplifiers. The neo-Nietzscheans ultimately all made a pact with the devil in search of a spontaneous life experience. They played with nihilism, one might say. However, there was no sevenfold loneliness, but first a pompous fanfare and then a long night.

The long night began on January 30, 1933 with Hitler's seizure of power, and it did not spare those many neo-conservatives who, in one way or another, had helped to bring it about. Once again the often-quoted words of Schiller applied: "The Moor has done his duty; the Moor can now go."[1] As the "national revolution" became the "National Socialist revolution," and as the Party gained control over the state and established itself in power, the intellectuals could be disposed of. For a party which was aiming at totalitarian rule they now constituted a threat. And in a totalitarian society there is no room for "deviations." Therefore, no one sang requiems for the "sulking clubs."[2]

But even in a totalitarian society, as we know now, there is a domain of freedom. Though it has no place for openly oppositional groups, it creates, in spite of itself, a realm for the individual sufferer. It must allow for the spiritual freedom of the one who has lost all but himself and who is beyond despair. Alongside the standard pattern of mass participation and conformance there develops what has been called an "inner emigration." This freedom created by totalitarian tyranny is as extreme as the oppression. It is ultimately transcendental; and it is the one force from

[1] Friedrich Schiller, *Verschwörung des Fiesco zu Genua* (1783), Act 3, Scene 4.

[2] Alfred Rosenberg, *Gestaltung der Idee* (7th edn., Munich, 1938), 17.

within a totalitarian society which can overcome it. It was the force which strengthened the German Resistance Movement against Hitler.

Between these two alternatives of conforming and non-conforming the neo-conservatives, one might say, were once more at the crossroads. But the situation was completely different from the early twenties. Now the decision they faced was of no immediate political nature. They had lost their political game. Now, for those who did not go into the "outer emigration," the decision was one of the individual conscience: whether to submit or to suffer. In a situation where so much was lost, where all of Germany was lost, partly due to their own doing, they had this other chance left, which was to suffer. In this direction, if in any, lay the path of rehabilitation for the neo-conservatives and their ideas.

A surface examination of the neo-conservatives' reactions to National Socialism does not show any essential change after January 30th. Their reactions varied widely. The record shows that while some few went abroad, others made their peace with the new regime in a more or less voluntary fashion, and still others chose the way of defiance. But it must be kept in mind that as there was less and less room for open opposition after the establishment of the dictatorship, society registered opposition all the more subtly. A given political position which meant one thing before the Nazis came to power could mean something quite different afterward. Indeed, whereas in the last years before 1933 any not-fully-disapproving attitude toward National Socialism tended to work in its favor, after January 1933 any not-fully-approving attitude tended to be considered hostile.

Considering this changed nomenclature of acceptance and rejection, the record of the neo-conservatives is quite remarkable. There were only a handful who went into exile, among them Otto Strasser and Treviranus. Otto Strasser, now more definitely the Trotsky of National Socialism, fled to Prague in the spring of 1933 and from there conducted his vigorous but hopeless campaign against National Socialism.[3] But it is interesting that after his emigration Otto Strasser, for whatever reasons, took pains to emphasize his conservative, anti-dictatorial, anti-totalitarian position. Treviranus was directly threatened by the Nazis on June 30, 1934 and managed to escape the Gestapo at the last minute.

Those who cooperated with the Nazis were, considering the pressures, surprisingly few in number. Surely, there was no future for any dissenting club or magazine—they were all earmarked for coordination (*Gleichschaltung*). The Herrenklub soon lost its identity by being put under the protectorate of Himmler. Its members went in all directions: Papen slid into utter moral and political bankruptcy; Edgar J. Jung, his secretary, geared himself for the role of a hero; Gleichen retired from the political scene. The *Deutsches Volkstum* found it necessary to emphasize in April 1933 that ever since the days of Brüning it had favored participation of the Nazis in government and that, indeed, it had "wanted the national revolution."[4] Stapel, moreover, hung onto his position until it had been made untenable by a series of attacks against him by the S.S.[5] A more pathetic victim of his own confusions was Othmar Spann, the theoretician of the corporative state. Scorning the corporative state which was being built in front of his

[3] His publication was *Die deutsche Revolution*, which at first carried the subtitle "Organ of the Black Front," and after June 1937 "European Publications of the Third Front." By publicizing expressions of opposition within Germany, like the ones by *Der Widerstand* and the *Deutsche Rundschau*, Otto Strasser did not always help the cause of those who stayed behind.

[4] *Deutsches Volkstum*, xxxv (1933), 311.

[5] In 1935 *Das Schwarze Korps*, the mouthpiece of the S.S., launched a number of caustic attacks against Stapel: "Herr Stapel entrüstet sich," "Hinter der freundlichen Maske," "Schluss mit der Frauenbewegung," "Ein letztes Wort, Herr Stapel," *Das Schwarze Korps*, I (April 24, July 10, July 24, August 7, 1935). In 1938 Stapel finally resigned. Later, in 1939, the name of the magazine was changed to *Monatsschrift für das deutsche Geistesleben*.

own eyes in Schuschnigg's Austria, he continued to court the Nazis in both Vienna and Berlin trying to sell his ware, and, furthermore, established close relations with Otto Strasser in Prague. When the German troops entered Vienna in March 1938 he gathered his family around him and opened a bottle of champagne to honor "the most beautiful day" of his life.[6] But the same day saw him also off to jail.

The *Nahe Osten* gave up the spirit before it actually suspended publication in 1936, in a sorry statement signed by Hans Schwarz and his coeditors: "The undersigned withdraw . . . their names from the cover of the *Nahe Osten*. They want thereby to express that the *Nahe Osten* is one with the great stream of the German revolution and has no intention of maintaining itself as an isolated circle at the fringes of German life. . . ."[7] Unlike the *Nahe Osten* the *Tat* voiced its determination to stay independent. "This independence has not been easy up to now, it has not become easier today, and it probably will be still more difficult in the future."[8] The way of the *Tat* Circle led both into forthright opposition and into collaboration. Zehrer had to abandon the direction of the *Tägliche Rundschau* in May 1933, and in August of the same year a "thorough reorganization" of the *Tat* Circle caused his resignation from the magazine. While Zehrer refused to come to terms with the Nazi Party—it is claimed that he rejected a Party membership book dated three years back[9]—Wirsing and Fried, hitherto unconnected with the Party, succumbed to it and climbed high in the Nazi intelligentsia. The name of the *Tat* magazine was finally changed in April 1939 to *Das Zwanzigste Jahrhundert*.

By contrast there were those who stood out firmly against Nazism in power, among them some of the most prominent neo-conservatives; besides Hans Zehrer, there were

[6] Von Salomon, *Der Fragebogen*, 214.

[7] "An unsere Leser," *Der Nahe Osten*, VI (1933), 298.

[8] Hans Zehrer, "25 Jahre Tat," *Die Tat*, XXV (1933-1934), 85.

[9] Heinrich Hauser, *Time Was; Death of a Junker* (New York, 1942), 229.

Oswald Spengler, Rudolf Pechel, Edgar J. Jung, and finally even Ernst Jünger. If they had lost one battle, they now proved that it was not courage which they lacked. Their record under the Nazi domination in some cases went beyond a mere "inner emigration" and led to outright defiance. It was largely their doing which forced the Nazis to define their own position. They warned and criticized. And when the counter-attack came against them on June 30, 1934 and, thereafter, in the form of murder, concentration camp, and abuse, these neo-conservatives regained one thing besides their integrity: a clearer view of where they stood. They thereby worked their way back again to the original premises of conservatism.

Spengler was the first to lead the attack, with his work *The Hour of Decision,* his last political book.[10] Based on a lecture given in Hamburg in 1929 under the title "Germany in Danger," it had been enlarged into book form in the winter of 1932-1933, and by January 30, 1933 a considerable portion of it was already printed. Offhand, there was nothing startlingly new about the book; none of the Spengleriana were missing: long-range predictions of a meeting between two "world revolutions"—white and colored— were coupled with sharp *aperçus* against democracy and Bolshevism. Even Spengler's new attacks against the Nazis did not outdo his earlier ones. He called them "everlasting 'Youths' . . . fired by uniforms and badges." And he ridiculed the "overcoming of individualism" by the "intoxication of mass-meeting oratory."[11] Only the path of a tough Bismarckian *Realpolitik,* Spengler kept insisting, would help Germany to tackle its "great problems" and to prove itself a leader of the white peoples and master the "colored menace."[12] In another passage, while discussing the polarization of political opinion into a radical Right and a

[10] Oswald Spengler, *The Hour of Decision* (New York, 1934); for a detailed discussion of the origins of the book cf. p. xv and Hughes, *Spengler,* 127f.

[11] Spengler, *The Hour of Decision,* 13.

[12] *Ibid.,* 202.

radical Left, he squarely rejected totalitarianism as an "infantile disease" of all revolutions. "One party is as impossible in a State as is one State in a stateless world."[13] Against such statements we have to hold in the line of Spengleriana the prediction that "armies, and not parties, are the future form of power."[14] If Spengler was pleading the case of diversity, would a balance of armies constitute the most creative diversity?

Spengler's attack against the Nazis would not have been dynamite had it not been for the changed situation. It is to Spengler's credit that he nevertheless published the book,[15] with a changed title—"to avoid misunderstandings"—a special Introduction, but nothing altered. In the Introduction Spengler defended his right of criticism. "No one," he claimed, had looked forward to the "national revolution" with "greater longing" than he, but "this was no victory, for opponents were lacking."[16] Germany, Spengler reemphasized, was still in danger. He went on record as opposed to the dictatorship of the masses whether it came from the Left or from the Right. In the fall of 1933 when 150,000 copies of the book were in print, it was these political passages rather than the tiring Spengleriana which were noticed by the public.

Just a fortnight before the appearance of the controversial book, in August 1933, Spengler had his one and only interview with Hitler.[17] Arranged by the Wagner family at the occasion of the Bayreuth Festivals, it turned into a monologue on the part of Hitler lasting an hour and a half. Like the earlier Hitler-Moeller meeting, this one turned out a failure. Surely the drummer turned chancel-

---

[13] *Ibid.*, 183.

[14] *Ibid.*, 202.

[15] As far as it had been in manuscript form as of the time of the revolution.

[16] *Ibid.*, IX, XI.

[17] For the information on this interview I am indebted to Dr. Georg Franz, Munich (letter of March 25, 1952) and to Oswald Spengler's niece and literary executor Dr. Hildegard Kornhardt, Munich (letter of August 29, 1954).

lor did not need Spengler. When later Spengler sent a copy of his book to Hitler, the mere receipt was acknowledged by the Chancellery.

The open break between the Nazis and Spengler was precipitated by Goebbels, angered by the fact that *The Hour of Decision* had escaped the attention of his ministry. Though another edition was allowed to appear in 1934, Nazi apologists, official and self-appointed, lost no time in accepting the challenge.[18] Spengler's admitted one-time reputation as "the strongest Rightist thinker in Germany"[19] had to be undone. He was now presented as a magician of decline, charlatan, Nietzsche plagiarizer, sadist, and decadent. Even though it was mainly hurt pride[20] which propelled these counter-attacks, they helped to draw the line somewhat more clearly between the conservative Spengler and the Nazi mass movement. Johann von Leers, who was one of the leading spirits in the Hitler Youth, stressed that Spengler and the Nazis had in common only the negative opposition to the Weimar regime. Otherwise Spengler was attacked for his "pseudo-Marxist" determinism,[21] his aristocratic bearing, and his denial of race. Von Leers summed up *The Hour of Decision* as "the first comprehensive attack against the National Socialist

[18] Arthur Zweiniger, *Spengler im Dritten Reich. Eine Antwort auf Oswald Spenglers "Jahre der Entscheidung"* (Oldenburg, 1933); Johann von Leers, *Spenglers weltpolitisches System und der Nationalsozialismus* (Berlin, 1934); E. Günther Gründel, *Jahre der Überwindung* (Berlin, 1934). It is interesting that in its issue of October 1, 1933 the Hitler Youth mouthpiece *Wille und Macht* carried a full-page photograph of a bust of Spengler accompanied by excerpts from *The Hour of Decision*. Also, it promised its readers an extensive discussion of the book in the following issue. The latter, however, made no mention of Spengler. On May 15, 1934, finally, *Wille und Macht* came out with a full-fledged attack upon Spengler; Kif, "Deutsche Jugend und Oswald Spengler," *Wille und Macht*, II (May 15, 1934), 25ff.

[19] Gründel, *Jahre der Überwindung*, 25.

[20] Zweiniger, *Spengler im Dritten Reich*, 22. Spengler had "failed . . . to present National Socialism as the fulfillment of his ideals."

[21] Von Leers, *Spenglers weltpolitisches System*, 12.

Weltanschauung" and pointed it out as "the master plan of counter-revolution."[21]

Whereas Spengler even in this last political move[23] protected himself with the immunity of the philosopher and never quite came down to earth, Edgar J. Jung, far less known all over Germany than Spengler, squarely challenged the Nazis. His attack against them was of considerable political consequence. When Papen had become chancellor in May 1932, Jung, upon the recommendation of Pechel, had moved to Berlin to serve as Papen's secretary. Warned about Papen's unreliability he had, nevertheless, accepted the position, his prime objective being the prevention of a National Socialist seizure of power. And he stayed on even after Papen had engineered himself into the position of vice-chancellor under Adolf Hitler.

In the days immediately following the revolution there was much to be said in favor of the many non-Nazi civil servants who remained in office keeping up their hopes to "harness" the revolution or to "prevent the worst." As yet National Socialism was many things: one party with one *Führer* but with a variety of factions. It had its Storm Troopers (S.A.) and its Black Shirts (S.S.) with their respective aims and interests. It had its conservative wing in people like Hermann Rauschning, the president of the Danzig Senate; its socialist wing in people like Gregor Strasser, who was no more in Hitler's best graces. The bulk of the Party constituted a broad indefinite middle ground. Under these circumstances it seemed but a matter of good political sense to encourage whatever one considered the "good" elements in the Party. But apparently such considerations gave way in Jung more and more to an under-

---

[22] *Ibid.,* 6f.

[23] A second volume of *The Hour of Decision,* which had been promised, was never written. After his last encounter with the Nazis Spengler sought refuge in prehistorical studies (cf. Hughes, *Spengler,* 133ff.). Though Spengler saw Gregor Strasser toward the end of 1933 and in the beginning of 1934, he was not implicated in the affairs of June 30, 1934. Spengler died on May 8, 1936.

standing of the basic gulf between National Socialism and conservatism. Precisely the Party's lack of direction was suspect to Jung. In a book which appeared after January 1933 and in which he voiced publicly the claims of those outside the Nazi Party who had contributed toward the German revolution,[24] he left none of his readers in doubt concerning his Girondist position toward the Party. Moreover, according to Pechel, Jung's one objective became the overthrow of the government.[25] He was in contact with Generals von Schleicher and von Bredow, with Brüning and Treviranus, with socialist and Christian union leaders, with industrialists and members of the German intelligentsia. We are even told that he had concrete ideas concerning the method of a coup as well as the composition of a future government.

Finally, with the famous Marburg address which Jung had drafted for Papen and which the latter agreed to deliver to the students of the University on June 17, 1934, Jung hoped to take his case to the public at large. It was a dramatic event, a last-minute attempt to force the revolutionary wave into conservative waters. No such clear and sober presentation of conservative principles had been given to the German people in the years before 1933. While accounting for the alliance between the conservatives and the Nazis which had led to the revolution Papen redefined conservatism as a philosophy of freedom. There was no longer any trace of the ambiguities of Moeller's style when Papen attacked the "rule of the catchword."

". . . There are . . . people who speak no single sentence without misusing the word "liberalistic." They are of the opinion that genuine humanitarianism (*Humanität*) is liberalistic whereas in reality it is a fruit of the classic and Christian tradition. They call freedom a liberal concept, whereas in reality it is an old Germanic tradition. They

[24] Edgar J. Jung, *Sinndeutung der deutschen Revolution* (Oldenburg, 1933).
[25] Rudolf Pechel, *Deutscher Widerstand* (Zurich, 1947), 76f.

attack equality before the judge, denouncing it as liberal degeneration, whereas in reality it is the basis for every just verdict.

"Those people suppress that very fundament of state which at all times, not only in liberal ones, has been called justice. Their attacks are directed against the security and freedom of the private sphere of life. . . ."[26]

The threat to freedom obviously came now from the Right. All the more vital was it for Papen to stress the difference between due, historically grown authority—at one point he even talked about the "divine order"[27]—and the totalitarian claims of the Party which he castigated as "Byzantinism."[28] The rule of one party, he added, appeared to him as "a transition stage."[29] Moreover, the totalitarian state endangered the prerogatives of religion. The faith of the new Reich was to be the Christian one and not a "half-religious materialism"[30] in the form of nationalism. In the midst of the revolutionary momentum Papen pleaded for reason. The conservatives had all along stressed life as against reason, but now it was obvious that reason was threatened. The danger now was the "confusion between vitality and brutality"[31] and, indeed, the fight against the intellect itself. In this connection he lashed out against Goebbels' methods of mass manipulation. The German people was too mature to be subjected to continual propaganda. Germany's mission in Europe, so Papen concluded, was too high a responsibility to be allowed to degenerate into "perpetual dynamism."[32] No "second [revolutionary] wave," about which everyone talked in the June days of 1934, could bring salvation, but only a return to the traditions of the past. "History waits for us, but only if we prove worthy of it."[33]

[26] "Rede des Vizekanzlers von Papen vor dem Universitätsbund, Marburg am 17 Juni 1934," *Trial of the Major War Criminals before the International Military Tribunal* (Nuremberg, 1949), XL, 555.
[27] *Ibid.*, 549.   [28] *Ibid.*, 555.   [29] *Ibid.*, 550.
[30] *Ibid.*, 552.   [31] *Ibid.*, 554.   [32] *Ibid.*, 556.
[33] *Ibid.*, 558.

After the mishandling of the Spengler affair, Goebbels now lost no time in talking counter-measures. The *Frankfurter Zeitung* of the same afternoon which brought excerpts from the speech was immediately confiscated. Except for an angry rejoinder which the next day's *Völkischer Beobachter* published, the speech remained suppressed. Only a few copies were printed by the *Germania* press and sent to the diplomatic corps, foreign correspondents, and a number of friends throughout Germany. However, the Marburg address had repercussions which exceeded Goebbels' competence as propaganda minister. Even though Papen prevented an open cabinet crisis, there remained, judging only from the widespread response which the speech found in Germany, the question of a conservative *fronde*. Along with the opposition from the restless S.A. and from the "Left" as represented by Gregor Strasser, it led directly into the events of June 30, 1934. As was to be expected, the *Herrenreiter*—Papen—himself, though he was put ignominiously under house arrest for four days, survived the crisis. But Jung, arrested by the Gestapo on June 25, was shot by the S.S. on the 30th; von Bose, Papen's press seceretary, was shot on the same day. Rudolf Pechel's untiring efforts to obtain information about his friend Jung were met by Gürtner, now German minister of justice, with a hint that it was best for Pechel himself to leave Berlin because the "action" was aimed at the "whole group."[34]

The Marburg address, then, did have political repercussions. Surely, if Jung had expected it to be a signal for resistance, he had greatly misjudged the domestic situation and, in particular, the power of the conservatives, who were completely disarmed. While June 30, 1934 was for the Nazis the "revolution after power,"[35] it meant for Jung and his political friends a defeat all over again. Something was accomplished, however, even if it was only a

[34] Pechel, *Deutscher Widerstand*, 283.
[35] Alan Bullock, *Hitler, A Study in Tyranny* (London, 1952), 229ff.

matter of bookkeeping. From June 30, 1934 the Party was definitely no longer the party toward which all the more or less confused conservatives could look. Indeed, there was no more confusion. The triumph of Hitler's elite army, the S.S., which was the final outcome of the complex pattern of June 30, 1934, shifted the basis of National Socialism from a political divide and rule and from an ideological eclecticism to a total reliance on its own power. The S.S. robots had no more room for ideas, and least of all for those with which in the past National Socialism had been connected. Under the prodding of the S.S., then, the Party went through a process of "debunking of ideas" (*Ideendämmerung*).[36]

Already in December 1933 Alfred Rosenberg, Nazi "philosopher," had come out in the *Völkischer Beobachter* against the various "untrusting and literary clubs" which claimed to be the fathers of National Socialism and even against the so far sacrosanct Moeller.[37] What bitter irony that the neo-conservatives who in the past had so glibly labeled their enemies as "eggheads" (*Literaten*),[38] were now the "eggheads" themselves. One of the favorite themes of *Das Schwarze Korps*, the new S.S. organ launched in 1935, was the attack against the "intellectuals."[39] Also from

[36] Karl O. Paetel, "Die S.S. Ein Beitrag zur Soziologie des National-sozialismus," *Vierteljahrshefte für Zeitgeschichte*, II (1954), 8. Paetel confirms that Heinrich Himmler "saw to it that neither Oswald Spengler nor Moeller van den Bruck nor Othmar Spann ever became ideologically important for the work of the Party."

[37] Alfred Rosenberg, "Gegen Tarnung und Verfälschung," *Völkischer Beobachter*, December 8, 1933, reprinted in Rosenberg, *Gestaltung der Idee*, 15ff.

[38] Cf. Thomas Mann's attack against his brother Heinrich as the "*Zivilisationsliterat*"; Thomas Mann, *Betrachtungen*, 14ff. Moeller, also focusing on Heinrich Mann, turned against the "*Revolutionsliteraten*" of 1918; Moeller, *Das dritte Reich*, 22. Spengler juxtaposed the "unbending reality of history" and mere "literature"; Spengler, *Preussentum*, 4.

[39] Cf. the articles against Stapel, supra, 204. Focusing on the *Tat*: "Literarisches Nachtwächtertum," *Das Schwarze Korps*, I (August 7, 1935). Focusing on Spann, "the pope of intellectualism" (Note: after

the S.S. came the first comprehensive attack against Moeller, by one of its members, Wilhelm Seddin. It appeared in the Hitler Youth periodical *Wille und Macht*.[40] "We have respected the author Moeller van den Bruck. . . . When, however, one starts constructing an ideology from his works and tying it up with National Socialism, we must turn our backs on Moeller and his epigones."[41] In short, Moeller also was an "egghead" and the connection between him and National Socialism was based on "artificial manipulations" of his "advertising manager" Hans Schwarz.[42] A point-by-point refutation of Moeller which carried the imprimatur of the Party came to the bold conclusion that "conservatism and nationalism in reality have different values." Moeller, indeed, was not the prophet of the Third Reich. He was the "last conservative."[43] The devil was kinder to Moeller than he deserved. One might say that at last Moeller was released from his original pact with the devil.

Directly or indirectly the story of Spengler and Jung, and of those who survived June 30, 1934 standing their ground, ties in with the Resistance against Hitler. Surely Jung's death served as an inspiration for the men of July 20, 1944. Moreover, in a very concrete sense the seeds were sown, however tentatively, for a broader opposition in later times.

An impressive stand was taken by Rudolf Pechel, who managed to utilize the *Deutsche Rundschau* as a moral and intellectual center for oppositional groups. A carefully

---

the *Anschluss*): "Einer wird herausgegriffen," *Das Schwarze Korps*, IV (December 8, 15, 22, 1938).

[40] Wilhelm Seddin, "Nachwort zu Moeller van den Bruck," *Wille und Macht*, III (December 1, 1935), 1ff. Cf. also Wilhelm Seddin, *Preussentum gegen Sozialismus* (Berlin, 1935), which was directed against all the non-party-line "intellectuals." Based on Seddin's attack: "Rechenschaft über Russland. Moeller van den Bruck," *Bücherkunde*, II (1935), 221f.

[41] Seddin, "Nachwort," *Wille und Macht*, III (December 1, 1935), 1.
[42] *Ibid.*, 1.
[43] Helmut Rödel, *Moeller van den Bruck* (Berlin, 1939), 162, 164.

developed camouflage allowed him to strike at the Nazi tyranny while featuring articles on tyrants of past times and remote parts of the world, on the late Roman emperors as well as on Genghis Khan and Francisco Solano López of Paraguay. He kept up contacts with some of the leading Germans in exile—Brüning and Rauschning—and among the inner circle of the conspirators he kept alive the ideas of freedom and justice and humanitarianism.[44] He was finally arrested in April 1942.

But how are we to assess the resistance which many leaders of the Youth Movement put up against being absorbed by the Hitler Youth,[45] or the stand which some of the more radical conservatives took against National Socialism? In fact, it is surprising to find muddleheads like August Winnig[46] and the National Bolshevist Ernst Niekisch go the way of opposition. The latter, in particular, had a valiant record during the twelve years of Nazi domination. He thought Hitler too "capitalistic," too pro-Western, too little Prussian. After January 1933 Niekisch, whose magazines were among the first to be suppressed by Goebbels, joined up with the conservative elements of the opposition against Hitler,[47] until arrested in 1937, prosecuted for high treason, and sentenced to life imprisonment. Others of similar persuasion—like Friedrich Hielscher[48] and Joseph (Beppo) Römer of the Oberland—played no less courageous parts, the latter paying with his life.[49]

[44] Pechel, *Deutscher Widerstand*, 277ff.

[45] For the many victims from oppression which the Youth Movement claimed and for its ties to the German Resistance see Günther Weisenborn, ed., *Der lautlose Aufstand* (2nd edn., Hamburg, 1954), 92ff.

[46] Cf. August Winnig, *Aus Zwanzig Jahren* (2nd edn., Hamburg, 1949).

[47] Fabian von Schlabrendorff, *They Almost Killed Hitler* (New York, 1947), 11.

[48] Cf. Winnig, *Aus Zwanzig Jahren*, 112, 153f., 175ff.; Friedrich Hielscher, *Fünfzig Jahre unter Deutschen* (Hamburg, 1954).

[49] Cf. Pechel, *Deutscher Widerstand*, 81ff.; Eberhard Zeller, *Geist der Freiheit. Der Zwanzigste Juli* (Munich, 1954), 117.

They all had for so long been in opposition and become so thoroughly alienated from "bourgeois" society that now not even revolution, and surely not Hitler's so-called "legal" revolution, would bring them into line. They were inveterate desperados and underground men. They were crude fellows but sincere ones, with better instincts than minds. They had, after all, a sense of honor, even though it was feudal. It steered them into a good fight and endowed them with a capacity for what Dostoevsky once called "exalted suffering."

Throughout the Nazi time Ernst Jünger was only indirectly connected with the Resistance. He kept aloof from political activities. His name appears somewhere in the Gestapo records of 1937 in connection with the activities of Niekisch,[50] but except for some official visits to his home, no action was taken against him. The years after 1933, in contrast to the earlier ones, were Jünger's "quiet" years: years of contemplation and of observation of his botanical specimens.[51] His joining up with the army in August 1939 was no evidence to the contrary. In Hitler's Germany, service with the army was for many a refuge from Party interference, even after Hitler had assumed personal command of the army in 1938. But what a transformation in Jünger! Whereas in 1914 he had volunteered to seek danger, he now sought refuge. He became for most of his army career court philosopher of the Paris Command under the military governor, General Karl Heinrich von Stülpnagel, and Rommel's chief of staff, General Hans Speidel, who were both deeply involved in the military resistance against Hitler. Jünger noted in his Paris diary that they lived "in the belly of Leviathan."[52] And

[50] Weisenborn, *Der lautlose Aufstand*, 197.

[51] "I have chosen for myself an elevated position from which I can observe how these creatures [the masses] devour each other," he is quoted as having said to Ernst von Salomon in 1937. And he continued imagining himself retired to a star—"to Mars or Venus; not to Saturn, which has rings around it; besides Spengler is sitting there already"; von Salomon, *Der Fragebogen*, 291.

[52] Ernst Jünger, *Strahlungen* (2nd edn., Tübingen, 1949), 64.

while Jünger's superiors prepared for the coup, he, who objected to political assassination,[53] was allowed to devote himself to his esoteric interests and tastes and to speculate about the sufferings of mankind.

Jünger's intellectual development during the years of Nazi rule had a distinct relevance to the Resistance nevertheless. The very fact that Jünger in 1939 came out with an anti-Hitler allegory[54] is important; it is a most involved allegory but, at the same time, obvious in its meaning. It is the story of the rise to power of a barbarous gang—the Mauretanians—under their chief ranger, and of the nature of tyranny. But Jünger's new "landscape" was no longer Mauretania—his "Mauretanian days" he now recognized as an error—but rather his beloved Marina with its Marble Cliffs. In this land he and his brother Otho[55] had lived in a seclusion given to their plants and books until attacked by the Mauretanians. After pitched battle between the forces of light and dark Marina was destroyed.

Everything was different for Jünger. Mauretania turned out to be an inferno; the Mauretanian war was no longer an exuberant "experience." When the second World War was nearing its end Jünger wrote, "In the previous war we told one another . . . about those wounded and killed in battle, in this one about those deported and murdered."[56] Therefore his admission: "I now loathe the uniforms, epaulettes, medals, the wine and the weapons whose splendor I so loved." At long last Jünger saw that "the old chivalry is dead."[57] His type was no longer the "soldier" or the "worker." Amidst all the suffering caused by his

[53] I am convinced . . . that by political assassination little is changed and above all nothing is helped"; *ibid.*, 540.
[54] Ernst Jünger, *Auf den Marmor-Klippen* (Hamburg, 1939). The book was temporarily suppressed in the spring of 1940, but not until after 35,000 copies had been printed. A new edition in 1941 brought the number of copies printed up to 62,000, many of which were especially distributed by the Paris Command to the soldiers.
[55] The poet Friedrich Georg Jünger.
[56] Jünger, *Strahlungen*, 336.
[57] *Ibid.*, 250.

warlord, Jünger's quest for heroism, which constitutes the continuity in his thought, took him now to the world of the civilian, the individual.[58] Jünger's new "type"—he called it in a later work the "woodsman"[59]—was the human being who kept his dignity in the face of oppression and destruction, the suffering, tragic hero. At last Jünger penetrated into the realm of the human and of ethics; at last he found out that "holier yet than life ought to be for us the dignity of man."[60]

The literary result of his new war experience was, besides his diaries, a booklet on which he had worked throughout his Paris time, *The Peace*,[61] which he described as the "turning point" in his life and a "voluntary linking up" with the "hierarchy of values."[62] It circulated in typescript among the German troops in the West in 1943. On July 16, 1944 General Speidel in good spirits assured Ernst Jünger that his pamphlet on peace was to appear in print soon. . . . [63]

The dilemma of conservatism in twentieth century Germany has turned out to be the drama of conservatism which had to take its course. The search for new ties which started with a harmless Youth Movement, in fact helped conjure up a stifling and monstrous monolithic society. But as much as the way of conservatism led toward National Socialism, it eventually led away from it. Conservatism in Germany finally emerged again out of the long night. Moeller, Spengler, and Ernst Jünger and their imitators will always remain controversial figures. Like those many intellectuals of the Left whose "God" failed, they are not on the side of the angels. Thrown into the turmoil of the twentieth century they all in one way or another expressed

[58] "I must never forget that I am surrounded by suffering people. That is far more important than all glory and fame and than the empty cheers of youth . . ."; *ibid.*, 144.

[59] Ernst Jünger, *Der Waldgang* (Frankfurt a.M., 1951).

[60] *Ibid.*, 68.

[61] Ernst Jünger, *The Peace* (Hinsdale, Ill., 1948).

[62] Jünger, *Strahlungen*, 377.

[63] *Ibid.*, 539.

the disillusionment with the values of the "bourgeois" civilization and its social order. And like so many other challenging minds of our century they gave way to an extremism which turned out to be an extremism of destruction. But what came after extremism, after destruction, is also historical reality. Through the bitter experience of the encounter with National Socialism the conservatives—the exceptions notwithstanding—became dedicated again to the cause of freedom and human decency, and conservatism became an ideological weapon against totalitarian tyranny. In the last analysis Jung died for a good cause. His ideas carried directly over to Count Helmuth von Moltke and his Kreisau Circle, one of the centers of the Resistance against Hitler. In the last analysis also the same Ernst Jünger who once had designed the "soldier-worker," the prototype of the S.S. man, came to devise the type of the "woodsman" who was none other than the partisan. Through trial and error the neo-conservatives in Germany were instrumental in establishing at least the basic differences between conservatism and National Socialism. They have after all saved conservatism from discredit. To each of those neo-conservatives who resisted National Socialism applies what Yeats wrote in tribute to the Irish rebels of 1916:

> He, too, has been changed in his turn
> Transformed utterly:
> A terrible beauty is born.

CONCLUSION

Yes, said I, what we are doing is probably foolish,
but it is necessary nevertheless. It is not good if
mankind overemphasizes reason and attempts to
solve things by means of reason which are not in
its domain. . . . The image of man, which was once
a high ideal, is about to become a cliché. *We fools*
shall perhaps ennoble it again.—HERMANN HESSE,
Der Steppenwolf *(Zurich, n.d.), 266.*

FROM T. S. Eliot to the Nazi poet Hanns Johst ("when-
ever I hear the word culture I cock my pistol") almost all
Western intellectuals of the twentieth century have had
in common the awareness of the crisis of our civilization.
They all were citizens of what Lewis Mumford called the
"night-time world"[1] of the twentieth century, with its catastrophes, be they war, revolution, inflation, or spiritual
crisis. They were in one form or another rebels against a
century which had failed them, against rationalism, against
the "bourgeois" order, against Victorianism, against the
modern city, against capitalism. Those in the nineteenth
century whose thought had been "out of season"—Dostoevsky, Marx, Burckhardt, Nietzsche, Kierkegaard—now moved
into their own and became the acknowledged fathers of the
rebellion. While with some, like Hofmannsthal, Eliot, and
Arnold Toynbee, it meant a return to a Christian conservatism, with others, like Johst, it appeared as the strong-armed
ethos of the storm trooper. It made some—namely, the
Communists—find a solution in the thick web of Marxian
dogmatism, and others—the T. E. Lawrences and Saint-
Exupérys—it sent into mere adventure or into the Resistance of the second World War. It was expressed equally
in the theological seriousness of a Reinhold Niebuhr and
a Tillich and in the affectations of the sidewalk-café crowd

[1] Lewis Mumford, "Mirror of a Violent Half Century," *New York
Times Book Review,* January 16, 1950.

on the left bank of the Seine. To use a distinction of Camus, it claimed its "rebels," or dissenters, like Camus himself, aiming at the liberation of man, as well as its "revolutionaries"—Stalin, Hitler—seeking political action and a new enslavement of man. In brief, it had its gentlemen and its brutes, its aristocrats and proletarians, its moderates and extremists, it "adorers" and "despisers." It was a symptom as much of anxiety and disintegration as of recovery.

Our conservatives were part of the rebellion against the past century. You will recognize among the neo-conservatives too representatives of each of these types. Between the groups of the "elders" and the "radicals" they also had their gentlemen and brutes, aristocrats and proletarians, moderates and extremists, "adorers" and "despisers." They were also a motley crowd and they constituted among themselves a microcosm, so to speak, of the whole rebellion with all its contrasts and incertitudes.

This study has been dealing with the conservative incertitudes, that is, with the dilemma of conservatism. In order to determine the full range of possibilities of a conservative policy in twentieth century Germany, it seemed reasonable to trace the neo-conservatives back to their nineteenth century antecedents. Surely, our conservatives were infinitely more history-conscious than the Nazi were. It is a fair assumption, therefore, that, unlike National Socialism, which was to a large extent a product of the immediate situation, the new conservatism had its historical roots in the early nineteenth century as well as in the later conservative opposition against the Second Reich.

On the other hand, there was the direct impact of the many crises starting with the first World War. In his *Doktor Faustus* Thomas Mann remarked that the defeated nations of 1918 saw more clearly than the victorious ones that 1914 meant the end of the "epoch of the middle class humanism."[2] While the Englishman was still protected by his

2 Mann, *Doktor Faustus*, 540.

traditional social order and while the Frenchman still had enough cause to persist in his faith in the rule of reason, the German—as also the Russian—saw obvious signs that the old world was crumbling. This is the reason for the intensity of the dilemma of the German conservatives and for their—paradoxical—tendency to seek revolutionary solutions.

Success or failure of the neo-conservative movement was primarily an intellectual matter and not a political one, and in those terms it ought to be measured. It could not at any time have been expected that a Stinnes dicatorship or a "New Front" or a "Third Front" would become a matter of reality. If the conservatives themselves thought so, they were foolish and they wasted their efforts dabbling in politics where they should have concentrated on clarifying their own position toward themselves and on propagating a true conservative spirit among their countrymen. In that case there would have been no need for a National Socialist "seizure of power."

The initial situation of the new conservatism starting with, say, 1914 was a complex but also a challenging one. While war, revolution, and inflation drew a sharp line under the past, they also exposed the inadequacies of the old German conservatism. The crises between 1914 and 1923, we might say, shook the conservatives into thinking along new lines.

The impact of the war upon conservative thought was, as we have seen, ambiguous. It brought vitality into conservatism. Rathenau and Moellendorff were the finest spokesmen for a German version of Tory democracy. Yet at the same time, and inevitably, the accent of the wartime conservatism was anti-Western. It seems a particular irony that Germany's new conservatism thus should have cut itself loose from England, a country whose conservative traditions served it well even in the twentieth century. After all, the "inner anglicization," against which even

Meinecke[3] had somewhat irresponsibly warned during the war, might have given direction to the German conservatives. The anti-French argument also kicked back when after the defeat the German conservatives, faced with the need of reconciling their views with a republican form of government, might well have learned a lesson or two from the Third Republic.

The decisive time in the history of twentieth century German conservatism turned out to be the years immediately following the revolution, decisive in terms of the conservatives' position toward the Republic and, more broadly, in terms of their own dilemma. Throughout our study the interrelatedness of these two issues has become increasingly evident. With the monarchy gone and ruled out as an issue even by the conservatives themselves, what was there left for the conservative other than either an acceptance of a republic or an open support of dictatorship? A republic is simply a government by law as opposed to a dictatorship, which is a government by force. And by these definitions a republic was the better bet for a conservative. In the twentieth century, republics have tended to be conservative while dictatorships have tended to be Jacobin. The choice, then, of our conservatives was between the new Republic and dictatorship, between free government and unfree government, and, ultimately, between conservatism and Jacobinism.

Our focus on the immediate years after the revolution has brought the neo-conservatives into a new perspective: not as villains, not as heroes, but instead faced by a challenge to which they did not measure up: to give a conservative foundation to the Republic. We have discovered that the Republic at first enjoyed the good will of sizable Rightist elements. And even though the "dreamland" psychology soon faded out, the June Club and the various journals such as the *Tat* and the *Deutsches Volkstum* remained for some time forums for a formulation of a con-

[3] Meinecke, *Die deutsche Erhebung*, 38.

servative policy within a republican framework. As long as the voice of the "elders" counted for something in these circles, the reforming zest of the neo-conservatives might have benefited the Republic. And it was only after the parting of the ways between the "elders" and the neo-conservative movement that the latter moved into the counter-revolutionary camp.

All this evidence suggests no plot on the part of a "Western" "bourgeois" Republic or a "semi-fascist" June Club. We cannot even speak of lost opportunities on the part of the Republican leadership, since its continuing Rightist support depended on a rejection of Versailles as well as on an aggressive socialization, neither of which would have been in the interest of sound statesmanship. The alienation of the neo-conservative movement from the Republic was mainly a symptom of a by then close to inevitable radicalization of the political temper in Germany; it was "outraged tradition." A note of the tragic was added by the fact that so many of the "elders"—Naumann, Troeltsch, Max Weber—died so soon and that Rathenau was killed. They might have given a "new faith" to the Republic. Instead the Republic became more and more the scapegoat for an unhappy generation which turned its eyes toward the promised "Third Reich."

Starting with the Youth Movement our conservatives had definitely achieved one thing. They had succeeded in overcoming the separation between the intellectual and politics, about which Hofmannsthal had talked. Surely, in the days of the Republic men like Moeller, Spengler, and Ernst Jünger represented an intelligentsia which had the ear of the people, and this in contrast to the Leftist intelligentsia, which was considered "Western" and "alien" by most. The alienation between the Republic and the neo-conservatives thus created a dangerous and paradoxical situation: a country with a republican government and with a predominantly anti-republican sentiment.

If such was the situation, the main function left to the neo-conservatives was to penetrate the Right with their thoughts. It was along these lines in particular that they failed. In spite of the example of Rathenau and Moellendorff they did not after all manage to outline a program on which they all could have agreed based on a German Tory democracy. This in itself would have been a constructive task. Naturally, the sectarian strife among the many groups and journals did not further this objective. Neither did the fact that German industry would hardly have supported a program of an even distantly socialistic nature, as had been shown already in 1919 in the experience of the "Solidarians" and as the Nazis found out later when they reinterpreted the "socialistic" points of their "program." However, the main cause of the failure lay in the neo-conservatives' abuse of their newly established oneness with public opinion. In spite of all the discussions in the halls of the Herrenklub about aristocracy, or in the more sociologically minded *Tat* about an "elite," despite the general condemnation of the plebeian nature of the Nazi Party among the neo-conservatives, there was among the latter an all too acute awareness of the need to win over the masses.[4] The style alone of the three heroes and saints of neo-conservatism gives them away: it was evasive to a point of being muddled, and designed to arouse emotion rather than to communicate ideas. All things considered, the positive message of a Rathenau and a Moellendorff had changed into a predominantly negative one. Political and social resentment and anti-intellectualism became the driving forces of the neo-conservatives. They lacked a sense of intellectual leadership and integrity. They were guilty of the crime which an unbending French rationalist, Julien Benda, has called the *trahison des clercs*.

We have started this study with a rigid separation between the worlds of conservatism and fascism. The material

[4] "We must try, we felt, to divide the masses. We must try to hold the masses in check through themselves. The masses could be tamed only by the masses. Political leadership could be won and kept only through the masses. The securing of the basis among the masses seemed to us to be the practical teaching of all political wisdom." Rauschning, *The Conservative Revolution*, 37.

collected in this book, however, has shown the conditions which made twentieth century conservatism and fascism converge. With the exodus of the "elders" the neo-conservative movement had lost much of its backbone and balance. Conservatism had lost its sense of "irony," for which Thomas Mann had pleaded during the first war. It had become pure dynamics, or, in Mann's terms, a "nihilistic Utopia." It therefore had to capitulate before the "fascinating potentialities of power."[5]

It is not in the province of the historian to indict or to absolve. Yet we can point out that in our story the elements of tragedy and guilt are mixed. The scene of tragedy was, above all, the immediate post-war period; the political and social conditions put on the German new conservatism the stamp of resentment and extremism from which it never recovered. Guilt, irresponsibility, *hybris* were rampant in the early thirties and most blatantly reflected in Zehrer's *Tat* and in the bloodthirsty writings of Ernst Jünger. These writers were thoroughly deceived in their assessment of the dynamism of the Nazi movement. Above all they failed to understand that nothing was to be gained from playing the role of what have been popularly called in Germany *Edelnazis* (respectable Nazis); they shied away from taking issue at a time when there was a need for decision. Finally, June 30, 1934 and July 20, 1944 were landmarks of redemption. The first of these two events was more than a bloody massacre, the second one more than senseless *fronde*. Edgar J. Jung and his friends and later the men of the Kreisau Circle have helped set the record straight again. Their thoughts, their upright rejection of the totalitarian state, and, in turn, the violent Nazi reaction against them have restated the case for conservatism as a force for freedom and for decency. They may not have solved the dilemma, but their example has demonstrated that, after all, conservatism, or in Hesse's terms, the business of "ennobling" the "image of man," is a task not for "fools" but for men.

[5] Rauschning, *Revolution of Nihilism*, 113.

POSTSCRIPT, 1968

No more than any study in intellectual history can this one be called definitive. It was first published more than a decade ago. Meanwhile, my thoughts on the subject have developed further, stimulated by the reviews of the book and by other more recent contributions to the literature on German conservatism of the twentieth century.[1] Yet I have decided to send out this 1968 edition without major revision, adding only this postscript, because I am persuaded that my book still holds its own, serving the purpose of defining and outlining the problems of Germany's new conservatism between the two World Wars.

The concept of the "conservative revolution," originally introduced in the scholarly literature of Armin Mohler, has found by now, to my regret, general acceptance among historians. As the reader may have noticed, I have never used the concept myself except with caution and, indeed, scepticism. It suggests a political self-consciousness, a voluntaristic side of the new conservatism, which in fact hardly existed. The new conservatism amounted to, above all, a broad current, an "experience" among German intellectuals, encompassing such diverse men[2] as Max Weber,

[1] Two outstanding general studies on the subject are Fritz Stern, *The Politics of Cultural Despair. A Study in the Rise of the Germanic Ideology* (Berkeley, 1961); and Kurt Sontheimer, *Antidemokratisches Denken in der Weimarer Republik. Die politischen Ideen des deutschen Nationalismus zwischen 1918 und 1933* (Munich, 1962). Among the monographs the following should be mentioned: Otto-Ernst Schüddekopf, *Linke Leute von rechts. Die nationalrevolutionären Minderheiten und der Kommunismus in der Weimarer Republik* (Stuttgart, 1960); Hans-Joachim Schwierskott, *Arthur Moeller van den Bruck und der revolutionäre Nationalismus in der Weimarer Republik* (Göttingen, 1962); and Hans-Peter Schwarz, *Der konservative Anarchist. Politik und Zeitkritik Ernst Jüngers* (Freiburg, 1962). See also in the periodical literature Kurt Sontheimer, "Thomas Mann als politischer Schriftsteller," *Vierteljahrshefte für Zeitgeschichte*, vi (1958), 1-44; Waldemar Besson, "Friedrich Meinecke und die Weimarer Republik," *ibid.*, vii (1959), 113-129; Kurt Sontheimer, "Der Tatkreis," *ibid.*, 229-260; and Walter Struve, "Hans Zehrer as a Neoconservative Theorist," *American Historical Review*, lxx (1965), 1035-1057.

[2] Cf. the critical remarks on this matter by various reviewers, such

POSTSCRIPT

Troeltsch, Meinecke, and Thomas Mann, as well as Moeller van den Bruck, Spengler, and Ernst Jünger. Writing about them, I have been guided by Meinecke's significant article about "three generations of German scholars' politics,"[3] describing the "atmosphere" of the generation which "since the nineties began to influence life in Germany." This was Meinecke's own generation, torn, and as Erich Heller put it, "disinherited."[4] Its style was "unharmonious." It left behind itself the "classic-romantic *Bildung*-ideal."

The generation which I mention here lacked the view of "wholeness," and it was more or less aware of this fact. Its new guiding stars were Burckhardt, the more clearly visible Nietzsche, and in a haze but nevertheless recognizable, Karl Marx. Its basic experience was one of malaise concerning the culture of the nineteenth century, the hothouse industrialization of Germany, and the impact of modern capitalism, as well as later on, of democracy, in Germany. It is important to stress that this basic experience was negative; it nevertheless had an intensity of feeling which overshadowed everything else. Impressed by the importance of this common experience, I may not have emphasized sufficiently the different responses which the crisis elicited from sober thinkers like Max Weber, Troeltsch, Meinecke, and Thomas Mann on the one hand, and from strange prophets like Moeller van den Bruck, Spengler, and Ernst Jünger on the other hand. I have taken more pains to stress the how and where of this parting of the ways and its consequences for the cause of the new conservatism.

Germany's new conservatism did not come to fruition; the "new middle ages" have come to naught. Partly for

as H. Stuart Hughes in *Commentary*, xxiv (November, 1957), 470-473; Minna Falk in *Journal of Central European Affairs*, xviii (July, 1958), 211f.; and Reginald H. Phelps in *Journal of Modern History*, xxiv (December, 1957), 402f.

[3] Friedrich Meinecke, "Drei Generationen deutscher Gelehrtenpolitik," *Historische Zeitschrift*, cxxv (1925), 248-283.

[4] Erich Heller, *The Disinherited Mind* (New York, 1959).

good reasons, I have been criticized for having given a too Platonic definition of nineteenth century conservatism and for having measured the German reality by an Anglo-Saxon Burkean ideal.[5] It had been my intention to work out an "ideal type" of European conservatism, such as that which served as a measure for men like Metternich, Gentz, Ranke, and Ernst Ludwig von Gerlach. The ideal conservative, fortunately, has never actually existed, either in England or in Germany. German conservatism in particular has been ailing since Bismarck. Constantin Frantz quite rightly observed that German conservatism had failed singularly over the German question. The few upright conservatives—such as Ernst Ludwig von Gerlach—had to give way to the Bismarckian policy of power interests and centralization, in short, to Bismarck's "crypto-conservatism" (Hans Joachim Schoeps). Ever since then Germany has witnessed a "crisis of conservatism" (Alfred von Martin) ; its conservatism has been one in name only. Austrian conservatism, however, has developed with less interruption; since there was no Bismarck, conservatism could develop in a more direct fashion, from Metternich and Gentz to Seipel, from Adam Müller and Friedrich Schlegel to Spann. But the dilemma of conservatism also affected the little Austria of the twentieth century, where Catholic romanticism became the basis of its own brand of dictatorship.

About German conservatism's deviation from the "ideal type," the following must be added. Its history exhibits German conservatism's failure to recognize the limits of conservatism. Conservatism without the ethos of liberty is no more conservative than a conservatism turned sentimental, passionate, or Jacobin. In the twenties and thirties there was much preaching about "allegiances," old and lost ones, new and to-be-found ones—about the "wholeness" which had been lost in the age of the bourgeoisie and

---

[5] Cf. the review by Carl E. Schorske, *The Yale Review*, XLVII (Winter, 1958), 276-281; and Klaus Epstein, "Neueres amerikanisches Schrifttum über die deutsche Geschichte im 20. Jahrhundert," in *Welt als Geschichte* (1960), 120-142.

was to be regained. There was too much preaching, too much marching and drumming, and too much intoxication. What had all this to do with conservatism?

Novalis once coined a beautifully conservative phrase to the effect that we "always go homeward." What did he mean by this? We might get an answer from his twentieth century disciple Hermann Hesse, a man who observed with considerable misgivings the new conservative trend between the wars. In his *Journey to the East* he writes about a league (*Bund*) of the sort of Hofmannsthal's "legion" of "seekers." The league moved to the East in search of the "home and youth of the soul," the "everywhere and nowhere," the "overcoming of all time." "According to the rules we lived as pilgrims, ignoring all devices which, connected with a world enslaved by money, numbers and time, deprive life of its content; specifically machines, railroads, watches were part of this world." But this "league," this "army," this "movement," which (Hesse remarked parenthetically) should have been put into the "service of republican politics," brought no relief. The league, after all, was an organization with its hierarchy. And Hesse's hero had to enter strange paths—from hybris which gave him the illusion of being part of a "whole," to despair (separation from the league), to finding himself in a renewed league which had no soldiers, no organization, no hierarchy, no new "allegiances," which had no rule other than the need to find and to know oneself. Novalis'-Hesse's "going homeward" then means not a losing of oneself but a finding of oneself; it means exploring the human condition. Certainly the function of conservatism in those years of mass hysteria should not have been to serve as an opiate for the people or to enter into a race with the pseudo-religions, whether National Socialism or Communism. Here the limits of conservatism should have been clearly drawn, but they were not sufficiently recognized.

If once again we look at all those conservative groups and circles, we find that they were conspirators, more or less saintly ones—crusaders, but mostly without the cross.

The militant conservatism of the twentieth century in Germany offered itself as a salvation-bringing quasi-church, indeed anti-church. This transgression, so to speak, this deviation from the "ideal type," was the hybris of the new conservatism.

It is imperative then, that the historian insist on correct conceptualizing and refrain from using the strangely tempting and paradoxical concept of the "conservative revolution." The radical pathos of the postwar prophets was Jacobin, not conservative. Furthermore, their message, as Stern and Sontheimer have convincingly demonstrated, added up to little more than tiredness, resentment, and cultural despair. The Third Reich of Moeller van den Bruck was less an outgrowth of the conservative tradition than it was a symptom of disinheritedness and crisis. After all, Georg Lukács' point[6] about the degeneration of German irrationalist thought in the nineteenth and twentieth centuries has a distinct bearing on our problem. In short, *la révolution conservative n'a pas eu lieu.*

The story of Germany's new conservatism remains one of lost opportunities, especially in its failure to buttress the Republic. While the neo-conservatives successfully undermined the Republic, they could not assert themselves against the National Socialist movement, which won over the masses. A dismal record indeed. By 1933 the new conservatism had lost its intellectual identity, moral dignity, and political viability. Only in the face of the extreme situation of experienced tyranny did it undergo a process of at least moral regeneration.

[6] Georg Lukács, *Die Zerstörung der Vernunft* (Berlin, 1955), 2.

BIBLIOGRAPHICAL ESSAY

THIS bibliography should be a guide for the reader through the materials which have served as a basis for my studies and conclusions. For a number of reasons, however, a critical commentary on the quality of the materials seemed preferable to a complete listing. The careful footnoting which has been observed throughout this book should in itself be a record of the sources, primary and secondary, for this study and should not be duplicated. Furthermore, for an excellent and fairly exhaustive bibliography on the subject, reference should be made to Armin Mohler, *Die Konservative Revolution in Deutschland 1918-1932* (Stuttgart, 1950), 212ff.

At any rate this study has not made use of any materials which were not available to the previous works on the subject, such as Walter Gerhart (pseud. for Waldemar Gurian), *Um des Reiches Zukunft. Nationale Wiedergeburt oder politische Reaktion?* (Freiburg, Br., 1932); Edmond Vermeil, *Doctrinaires de la Révolution Allemande 1918-1938* (Paris, 1938); Aurel Kolnai, *The War against the West* (New York, 1938); and Mohler, *Die Konservative Revolution*. The historian of neo-conservatism in Germany is faced with an abundance rather than with a dearth of documents, and his task is one of selection from among a vast publicistic literature. He has to live with a whole lot of rather second-rate thinkers, more or less terrible *simplificateurs* who repeated their platitudes over and over again, with whom he may be in violent disagreement. It is all the more important that he live himself into his subject with a historian's sense of sympathy. No historical problem should be approached with political and moral bias alone; it calls for an imaginative understanding on the part of the historian as well.

Among the existing studies on the new conservatism these two approaches are combined to a varying degree. While Vermeil and Kolnai, writing during the height of

the Nazi threat, had little patience with the neo-conservatives, who so clearly had failed, Mohler, a Swiss historian
and secretary of Ernst Jünger, writing after the war, has
approached the "Conservative Revolution" with too much
reverence. He has tended to ignore the extent to which
the new conservatism was a poor man's Nietzsche and
pseudo-conservatism. Gurian, writing during the critical
years before 1933 and concerned about the growing extremism of what he called the "new nationalism," came close
to striking a balance between the two approaches. Quite
sui generis are Hermann Rauschning, *The Revolution of
Nihilism. Warning to the West* (New York, 1939) and *The
Conservative Revolution* (New York, 1941) and Ernst Robert Curtius, *Deutscher Geist in Gefahr* (Stuttgart, Berlin,
1932), inasmuch as they are obviously based on first-hand
experience rather than research; but as such they are in-
valuable to the historian of conservatism between the wars.

The approach of this study, tracing and measuring the
gulf between the logic and politics of conservatism, necessarily involved a going back to a consideration of the early
nineteenth century background. The best comprehensive
studies on nineteenth century conservatism in Germany are
Alfred von Martin, "Weltanschauliche Motive im altkonservativen Denken," *Deutscher Staat und deutsche Parteien.
Beiträge zur deutschen Partei- und Ideengeschichte. Friedrich Meinecke zum 60. Geburtstag dargebracht* (Munich,
Berlin, 1922), 342-384; Karl Mannheim, "Conservative
Thought," *Essays on Sociology and Social Psychology* (ed.
Paul Kecskemeti, London, 1953); and Sigmund Neumann,
*Die Stufen des preussischen Konservatismus. Ein Beitrag
zum Staats- und Gesellschaftsbild Deutschlands im 19. Jahrhundert* (Berlin, 1928)—the first two dealing particularly
with the weaknesses of the German conservative tradition.

It is interesting that so much more work should have
been done on National Socialism than on conservatism.
Konrad Heiden's *Adolf Hitler. Das Zeitalter der Verant-
wortungslosigkeit. Eine Biographie* (Zurich, 1936), his *Der*

Führer. Hitler's Rise to Power (New York, Boston, 1941), and the other editions by the same author are still unsurpassed. Even the more recent work by Alan Bullock, *Hitler. A Study in Tyranny* (London, 1952), is in many instances based on Heiden. On this subject also Rauschning's work is of great help. As an analysis of the structure of National Socialism, Franz Neumann, *Behemoth. The Structure and Practice of National Socialism 1933-1944* (Toronto, New York, London, 1944) is excellent. Much of the work done in Germany since the second World War in connection with the Institut für Zeitgeschichte in Munich has appeared in the *Vierteljahrshefte für Zeitgeschichte;* among its articles the one by Hermann Mau, "Die 'Zweite Revolution'—Der 30. Juni 1934," *ibid.,* I (April 1953), 119-137 is of particular relevance to an understanding of the nature of National Socialism. A most uneven work is the recent *The Third Reich* (ed. UNESCO, London, 1955); however, it contains some very valuable contributions, particularly Karl O. Paetel, "The Reign of the Black Order: The Final Phase of German National Socialism: The SS Counter-State," *ibid.,* 633-677, which originally had appeared in the *Vierteljahrshefte.* A stimulating introduction to the comparison between conservatism, an essentially nineteenth century political idea, and National Socialism is offered by Isaiah Berlin, "Political Ideas in the Twentieth Century," *Foreign Affairs,* XXVIII (April 1950), 351-385.

As this study has emphasized the connection of the dilemma of conservatism with the structure of modern society, it has benefited much from works such as Hendrik de Man, *Sozialismus und Nationalfascismus* (Potsdam, 1931), a pioneering study in the field of sociological history which, so it seems, greatly influenced the suggestive book by Erich Fromm, *Escape from Freedom* (New York, 1941). Unfortunately, Fromm makes no attempt to differentiate between conservatism and National Socialism. Both Wilhelm Röpke, "Die proletarisierte Gesellschaft," *Der Monat,* II (June 1950), 227-231 and Karl Mannheim, *Freedom,*

Power and Democratic Planning (New York, 1950), however different their approaches, try to cope with the problem of saving freedom in an age of the masses. An interesting discussion of the intellectual and social scene in Germany since 1870 is contained in Georg Steinhausen, *Deutsche Geistes- und Kulturgeschichte von 1870 bis zur Gegenwart* (Halle, 1931). However, most of all have I benefited from the reading of two great German men of letters, Friedrich Meinecke, who toward the end of his life attributed increasing importance to the social factor in history, and Thomas Mann, whose work is no doubt one of the best commentaries on modern German social history.

While a discussion of the Youth Movement and of the "ideas of 1914" was imperative, these form merely the background for neo-conservatism in modern Germany. In its essence this study aspires to be a contribution to our knowledge of the Weimar Republic. An excellent general introduction to the problems of research in the latter field is Karl Dietrich Erdmann, "Die Geschichte der Weimarer Republik als Problem der Wissenschaft," *Vierteljahrshefte für Zeitgeschichte*, III (January 1955), 1-19. I have benefited much from the standard works by Arthur Rosenberg, *The Birth of the German Republic 1871-1918* (London, 1931) and *A History of the Weimar Republic* (London, 1936); Arnold Brecht, *Prelude to Silence* (New York, 1944); Ferdinand Friedensburg, *Die Weimarer Republik* (Berlin, 1946); S. William Halperin, *Germany Tried Democracy* (New York, 1946); and Erich Eyck, *Geschichte der Weimarer Republik. Vom Zusammenbruch des Kaisertums bis zur Wahl Hindenburgs*, Vol. I (Erlenbach-Zurich, Stuttgart, 1954). I am certainly not prepared to agree with Mohler's estimate of Hermann Ullmann, *Durchbruch zur Nation. Geschichte des deutschen Volkes 1919-1933* (Jena, 1933) as the most satisfactory history of the Weimar Republic; at best the book represents a neo-conservative's view with all its prejudices and deceptions, and it is more a political tract than a history book. Much more original and valuable as interpretations of the Weimar Republic by Rightist intellectuals are Ernst von Salomon, *Nahe Geschichte. Ein Überblick* (Berlin, 1936) (for the early period) and Frank Thiess, "Die unsichtbare Revolution," *Wiedergeburt der Liebe. Die unsichtbare Revolution* (Berlin, Vienna, Leipzig, 1931) (for the trends among the young generation in the nineteen thirties). Of great value are the accounts of the 1918-1919 Revolution by two observer-historians, Ernst Troeltsch, *Spektator-Briefe. Aufsätze über die deutsche Revolution und die Weltpolitik, 1918-1922* (ed. Hans Baron, Tübingen, 1924) and Ralph Haswell Lutz, *The German Revolution 1918-1919* (Stanford University, 1922), and the observations on the state of Germany between the wars by three scholars—Willy Hellpach, *Politische Prognose für Deutschland* (Berlin, 1928); Eugen Diesel, *Die deutsche Wandlung. Das Bild eines Volkes* (Berlin, 1929); and Ernst Robert Curtius, *Deutscher Geist in Gefahr* (Stuttgart, Berlin, 1932)—and by the American journalist Edgar Ansel Mowrer, *Germany Puts the Clock Back* (Harmondsworth, 1939). On the political parties there are Ludwig Bergsträsser, *Geschichte der politischen Parteien in Deutschland* (Mannheim, 1932) and Sigmund Neumann, *Die deutschen Parteien. Wesen und Wandel nach dem Kriege* (Berlin, 1932); on the German economy Werner F. Bruck, *Social and Economic History of Germany from William II to Hitler, 1888-1938* (Cardiff, 1938) and Gustav Stolper, *German Economy, 1870-1940* (London, 1940). A good survey of the German para-military organizations is Ernst H. Posse, *Die politischen Kampfbünde Deutschlands* (2nd edn., Berlin, 1931) and of the political periodicals Helmut Hüttig, *Die politischen Zeitschriften der Nachkriegszeit in Deutschland* (Magdeburg, 1928). An excellent essay on the problem of the German intelligentsia between the two wars is Golo Mann, "The German Intellectuals," *Encounter,* IV (June 1955), 42-49.

Erdmann's observation that the research in the history of the Weimar Republic is only in its initial phase applies in particular to the field of conservatism, in which little work as yet has been done. Among the few studies in this area are Walter H. Kaufmann, *Monarchism in the Weimar Republic* (New York, 1953) and Lewis Hertzman, *The German National People's Party (D.N.V.P.) 1918-1924* (Ph.D. thesis, Harvard University, 1954). The main scholarly works on the neo-conservative movement have been discussed in the text and above in this essay. Further interesting—mostly contemporary—discussions of one or another aspect of the movement are contained in Kurt Hiller, *Der Sprung ins Helle* (Leipzig, 1932); Wilhelm Röpke, *The Solution of the German Problem* (New York, 1947); Josef Winschuh, "Die Rolle der Sozialpolitik in den neueren politischen Strömungen," *Der Arbeitgeber,* xx (1930), 214-218; Georg Schröder, "Der Sozialismus der nationalen Jugend," *ibid.*, 218-221; various articles by Erich Tross in the *Frankfurter Zeitung* of August 26, 1929 (morning edn.), October 21, 1929 (evening edn.), and December 16, 1929 (evening edn.), and by Karl O. Paetel in *ibid.* of August 26, 1929 (evening edn.); Heinz Gollong, "Nationalisten," *Die Literarische Welt,* viii (1932), 5-6; Alex M. Lipiansky, "Pour un communisme national," *Revue d'Allemagne et des Pays de Langue Allemande,* vi (1932), 849-867; and Otto Friedländer, "Die ideologische Front der nationalen Opposition," *Sozialistische Monatshefte,* xxxv (1929), 207-212.

The best direct introduction to the mentality of the neo-conservative movement are symposia such as Moeller van den Bruck, Heinrich von Gleichen, and Max Hildebert Boehm, *Die neue Front* (Berlin, 1922); Ernst Jünger, ed., *Krieg und Krieger* (Berlin, 1930); Goetz Otto Stoffregen, ed., *Aufstand. Querschnitt durch den revolutionären Nationalismus* (Berlin, 1931); and Albrecht Erich Günther, ed., *Was wir vom Nationalsozialismus erwarten* (Heilbronn, 1932). Focusing on the problem of the "young generation" is E. Günther Gründel, *Die Sendung der jungen Generation* (3rd edn., Munich, 1933). Informative, though exaggerating the central role among the neo-conservatives of Otto Strasser's Black Front, is Adolf Ehrt, *Totale Krise—totale Revolution? Die "Schwarze Front" des völkischen Nationalismus* (Berlin, 1933). Ernst von Salomon, *Der Fragebogen* (Hamburg, 1953), a book which has been so negatively received in this country, serves nevertheless as an important document of the aspirations, deceptions, and disappointments of the neo-conservatives.

It ought to be noted here that the cause of the neo-conservatives was greatly furthered by the work of various publishers, namely the Eugen Diederichs Verlag, the Hanseatische Verlagsanstalt (owned by the D.H.V.), the Wilh. Gottl. Korn Verlag, and the Verlag Gerhard Stalling. However, their lists of publications included Nazi writers as well and confirm the degree to which the two movements, neo-conservative and Nazi, were interwoven.

The number of periodicals backing the cause of the neo-conservatives is legion. Once more the main problem of the scholar in this field is selectivity among the abundance of material. The only periodicals which I wanted to consult and which have been unavailable to me are the *Volkskonservative Stimmen* and the *Politische Wochenschrift*, both connected with the Young Conservatives. Otherwise an attempt has been made in this study to include a fair representation of magazines for both the early phase (up to 1928) and the later phase of the Republic and to account for the various shades of opinion. The magazines themselves have been amply discussed in the text; the following list should primarily serve to point out some selected articles in them:

Deutsche Arbeit. Monatsschrift für die Bestrebungen der christlich-nationalen Arbeiterschaft.

Die deutsche Revolution. Organ der Schwarzen Front.

Deutsche Rundschau.
Moeller van den Bruck, "Das Recht der jungen Völker," *ibid.*, CLXXVII (1918), 220-235.

————, "Der Untergang des Abendlandes. Für und wider Spengler," *ibid.*, CLXXXIV (1920), 41-70.

Heinrich von Gleichen, "Das Politische Kolleg," *ibid.*, CLXXXVII (1921), 104-109.

Franz Fromme, "Die neue Front," *ibid.*, CXCI (1922), 314-320.

Edgar J. Jung, "Aufstand der Rechten," *ibid.*, CCXXIX (1931), 81-88.

————, "Neubelebung von Weimar?" *ibid.*, CCXXXI (1932), 153-162.

————, "Einsatz der Nation," *ibid.*, CCXXXIV (1933), 155-160.

Paul Fechter, "Das Leben Moellers van den Bruck," *ibid.*, CCXXXIX (1934), 14-21.

Deutsches Volkstum. Monatsschrift für das deutsche Geistesleben.

Wilhelm Stapel, "Die Zukunft der nationalen Bewegung," *ibid.*, XXVI (1924), 1-8.

Hans Schwarz, "Über Moeller van den Bruck," *ibid.*, XXVIII (1926), 205-211.

Ernst Jünger, "Die Geburt des Nationalismus aus dem Kriege," *ibid.*, XXXI (1929), 576-582.

Hans Schwarz, "Über Moeller van den Bruck," *ibid.*, XXXIV (1932), 689-692.

Max Hildebert Boehm, "Moeller van den Bruck im Kreise seiner politischen Freunde," *ibid.*, XXXIV (1932), 693-697.

Erich Müller, "Zur Geschichte des Nationalbolschewismus," *ibid.*, XXXIV (1932), 782-790.

Wilhelm Stapel, "Zwanzig Jahre *Deutsches Volkstum*," *ibid.*, XL (1938), 795-810.

Das Dritte Reich. Blätter für Freiheit und Gemeinschaft. Mouthpiece of the Bund Oberland; absorbed in January 1933 by the *Widerstand.*

Freideutsche Jugend. Eine Monatsschrift.

Gewissen. Wochenzeitung für Politische Bildung.

Hans Heinrich Schraeder, "Max Weber als Politiker," *ibid.*, III (March 2, 1921). A positive evaluation.

Moeller van den Bruck, "Stellung zu Amerika," *ibid.*, III (April 15, 1921).

Otto Werner, "Mann über Bord," *ibid.*, IV (October 23, 1922). An attack against Thomas Mann's address *Von deutscher Republik*.

Moeller van den Bruck, "Der Wanderer ins Nichts," *ibid.*, V (July 2, 1923).

————, "Der dritte Standpunkt," *ibid.*, V (July 16, 1923).

————, "Wirklichkeit," *ibid.*, V (July 30, 1923).

Erich Brock, "Thomas Manns Manifest zum Schutze der Republik," *ibid.*, V (July 23, 1923).

Otto Strasser, "Pazifismus, Judentum und nationaler Wille," *ibid.*, VI (November 3, 1924).

Erich Brock, "Thomas Mann als Prophet des Westens," *ibid.*, VII (June 8, 1925). An attack against Mann and Troeltsch.

Ernst Jünger, "Revolution und Frontsoldatentum," *ibid.*, VII (August 31, 1925).

Erich Brock, "Die Brüder Mann auf der Wallfahrt nach Europa," *ibid.*, VIII (April 5, 1926).

Die Grenzboten. Zeitschrift für Politik, Literatur und Kunst.

Max Hildebert Boehm, "Oswald Spengler, *Preussentum und Sozialismus*," *ibid.*, LXXIX, 1/4 (1920), 60-62.

Cf. also the articles by Moeller van den Bruck of the year 1920.

Der Nahe Osten.

Moeller van den Bruck, "Abrechnung mit der Innenpolitik," *ibid.*, III (1930), 164-166.

Lucy Moeller van den Bruck, "Erbe und Auftrag," *ibid.*, V (1932), 429-436. An interview by the widow of Moeller on his person and views.

Hans Schwarz, "Anfang 1933," *ibid.*, VI (1933), 1-9.

Erich Müller, "Heroischer Nihilismus. Zu Ernst Jüngers Buch *Der Arbeiter*," *ibid.*, VI (1933), 110-115.

Preussische Jahrbücher.
Oswald Spengler, "Pessimisus?" *ibid.*, CLXXXIV (1921), 73-84.
Hermann Haering, "Die neue Front," *ibid.*, CXC (1922), 91-103.
Escherich (Forstrat), "Die Tragödie des Mittelstandes," *ibid.*, CXC, 119-133.

Der Reichswart. Parteilose Wochenschrift.
"Nationalbolschewismus," *ibid.*, I, No. 6 (1920), 6-9.

Der Ring. Konservative Wochenschrift.

Die Schwarze Front. Kampforgan für die deutsche Revolution.

Die Sozialistische Nation. Blätter der deutschen Revolution.

Süddeutsche Monatshefte.
Max Hildebert Boehm, "Die Front der Jungen," *ibid.*, XVIII, Vol. 1 (1920-1921), 8-12.

Die Tat.
Moeller van den Bruck, "Schönheit," *ibid.*, III (1911-1912), 138-142.
————, "Der Kaiser und die architektonische Tradition," *ibid.*, V (1913-1914), 595-601.
Hans Siegfried Weber, "Überwindung des Marxismus (Karl Marx und Paul Lensch)," *ibid.*, XIX (1927-1928), 756-765.
Wilhelm Rössle, "Sozialismus auf dem Papier," *ibid.*, XXII (1930-1931), 903-913. About the failure of socialization.
Wilhelm Wunderlich, "Die Spinne," *ibid.*, XXIII (1931-1932), 833-844. Biased and unreliable information about the June Club.

Graf Ernst Reventlow, " 'Ein Stück Wegs?' " *ibid.*, XXIII (1931-1932), 989-993. Reventlow reconsidering Radek's offer.

F. W. Eschmann, "Nationale Planwirtschaft: Grundzüge," *ibid.*, XXIV (1932-1933), 225-243. From the war economy to the *Gemeinwirtschaft*.

Hermann Curth, "Das erste Scheitern des deutschen Sozialismus," *ibid.*, XXIV (1932-1933), 593-606. On Moellendorff.

Wolfgang Herrmann, "Moeller van den Bruck," *ibid.*, XXV (1933-1934), 273-297. Quite inaccurate.

Cf. also the many articles by Hans Zehrer, Giselher Wirsing, and Ferdinand Fried.

Widerstand. Zeitschrift für national-revolutionäre Politik.
Ernst Niekisch, "Die antiimperialistische Situation," *ibid.*, VIII (1933), 129-136.

Among the exponents of neo-conservatism the choice of Moeller van den Bruck, Spengler, and Ernst Jünger was an obvious one. However, the following list of selected authors and books should give the reader a concrete idea concerning the widespread publication of neo-conservative literature between the two wars:

Max Hildebert Boehm, *Was uns not tut* (Berlin, 1919). Close to the June Club.

Hans Bogner, *Die Bildung der politischen Elite* (Oldenburg (1932). Close to the Herrenklub.

Eugen Diederichs, *Aus meinem Leben* (2nd edn., Leipzig, 1938). An autobiography of the publisher.

Eugen Diederichs. Leben und Werk (ed. Lulu von Strauss und Torney-Diederichs, Jena, 1936).

Eugen Diederichs, *Politik des Geistes* (Jena, 1920). A collection of Diederichs' articles in the *Tat* between 1915 and 1919.

Leopold Dingräve (pseud. for Ernst Wilhelm Eschmann), *Wo steht die junge Generation?* (Jena, 1931). Close to the *Tat* Circle.

————, *Wohin treibt Deutschland?* (Jena, 1932).

Carl Dyrssen, *Die Botschaft des Ostens* (Breslau, 1933). close to *Der Nahe Osten.*

Hans Freyer, *Revolution von rechts* (Jena, 1931). Close to the *Tat* Circle.

Ferdinand Fried (pseud. for Friedrich Zimmermann), *Autarkie* (Jena, 1932). Close to the *Tat* Circle.

————, *Das Ende des Kapitalismus* (Jena, 1931).

Henrich von Gleichen, *Freies Volk* (Charlottenburg, 1919). A political pamphlet by the head of the June Club.

Friedrich Hielscher, *Das Reich* (Berlin, 1931). A much-discussed pseudo-historical tract. Hielscher was close to Ernst Jünger.

Edgar J. Jung, *Deutsche über Deutschland* (Munich, 1932). Close to the Herrenklub.

————, *Die Herrschaft der Minderwertigen. Ihr Zerfall und ihre Ablösung durch ein neues Reich* (3rd edn., Berlin, 1930).

————, *Sinndeutung der deutschen Revolution* (Oldenburg, 1933).

Harald Laeuen, *Östliche Agrarrevolution und Bauernpolitik* (Berlin, 1929). Close to *Der Nahe Osten.*

Weigand von Miltenberg (pseud. for Herbert Blank), *Adolf Hitler Wilhelm III* (Berlin, 1931). Close to the Black Front.

Ernst Niekisch, *Hitler—ein deutsches Verhängnis* (Berlin, 1932). A pamphlet by the leader of the Resistance Movement (Widerstandsbewegung); anti-Nazi though outdoing the Nazis in its extremism.

————, *Politik und Idee* (Dresden, 1929).

————, *Der Weg deutschen Arbeiterschaft zum Staat* (Berlin, 1929).

Karl Otto Paetel, *Das geistige Gesicht der nationalen Jugend* (Flarchheim, 1930). A National Bolshevik publication by the editor of *Die Sozialistische Nation.*

————, *Sozialrevolutionärer Nationalismus* (Flarchheim, 1930).

Georg Quabbe (pseud. for Theodor Böttiger), *Tar a Ri. Variationen über ein konservatives Thema* (Berlin, 1927). Close to the Herrenklub.

Richard Schapke, *Aufstand der Bauern* (Leipzig, 1933). Close to the Black Front.

————, *Die Schwarze Front* (Leipzig, 1932).

Franz Schauwecker, *Aufbruch der Nation* (Berlin, 1930). Close to the radical conservatives.

Friedrich Schinkel, *Polen, Preussen und Deutschland* (Breslau, 1932). Close to *Der Nahe Osten*.

————, *Preussischer Sozialismus* (Breslau, 1934).

Walther Schotte, *Das Kabinett Papen Schleicher Gayl* (Leipzig, 1932). Close to the Herrenklub.

————, *Der neue Staat* (Berlin, 1932).

Wilhelm von Schramm, *Radikale Politik. Die Welt diesseits und jenseits des Bolschewismus* (Munich, 1932). A Catholic approach to neo-conservatism. Close to the Herrenklub.

Othmar Spann, *Der wahre Staat. Vorlesungen über Abbau und Neubeu der Gesellschaft* (Munich, 1932). This book exercised a considerable influence upon the Young Conservatives.

Eduard Stadtler, *Als Antibolschewist 1918-1919* (Düsseldorf, 1935). Autobiographical; pompous and egocentric. Close to the June Club.

————, *Der Bolschewismus und seine Überwindung* (Berlin, 1918).

————, *Der Bolschewismus und das Wirtschaftsleben* (Berlin, 1919).

————, *Die Diktatur der sozialen Revolution* (Leipzig, 1920). Contains much information about the forces and aims of neo-conservatism.

————, *Als politischer Soldat 1914-1918* (Düsseldorf, 1936). Autobiographical; pompous and egocentric.

————, *Die Revolution und das alte Parteiwesen* (Berlin, 1919). The clearest statement by Stadtler on the November Revolution and Bolshevism.

————, *Die Weltkriegsrevolution* (Leipzig, 1920). Public addresses, 1917-1919.

————, *Weltrevolutionskrieg* (Düsseldorf, 1937). Stadtler all over.

Wilhelm Stapel, *Der christliche Staatsmann. Eine Theologie des Nationalismus* (Hamburg, 1932). The main work by the editor of the *Deutsches Volkstum*.

Alexander Stenbock-Fermor, Graf, *Deutschland von unten. Reise durch die proletarische Provinz* (Stuttgart, 1931). Close to the *Tat* Circle. Stenbock-Fermor joined the Communists in 1931.

————, *Meine Erlebnisse als Bergarbeiter* (Stuttgart, 1928).

Otto Strasser, *Aufbau des deutschen Sozialismus* (2nd edn., Prague, 1936). The main work by the leader of the Black Front. The first edition appeared in Berlin in 1931.

————, *Die deutsche Bartholomäusnacht* (Prague, 1938).

————, *History in My Time* (London, 1941). Autobiographical.

————, *Wissen Sie das auch schon?* (Berlin, 1928).

Kurt van Emsen (pseud. for Strünckmann), *Adolf Hitler und die Kommenden* (Leipzig, 1932). Close to the Black Front.

Otto Weber-Krohse, *Landschaftliche Politik* (Breslau, 1932). Close to *Der Nahe Osten*.

August Winnig, *Frührot. Ein Buch von Heimat und Jugend* (Stuttgart, Berlin, 1926). Autobiographical.

————, *Heimkehr* (3rd edn., Hamburg, 1935). Autobiographical; covering Winnig's East Prussian experiences.

————, *Vom Proletariat zum Arbeitertum* (Hamburg, 1930).

————, *Das Reich als Republik, 1918-1928* (2nd edn., Stuttgart, Berlin, 1929).

————, *Der weite Weg* (4th edn., Hamburg, 1932). Autobiographical.

—————, *Wir hüten das Feuer. Aufsätze und Reden aus zehn Jahren (1923-1933)* (Hamburg, 1933). Containing some of Winnig's articles from the *Berliner Börsen-Zeitung* and *Der Firn.*

Giselher Wirsing, *Zwischeneuropa und die deutsche Zukunft* (Jena, 1932). Close to the *Tat* Circle.

While all the above-listed periodicals and authors are evidence of the complex and muddled ideas of the neo-conservatives about National Socialism, the following books and periodicals reflect the confusion prevailing within the German Right, including the Nazis themselves, concerning the Nazis on neo-conservatism:

Reinhard Adam, *Moeller van den Bruck* (Königsberg, 1933). Friendly.

E. Günther Gründel, *Jahre der Überwindung* (Breslau, 1934). Hostile.

Johann von Leers, *Spenglers weltpolitisches System und der Nationalsozialismus* (Berlin, 1934). Hostile.

Helmut Rödel, *Moeller van den Bruck* (Berlin, 1939). Hostile.

Alfred Rosenberg, *Der Mythus des 20. Jahrhunderts* (Munich, 1930). Hostile.

Herbert Schack, *Denker und Deuter. Männer von der deutschen Wende* (Stuttgart, 1938). Friendly.

Eugen Schmahl, *Der Aufstieg der nationalen Idee* (Stuttgart, 1933). Friendly.

Erich Unger, *Das Schrifttum des Nationalsozialismus von 1919 bis zum 1. Januar 1934* (Berlin, 1934). Including works by Jung, Ernst Jünger, Moeller van den Bruck, Spann, Stapel.

Arthur Zweiniger, *Spengler im Dritten Reich. Eine Antwort auf Oswald Spenglers "Jahre der Entscheidung"* (Oldenburg, 1933).

Nationalsozialistische Monatshefte.
Alfred Rosenberg, "Oswald Spengler," *ibid.*, I (July 1930), 180-184. Hostile.

"Das Recht der jungen Völker," *ibid.*, III (June 1932), 267-271. Friendly.

Heinrich Härtle, "Othmar Spann, der Philosoph des christlichen Ständestaates," *ibid.*, IX (August 1938), 690-698. Hostile.

Das Schwarze Korps.

"Herr Stapel entrüstet sich," *ibid.*, I (April 24, 1935), 12.

"Hinter der freundlichen Maske," *ibid.*, I (July 10, 1935), 9.

"Schluss mit der Frauenbewegung," *ibid.*, I (July 24, 1935), 10.

"Ein letztes Wort, Herr Stapel," *ibid.*, I (August 7, 1935), 9f.

"Literarisches Nachtwächtertum," *ibid.*, I (August 7, 1935), 12.

"Einer wird herausgegriffen," *ibid.*, IV (December 8, 15, 22, 1938), in each case 13f.

All hostile.

Völkischer Beobachter.

Alfred Baeumler, "Revolution—von ferne gesehen. Zu Oswald Spenglers neuer Schrift," *ibid.*, August 31, 1933. 1931.

Alfred Rosenberg, "Gegen Tarnung und Verfälschung," *ibid.*, December 8, 1933.

Walther Schmitt, "Gegen Verfälschungen," *ibid.*, January 18, 1934.

All hostile.

Wille und Macht.

Kif, "Deutsche Jugend und Oswald Spengler," *ibid.*, II (May 15, 1934), 25-28.

Karlheinz Rüdiger, "Klarheit über Othmar Spann," *ibid.*, IV (January 15, 1936), 12-17.

Both hostile.

INDEX

Acton, Lord, 35
Albers, August, 171
Alvensleben, Count Bodo von, 121
Anti-Bolshevik Movement, 104-107, 113, 141
Antibolschewistische Korrespondenz, 106
Arbeitsgemeinschaft, 81-83, 85, 166
Association of German Scholars and Artists, 49, 104, 142

Balzac, Honoré de, 19
Bauer, Gustav, 87
Bebel, August, 177
Benda, Julien, 225
Berliner Börsen-Zeitung, 108n, 110
Bernhard, Georg, 108
Bernstorff, Count Johann Heinrich von, 106
Binding, Rudolf, 48
Bismarck, Prince Otto von, 34-36, 37-38, 41, 45, 55, 58, 65, 73, 74, 155, 157, 164, 184, 206
Black Front, 108, 135-138, 148n, 149
Bloch, Joseph, 85n
Blüher, Hans, 101n
Boehm, Max Hildebert, 106n, 107, 109, 110, 162
Bogner, Hans, 200n
Borsig, Ernst, 105n
Bose, von, 212
Bossuet, Bishop of Meaux, 19
Böttiger, Theodor, 123, 124, 129
"bourgeois," *see* middle classes
bourgeoisie, *see* middle classes
Brandes, Georg, 39
Brauweiler, Heinz, 99n, 107, 110, 111n, 120n, 123
Bredow, Kurt von, 210
Brentano, Lujo, 101
Brockdorff-Rantzau, Count Ulrich von, 89, 139
Brüning, Heinrich, 108, 120, 128, 129, 131, 193n, 194n, 204, 210, 215
Budenny, Marshal S. M., 143-144
Bukharin, Nikolai, 142n, 145
Bündische Jugend, 97, 137

Burckhardt, Jakob, 6, 8, 36, 37, 40, 52, 58, 155, 171, 196, 197, 202, 220
Burke, Edmund, 18-20, 23-25, 27-30, 33, 34, 41, 163
Burschenschaften, 44

Camus, Albert, 221
Carr, E. H., 11n
Center Party, 68, 104, 108, 109
Central Europe, 50, 55-56, 130, 134
Chamberlain, Houston Stewart, 196
Christian National Peasant's Party, 128
Christian Socialist People's Service, 128, 131
Christlichsozialer Volksdienst, *see* Christian Socialist People's Service
Clausewitz, Carl von, 160
Cohen-Reuss, Max, 85n, 106n
Coleridge, Samuel Taylor, 21n
Comintern, 142, 145
Communist Party, 71, 72, 80, 128; and National Bolshevism, 143ff
Communist Workers' Party of Germany, 143
conservatism: and Ancien Régime, 19, 26; concept of change, 21-24; concept of freedom, 24-26; and constitutions, 23-24; definition of, 17-32; dilemma of, 3-4, 7-9, 12-13, 32, 39, 42, 59, 73, 80, 92-93, 112, 116, 117, 163, 179, 186, 191-192, 218, 221, 226; and freedom, 7, 8; and French Revolution, 4, 18-20, 23, 24, 25, 74; genesis of dilemma, 33-42; German, 33-36, 40, 42, 53; and irrationalism, 26-28; and liberalism, 5, 19-21, 24, 26-28, 30-32, 44; and National Socialism, 26-32, 42n, 124, 210, 225; and nihilism, 7, 36ff, 42; and pessimism, 28-31, 38; philosophy of acceptance, 20, 31, 171; and reaction, 5, 21-22; and romanticism, 27, 113; and royalism, 19;

INDEX

Other Titles in European History
and International Affairs
Available in Princeton Paperback